kid chef bakes

kid chef
BAKES

The KIDS COOKBOOK
FOR ASPIRING BAKERS

Lisa Huff

ROCKRIDGE
PRESS

For general information on our other products and services or to obtain technical support, please contact our Customer Care Department within the U.S. at (866) 744-2665, or outside the U.S. at (510) 253-0500.

Rockridge Press publishes its books in a variety of electronic and print formats. Some content that appears in print may not be available in electronic books, and vice versa.

All photography © Hélène Dujardin/Food styling by Tami Hardeman/prop styling by Angela Hall except pages 34, 72 & 83: © Jennifer Davick; pages 67, 77, 79, 93, 117, 125, 135, 145, 151, 163, 173, 177 & 187: © Lisa Huff; page 133: Ellie Baygulov/Stocksy. Illustrations: TongSur/iStock, pages 11-13.
Author photo © Andrea Topalian

ISBN: Print 978-1-62315-942-9 | eBook 978-1-62315-943-6

To my kids, Jordan and Cora,
and all other kids learning to bake.
Keep baking, and may all your
dreams come true!

CONTENTS

....

INTRODUCTION

....

Welcome to the world of baking! Okay, you may have been baking in the kitchen for years with your grandparents, parents, older siblings, or maybe even all by yourself. So now you have this book—with all these tools, you're off to a great start! If you're just getting started baking in the kitchen, that's awesome, too! This fun book will teach you baking basics, and also help you master some more advanced baking techniques.

When we think of baking, most of us conjure up images of cookies, breads, cakes, pies—well, desserts! That's definitely part of it, but other baking options that we'll explore include appetizers, pizzas, and quiche, to name a few. At its core, baking is the act of cooking something, usually flour-based foods, with dry heat (like in an oven). Baking is a little different than cooking, and sometimes trickier! With many baking recipes, there is a science behind the recipe. Finding the right balance between ingredients can be a challenge. Like, when I was a kid, I thought I could substitute melted butter for softened butter in one of my favorite cookie recipes. What a disaster—my cookies turned out flat and mushy and fell apart! I quickly learned that shortcuts aren't always a great idea when baking. I'll share some of my funny and memorable lessons with you so you can hopefully learn from my mistakes, which, by the way, weren't so funny at the time.

This book will help you learn lessons for baking success, as well as many baking tricks and tips along the way that might surprise your older family members, as well! Get ready to:

- Explore your kitchen and learn what baking tools, appliances, bakeware, cookware, and pantry items can really help make you a baking pro.

- Master baking skills such as how to measure ingredients, mix and fold, cream butter and sugar, create perfect dough, and melt chocolate, so you'll be ready to move onto more advanced baking recipes in no time.

- Discover a world of sweet and savory baking recipes you can try, from basic to more advanced delicacies, as well as classics to new favorites.

Let's get baking—you'll soon see it's "a piece of cake!"

PART ONE

welcome to baking school!

1

in the baker's kitchen

Your mouth may be watering with the idea of yummy baked goods, but first, let's make sure you have everything you need in your kitchen to get started, including basic baking equipment, ingredients, and some general rules and tips to get you prepared and keep you safe. I'm also sharing some of my favorite baking gear and tool ideas, and I hope you'll discover some of your own favorites, as you begin to explore the joys of baking.

KITCHEN RULES

Rules aren't fun, but these few simple rules will keep you safe and avoid another irksome fate—unnecessary cleanup! Here's a quick list of things to keep in mind before you start baking.

1. **Check in with an adult.** Before you start baking, check in with an adult. It's a good idea for someone to know what you're doing and where you are, especially in case of an emergency.

2. **Wash hands.** Every good chef makes a habit of washing their hands with warm soapy water before getting started in the kitchen, and then again before and after handling raw meat (and of course when their hands get messy while baking). I realize that it's tough to resist licking frosting off your fingers; just make sure you're done handling the food before you reward yourself with that treat!

3. **Prepare a chef-worthy work area.** Find a counter or table that has plenty of room to work at and to hold your ingredients and tools. Give the area a quick cleaning with a warm soapy sponge and dry with a clean towel.

4. **Wash ingredients.** Washing and drying any fresh fruit or vegetables will get rid of some of the dirt, germs, and chemicals used in farming. Some produce might require scrubbing the dirt off with a soft brush.

> **KID CHEF TIP:** Keep baking soda nearby, as it can also serve as a fire extinguisher. Pouring baking soda on a small oven fire can smother the blaze.

5. **Prep like a pro.** Give your recipe a quick read through and make sure you understand all the steps in the recipe. Ensure that you have everything you need by gathering your ingredients, bakeware, and tools. This is known as *mise en place* (pronounced MEEZ ahn plahs), French for "everything in its place."

6. **Clean as you go.** I hate cleaning, too, but if you keep your work area clean as you go, it will mean less cleanup when you're done baking.

7. **Be prepared for an emergency.** Talk with an adult about what to do in case of a fire or an emergency in the kitchen. It's good to know where the fire extinguisher is located and how to use it, just in case it's needed.

BAKER'S PANTRY

Your pantry is where the ingredients await! And the first rule of thumb for delicious baked goods: start with quality ingredients. It's important to have the right ingredients, but it's just as important that your ingredients are fresh and of the best quality. In some cases, you can substitute ingredients when you don't have the right thing, but sometimes substituting ingredients in baked goods can have disappointing results. Here are some common ingredients used in many baking recipes.

Baking Powder

This powder is a leavening agent—it makes baked goods rise. Store this in a dry, dark, cool place. You can check the expiration date, but it should usually be replaced every six to twelve months. Here's a fun experiment to test if baking powder is still good: Stir about 1 teaspoon baking powder into 1/3 cup hot water. If the mixture produces a lot of bubbles, the baking powder is still good to use.

Baking Soda

Similar to baking powder, baking soda is a leavening agent used to make baked goods rise. Baking soda and baking powder are not the same and can't be substituted for one another. Unlike baking powder, baking soda needs an acid in the recipe to make it work. You can check the expiration date, but baking soda also needs to be replaced every six to twelve months. A fun way to test if baking soda is still good: Stir about 1 teaspoon of baking soda into 1/3 cup of something acidic, such as lemon juice or vinegar. If the mixture produces lots of bubbles, the baking soda is still good to use.

Butter

Butter is used in many baking recipes. There are two main types of butter, unsalted and salted. Most baking recipes will call for unsalted butter, so you can control the amount of salt by adding it separately. Check your recipe to see if the butter should be cold, softened to room temperature, or melted. Don't substitute one for another, even if you're in a hurry. Also, don't substitute margarine or oil for butter unless the recipe says it's okay. Butter can be kept at room temperature for a short amount of time, but generally should be kept refrigerated.

Chocolate

This wildly popular delicacy comes in many types: unsweetened, dark, bittersweet, and semisweet are some of the most common. Unsweetened chocolate (which doesn't taste so great by itself) usually comes in bar form, while dark, bittersweet, and semisweet can be found as chips or bars. Unsweetened cocoa powder is called for in some baking recipes. This is a powder and contains no sugar. Chocolate lasts for a long time, but for best results, it should be stored in a dry, dark, cool place. Storing chocolate in the fridge is not recommended because the chocolate may "bloom," forming a gray film on the outside caused by the cocoa butter separating from the chocolate. It's safe to eat, but not so pretty to look at!

Cream and Milk

Whipped cream, made from cream, is a yummy and festive addition over many baked goods. If you're not familiar with cream, look out for the different types of cream next time you're in the grocery store. Heavy cream is the richest type of liquid cream, made up of at least 36 percent fat. Whipping cream has a fat content between 30 and 36 percent. Heavy cream and whipping cream should both be stored in the refrigerator. Either can be used in most cases, but whipping heavy cream will result in a more stable, slightly thicker whipped cream.

Milk also comes in different fat contents. Whole milk is the highest in fat, followed by 2 percent, 1 percent, and then skim (fat-free). When baking with milk, a higher fat content milk will result in a moister and finer-textured baked good.

With both cream and milk, check the expiration date on the container before using; a sniff test will also tell you if your dairy is past its freshness. In general, both cream and milk should be used within two weeks of opening.

SEASONAL FOOD CHOICES

There's a good reason apple pie is associated with fall: apples are simply at their best, so crispy and juicy! This formula holds true for all kinds of baked goods—everything has its season. Whenever possible, use fresh fruits and vegetables in your baked goods. You can sometimes substitute frozen or canned, but for best results, there's nothing like fresh produce, and especially when it's in season. When choosing fresh produce, look for fruits and vegetables that are ripe and free of wrinkles and blemishes. Most produce can be found in grocery stores year-round, but here's a quick list of some popular baking produce and their peak seasons throughout the year.

FALL
- Apples
- Bananas
- Cranberries
- Pears
- Pineapple
- Pumpkins
- Sweet Potatoes

WINTER
- Bananas
- Lemons
- Pears
- Sweet potatoes

SPRING
- Apricots
- Bananas
- Mangos
- Pineapple
- Rhubarb
- Strawberries

SUMMER
- Apricots
- Bananas
- Blackberries
- Blueberries
- Cherries
- Peaches
- Plums
- Raspberries
- Strawberries
- Zucchini

Eggs

Eggs add so much to baked goods, including richness, color, strength, and structure. Eggs come in different sizes (medium, large, X-large, jumbo, etc.) and colors (brown and white). The standard egg size for most baking recipes is large unless otherwise directed. Egg color does not matter—white and brown eggs can be used interchangeably. Eggs may also be pasteurized or unpasteurized. Unpasteurized eggs may contain bacteria, so they should never be consumed raw. Use pasteurized eggs for any recipe in which the eggs are not fully cooked. Store eggs in the refrigerator and check the expiration date on the egg carton before using.

KID CHEF TIP: Check an egg's freshness with a float test. Place the egg in a container of cold water. If the egg lies at the bottom on its side, it's really fresh. If it stands in the bottom, it's still fresh enough to use. If it floats to the top, it's no longer fresh enough to eat.

Flour

Flour is not just flour anymore! Many types of flour are sold today including all-purpose (bleached or unbleached), bread, cake, and whole-wheat, as well as specialty flours such as almond, coconut, etc., which are not made of grains. The type of flour to use is usually stated in the recipe (this cookbook mostly calls for all-purpose flour), and other types shouldn't be used interchangeably unless the recipe specifies it's okay.

Sifting flour (running the flour through a sieve or sifter) will break up any lumps and it also aerates (adds air to) the flour. This extra step is mostly unnecessary for everyday baking, but it can be helpful for delicate baked goods such as angel food and sponge cakes.

Flour should be stored in an airtight container in a dark, dry, cool place. Whole-grain flours, if not being used for a while, can be stored in the freezer to prolong shelf life and keep the oils from going bad.

Spices

Spices are fun because they add unique flavors and aromas to baked goods. These can remind us of holidays as they fill our homes with their delightful scents! Some of the most common spices used for baking include cinnamon, cloves, ginger, nutmeg, allspice, and even salt. There are also spice blends that are worth discovering and great for baking, such as apple pie and pumpkin pie spice. Many spices can be used interchangeably, but your baked treat will have a different taste depending on what you use. Ground dried spices may start to lose some of their flavor after about six months, but are still safe to use. Spices should be stored away from heat in a dry, dark, cool place.

Sugar

Like flour, sugar comes in many types, such as granulated, confectioners' (powdered), light and dark brown, and even some more exotic varieties like turbinado and muscovado. Granulated, powdered, and brown sugar are the most well-known and commonly used in everyday baking. Light and dark brown sugar can be used interchangeably, but dark brown sugar will give your baked goods a stronger molasses flavor. Sugar should be stored in airtight containers in a dry, dark, cool place.

Vanilla

Vanilla extract is great for everyday baking since it's a quick and easy way to add deeper flavor. Vanilla extract is made by infusing vanilla beans into alcohol—this is why vanilla extract smells great but tastes pretty terrible by itself! Vanilla beans can also be used. They are more expensive, but are great to use in recipes if you want a stronger vanilla flavor. Both vanilla extract and vanilla beans should be stored in a dry, dark, cool place.

BAKING EQUIPMENT

I'm going to share some of my favorite cookware, bakeware, tools, utensils, and small appliances with you. I've accumulated them over the years, but these are all good basics to start with on your way to becoming a baking pro. There is also a world of cool specialty bakeware items and equipment that are fun and unique, but the following items will help you get started.

COOKWARE AND BAKEWARE

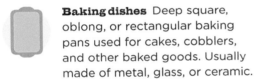 **Baking dishes** Deep square, oblong, or rectangular baking pans used for cakes, cobblers, and other baked goods. Usually made of metal, glass, or ceramic.

Baking sheets Large, flat, rectangular metal pans (preferably rimmed to avoid dripping) for baking cookies, pastries, biscuits, and other baked goods. Baking sheets come in full, three-quarter, half, and quarter sizes. I prefer the half size (13-by-18-inch) for most baking jobs, and it fits most conventional ovens.

Cake pans Round metal pans normally used to bake cakes. They may also be used to bake other things that cook snugly together, such as cinnamon rolls.

 Double boiler Two saucepans fitted together with boiling water in the bottom pan. Typically used for melting chocolate, as well as making custards and some sauces. (See Make Your Own Double Boiler, page 53.)

 Loaf pans Deep, narrow, rectangular pans generally used to bake—you guessed it—breads and loaf cakes. Loaf pans can be made out of metal, glass, or ceramic, and your results may vary depending on the type of loaf pan you use.

 Muffin pans Baking pans with built-in cups, primarily for making muffins and cupcakes, but sometimes even cookies. Usually made out of metal or silicone, these come in different sizes, including mini, standard, and jumbo.

 Pie pans Round baking pans made out of metal, glass, or ceramic. Generally used to make pies and quiches, but may also be used for other baked goods.

 Ramekins Small dishes made out of ceramic or sometimes glass. Used for making individual portions.

Skillet A shallow metal pan with many uses, including cooking food on the stovetop or baking in the oven. Cast-iron skillets are my personal favorite because they retain heat well and can be used both on the stovetop and in the oven. They are, however, pretty heavy.

 Tube pan A deep, metal, circular-shaped baking pan with a hole in the middle. Mostly used to bake cakes such as angel food and coffee cakes.

TOOLS & UTENSILS

 Cookie cutters You can find cookie cutters in almost every theme, from holidays to animals. Besides all the fun shapes and sizes out there, round and square cookie cutters in various sizes come in handy for cutting out cookies, pastries, and even biscuits.

 Grater A tool with many small blades on its surface. Used for shredding cheese, vegetables, and other foods.

 Measuring cups Cups of various sizes used to measure liquid or dry ingredients.

 Measuring spoons Spoons of various sizes used to measure small amounts of liquid or dry ingredients.

 Mixing bowls Bowls of different sizes, used to mix and combine ingredients together.

 Pastry brush A small, flat brush used for jobs like brushing butter or eggs onto baked goods, or brushing crumbs off cakes before frosting.

 Pastry cutter A tool, generally made of narrow metal strips attached to a handle, used to mix or "cut" butter or shortening into flour to make biscuits, pie crusts, and pastry dough. (See Cutting in Butter, page 42.)

 Peeler A small kitchen tool with a sharp blade that peels skin off vegetables or fruit.

 Rolling pin A long cylinder-shaped kitchen tool with handles, used for rolling out dough for cookies, pies, and pizza.

 Spatula A flat, handled kitchen utensil that comes in a variety of shapes and sizes. Used for spreading and mixing, or lifting baked goods. Heat-resistant spatulas are best for baking.

Spring-loaded scoops A utensil with a trigger release that is perfect for scooping equal-sized measurements of batter and dough for such things as cookies, cupcakes, and muffins. It's nice to have a small and large one.

 Whisk A kitchen utensil with wire loops held together by a handle, used for beating, whipping, or mixing ingredients.

 Wooden spoon A strong spoon perfect for scraping and mixing in ingredients that can't be beaten in with an electric mixer.

 Zester A sharp kitchen utensil used to take the zest off citrus fruit or grate whole spices.

APPLIANCES

 Blender An electric appliance with a tall glass or plastic container that has sharp blades at the bottom, used to purée, chop, or mix foods. A great tool to make quick fruit sauces for baked goods.

 Food processor An electric appliance with a holding canister and interchangeable blades, used for slicing, shredding, and chopping. Useful for quickly mixing dough and chopping nuts, cookies, and crackers into crumbs.

 Hand mixer A small handheld electric appliance with a set of rotating beaters. Used to beat, whip, and mix ingredients. Great for more control and speed in beating your ingredients.

 Stand mixer An electric appliance with a mixer over a bowl on a platform that comes with a variety of attachments, such as beaters, dough hooks, spatulas, and whisks for hands-free mixing. Great choice for recipes that require long mixing times.

KNIVES AND OTHER SHARP TOOLS

To make your work easier, you'll need a few good knives and sharp tools in your kitchen. It's helpful to know the best uses for different types of knives, as well as other sharp tools such as graters and peelers. Good kitchen tools can make things quicker and easier in the kitchen, but discuss their use with an adult beforehand, and then use caution when handling.

KID CHEF TIP: Place a damp cloth or towel under your cutting board to prevent it from sliding while cutting.

Know Your Knives

There are four types of knife that will help you with your baking. Each one has a special use, and you will find that using the right knife can make your job easier.

- **Butter knife** A small knife with a blunt-edge blade. Great to use for slicing soft food or spreading foods such as peanut butter, butter, cream cheese, etc.

- **Chef's knife** An all-purpose knife with a large, sharp, straight-edge blade. Used for a wide variety of purposes such as chopping, dicing, and slicing food.

- **Paring knife** A small knife with a sharp, straight blade. Generally used for peeling and coring food. Also good for finely cutting small amounts of food such as fresh fruits, vegetables, and herbs.

- **Serrated knife** A knife with a sharp saw-like edge. Typically used to slice through bread. Smaller versions can also be used to slice through such food as tomatoes and pineapple.

CUTTING STYLES

A   **Chop.** To cut food into small, similar-sized pieces. Chopped food should be uniform in size and may be finely chopped (small pieces) or coarsely chopped (larger pieces), depending on the recipe.

B   **Dice.** To cut food into small cubes. Size may vary but generally from about ¼-inch to ¾-inch in diameter.

C   **Julienne.** To cut food into long thin uniform sized strips, like matchsticks.

D   **Mince.** To cut food into very small similar sized pieces and smaller than chopped food.

E   **Slice.** To cut food into thin pieces that are similar thickness.

How to Use a Knife

Learning how to hold and use a knife can take some practice. If you're just starting out, ask an adult to help you get started and demonstrate how to hold and use a knife properly.

- **Choose the right knife for the job.** Different knives have different jobs (see Know Your Knives, page 14), so be sure you have the correct size and shape when starting.

- **Use two hands.** Are you a righty or a lefty? Your dominant hand should hold the knife, while your less dominant hand carefully holds the food in place.

- **Hold the knife based on its size.** For larger knives, wrap your fingers around the handle, curling your pointer finger up against the blade for better control. For smaller knives, wrap your fingers around the handle, and if it helps, place your pointer finger on top of the knife for better control.

KNIFE SAFETY

- **Sharpen knives.** Does your home have a knife sharpener? Sharpening knives ensures easy food preparation and can even prevent accidents such as knives slipping while cutting.

- **Use a cutting board.** Don't hold food in your hands while you try to cut it. A cutting board will help prevent the knife from slipping while cutting, and of course, you want the knife to connect with the board—not with your skin!

- **Watch your fingers.** Keep your fingers tucked in and focus on what you're doing to prevent injuries.

- **Carry and store knives correctly.** Carry knives by the handle with the tip down and blade facing away from you and others. Knives should be stored in a knife rack or knife drawer.

- **Keep your knives clean.** Make sure your knives are clean and handles are dry and free from anything greasy. Take care not to leave knives in the sink or where someone could grab them accidentally.

- **Read what size to cut.** Check the recipe to see what needs to be chopped, minced, or sliced (see Cutting Styles, page 15).

- **Watch your fingers!** When you're slicing, tuck in your fingers and place your knuckles against the knife to steer it. Keep your hands and fingers stable to make even slices, and call on a grown-up to help if you need assistance—hard foods like carrots can be tough to cut through.

USING THE STOVE

Every stove is a little different. If you are unsure how to use your specific stove, ask an adult or parent for help—they will probably be able to tell you more about your stove. Gas (which have a stovetop flame) and electric stoves (which have a coil or surface that turns red hot) are also a little different from each other in the way they cook.

Always make sure your stovetop is clean before you turn it on. A dirty stovetop with grease or leftover food can start a fire. It's also best to place your pot or pan on the burner before lighting or turning it on.

Heat for the stovetop is usually controlled by a knob or digital panel on your stove for each specific burner. Heat can range between low (or 1) and high (or 10). Gas stoves have pilot lights, which are flames that burn continuously under the surface of the stovetop. To light the burner, turn the knob to "light" until you hear a clicking sound and see a flame. Now you can adjust the heat. If the gas burner doesn't light right away, turn it off for a few moments so you don't let gas escape—this can cause a fire and release harmful carbon monoxide.

Whether you have a gas or electric stove, there are some safety tips that even the most seasoned chefs follow:

- Make sure handles from pots and pans are always facing in, and not over the edge of the stove, where someone can accidentally knock them over or smaller children can grab them.

- Know where the fire extinguisher is kept. If you put water on a grease fire, it can get bigger and spread, so when in doubt, use a fire extinguisher or even baking soda if needed.

- Use sturdy oven mitts or potholders to prevent burns when handling or working with hot pans and pots. Also use mitts or potholders when stirring with metal spoons or utensils—they can quickly heat up when in contact with something hot.

- Pull your hair back, and make sure you are not wearing any loose clothing, long sleeves, or jewelry that may catch fire or get caught.

- Don't get distracted! Even the best chefs have learned from experience—never leave a pan unattended on the stove. Keep an eye on whatever you are cooking.

USING THE OVEN

Just like stovetops, every oven can be a little different depending on age, model, and type. There are two major types: conventional and convection. A conventional oven is designed with two heating elements: one for baking and one for broiling. A convection oven uses circulating hot, dry air to create a more even heat and faster baking times, and is generally used for baked items. The times and temperatures in these recipes are designed for conventional ovens, so if you're using a convection oven, you may need to adjust your baking temperature and/or time for many of the recipes.

Before you use the oven, do a quick inspection to make sure the inside of your oven is clean and nothing has been left inside such as pans, food, or anything that could catch fire or burn. After your inspection, adjust the oven racks to wherever you would like them. Typically, placing your rack in the middle of the oven, and placing the pan in the middle of that rack results in the most even heat. However, if you need to put more than one pan in the oven and need more than one rack, you can place two oven racks equally apart and, if you wish, rotate pans halfway through baking for more even cooking and browning.

When you're ready to turn on the oven, look at the panel on top of the stove. Many ovens now have a digital panel. Either way, enter or turn

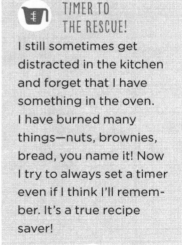

TIMER TO THE RESCUE!

I still sometimes get distracted in the kitchen and forget that I have something in the oven. I have burned many things—nuts, brownies, bread, you name it! Now I try to always set a timer even if I think I'll remember. It's a true recipe saver!

the dial to the desired temperature, and fully preheat your oven before placing your baked goods inside. After you place your baked goods in the oven, use a timer to remind you to check on your food—it's easy to forget something's baking!

Every oven is different. Baking and cooking times listed in a recipe are reasonable suggestions, but can vary by a few minutes or more. For best results, keep an eye on what you're baking and check on it every few minutes.

Don't worry if you need to bake things a little less or a little longer on occasion than what is suggested in the recipe. However, if you feel that your oven always seems to be baking things much quicker or slower than it should, an inexpensive oven thermometer will allow you to double-check that your oven is heating correctly.

Just like when using the stovetop, a few basic safety guidelines can prevent oven fires and accidents:

- Know where a fire extinguisher is stored (or baking soda).

- Stand back when opening the door to a hot oven. The steamy air coming out of the oven can be quite hot.

- Make sure no small children are nearby when opening the oven.

- Use oven mitts or potholders whenever placing pans in the oven or taking them out.

- Keep pans and food away from the heating elements in the oven. If things are too close to the heating elements, they can catch fire.

- Make sure anything you put in the oven, such as pots, pans, paper liners, etc., are oven-safe for use at high temperatures.

- Be careful when dealing with hot objects in the kitchen. Good oven mitts are essential so you don't burn yourself, but also use caution when placing hot objects on other surfaces like countertops, tables, or surfaces that may crack, stain, etc.

MY BAKER'S DOZEN TIPS

A baker's dozen is 13. If you're in a bakery that offers a baker's dozen, that means you'll get one free when you order 12 of something. That said, here are 13 of my overall top tips to help you become a baking pro!

1 **Buy the freshest and best quality ingredients you can.** The better the ingredients, the better your results will be. It makes sense—if you're starting with ingredients that don't taste good, your baked goods won't taste good either!

2 **Start with easy recipes.** Begin with ones that you are comfortable with, and then step up to recipes that are a little bit more challenging each time you bake.

3 **Read through the recipe before starting.** Make sure you understand every step and have all the ingredients, bakeware, and tools needed to complete the recipe.

4 **Ask questions.** If you don't understand the recipe or how to do something directed in the recipe, ask an adult for help.

5 **Find a work area that has plenty of room.** Clean your hands and your work area before starting, and keep the area clean as you go.

6 **Put safety first.** Practice good safety skills and keep an eye on what you're doing to prevent accidents and fires.

7 **Get organized.** Remember *mise en place*, "everything in its place?" It's a great skill to practice—pretend you're on a cooking show! Get all your ingredients, bakeware, and tools in order before starting. Prep all your ingredients so you're ready to go.

10 **Be watchful.** Cooking times can vary so keep an eye on things. Look for visual clues like browning or bubbling, or try inserting a toothpick into the middle of some baked goods, like brownies or cakes, to see if they're done.

11 **Use a timer.** Let it help remind you when to check on what you're baking.

12 **Don't get frustrated.** If things don't turn out quite as you planned, take a deep breath. It's okay, mishaps will occur—remember my mushy cookie story? Learn from what went wrong, and try again.

13 **Have fun!** Baking should be an enjoyable adventure!

8 **Be cautious when substituting ingredients.** Baking is a science. Not all ingredients can be substituted for others with similar results. Sometimes an Internet search will offer suggestions for a reasonable substitution, but the results will vary depending on what you're making.

9 **Measure with care.** Take your time and look at your measuring cup with a level eye. An inaccurate measurement can mean the difference between yum and yuck!

2

baking skills

Now that you have done inventory of your basic cookware, bakeware, utensils, and tools, let's discuss how you can use some of them. There is definitely some science and chemistry involved with baked goods— remember those fun experiments to see if your baking soda and powder are still good? You'll be prepared to make perfectly baked goods after we explore some basic techniques, such as how to measure ingredients, cream butter and sugar, melt chocolate, and more!

THE BASICS

Before we get to mixing and baking, it's good to know a few basics. One of the most important things to know is how to measure liquid and dry ingredients. It's also good to know other tricks, such as preparing different temperatures of butter, greasing a pan, and knowing when your baked goods are done.

Measuring Liquids

Transparent measuring cups are best to use for larger amounts of liquids; measuring spoons work for smaller amounts. Pour liquids directly into the measuring cup and place on a flat surface such as your counter. Here's the trick: To check your measurement, be sure to bend down and look at the liquid at eye level. Looking from below or above can result in a miscalculation. When using measuring spoons, fill the spoon until it's level and flat all the way across.

Measuring Dry Ingredients

The most accurate method for measuring dry ingredients is by using a scale and measuring by weight, not volume, especially for flour. However, most recipes call for measuring by volume (including those in this book). Use dry measuring cups for larger amounts of dry ingredients, and measuring spoons for smaller amounts. Dry measuring cups are typically opaque (not transparent) and made of metal or plastic.

To measure flour, lightly spoon the flour directly into the measuring cup. Using the flat side of a butter knife, gently scrape the excess off so the flour is level with the measuring cup.

Brown sugar is usually measured by packing the brown sugar into the measuring cup tightly, unless otherwise noted. You can press it down so it's level, or with the flat side of a butter knife, gently scrape off the excess to make it level.

For most other dry ingredients, you can use the measuring cup to scoop up the ingredients and shake it a bit until level with the measuring cup.

KID CHEF TIP: For sticky liquids such as honey or molasses, spray your measuring cup or spoon with a little nonstick spray before measuring to keep the liquid from sticking. It should pour right out into your mixing bowl.

Melting or Softening Butter

When using butter, check to see if the recipe calls for cold, melted, or room-temperature softened butter. They should not be used interchangeably.

- **Melted.** Butter can be melted in a small saucepan on the stove, or in the microwave in a microwave-safe container lightly covered to prevent spattering—you won't want to clean *that* up!

- **Softened.** For room-temperature butter, let the butter sit on the counter for at least a half hour, or until it's soft to the touch. Some microwaves even have a "soften" setting.

- **Cold.** Leave the butter in the fridge until ready to use. Most times, you'll need to cut the butter into small cubes if using it cold.

Greasing a Pan

Recipes generally call for either a greased or ungreased pan. Depending on your pan, how you grease it may vary. Nonstick and silicone bakeware do not usually need to be greased. For other pans, there are several options. You can lightly spray the pan with a nonstick spray. You can lightly spread some room-temperature butter or shortening on the pan with a paper towel. Or you can line the pan with parchment paper or nonstick foil. Greasing or lining a pan keeps cookies and biscuits from sticking to the pan and makes baked goods such as cakes, bars, and brownies easier to remove.

Some recipes, such as cakes and brownies, may direct you to butter *and* flour the pan. First, grease the pan with butter or shortening on a paper towel. Then lightly spoon some flour over the pan and gently shake it around until it's well coated. Turn the pan upside down over a sink and lightly tap the pan on the sink to remove excess flour.

KID CHEF TIP:
DO: If you're making a chocolate baked good, you can add a little cocoa powder to the flour, before flouring the pan. **DON'T:** When making Angel Food Cake (page 90), don't grease the pan. The cake needs to stick to the sides in order to rise!

very berry granola bars

PREP TIME: 20 minutes

COOK TIME: 34 minutes

YIELD: 8 bars

TOOLS/EQUIPMENT

- 8-inch square baking pan
- Parchment paper or aluminum foil
- Large saucepan

⅓ cup unsalted butter

⅓ cup honey

2 tablespoons brown sugar

1 teaspoon vanilla extract

¼ teaspoon table salt

2 cups quick rolled oats

½ cup chopped almonds (see Pro Tip)

¾ cup chopped dried chewy fruit

Preheat the oven to 350°F.

Line an 8-by-8-inch square baking pan, including sides, with parchment paper or aluminum foil.

Melt the butter and sugar.

In a large saucepan over medium heat, heat the butter, honey, brown sugar, vanilla, and salt. Cook 3 to 4 minutes, stirring occasionally, until blended and smooth.

Add the oats.

Remove the pan from the heat. Add the oats, almonds, and dried fruit to the pan, stirring to combine.

Bake the bars.

Spoon the mixture into the prepared pan. With the back of a fork, firmly press down on the mixture to form an even layer in the pan. Bake for 25 to 30 minutes, or until brown and toasted.

Cool and cut the bars.

Remove the pan from the oven. Press firmly again on the mixture with the back of a fork. Cool completely overnight, covered. Remove from pan and cut into bars.

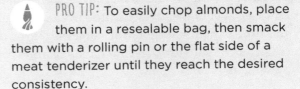 **PRO TIP:** To easily chop almonds, place them in a resealable bag, then smack them with a rolling pin or the flat side of a meat tenderizer until they reach the desired consistency.

CRACKING AND SEPARATING EGGS

If you've never cracked an egg, it's a great skill to practice since so many recipes require eggs. There are several methods that can be used to crack eggs—even one-handed, if you practice! Some recipes may also call for egg whites and/or egg yolks, so learning how to separate eggs is also an egg-ceptional skill for any young chef.

Room-Temperature Eggs

It's usually best to crack and separate eggs straight out of the fridge, while the eggs are still cold. After you crack or separate your eggs into a bowl, let them sit on the counter for about a half hour to reach room temperature. Room-temperature eggs and egg whites will become a little fluffier when whipped, so if you have the time, test whipping room-temperature eggs versus cold ones and see if you notice a difference.

Cracking Eggs

There are several popular ways to crack an egg. One way is to crack it on the side of a bowl. Separate the shell at the crack and pour the egg into a bowl. Another method is to tap the egg gently on a flat, hard surface to crack the egg and then pour the egg into a bowl.

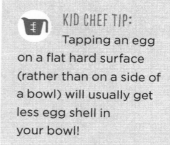

KID CHEF TIP: Tapping an egg on a flat hard surface (rather than on a side of a bowl) will usually get less egg shell in your bowl!

It's also a good idea to crack your eggs over a separate bowl, rather than over a mixing bowl containing other ingredients. It's easier to get the shell out of a little bowl with nothing else in it than from a mixing bowl with other ingredients. To remove the shell, you can use a small spoon or fork, or wet your finger with a little water and pull the shell pieces out. With a little patience, it should all come out. If you use your finger to get the shell out, be sure to wash your hands again so you don't get bacteria on your hands.

Separating Eggs

Some recipes may require just egg whites or egg yolks, rather than the whole egg. You can use specialty tools to separate eggs, but it's a fun trick to just use the egg shell. Here's how: Start with cold eggs because they are easier to separate. Crack the egg in the middle of the shell, then gently open the egg over a bowl, letting the yolk rest in one side of the shell while the whites drip over the edge of the shell into the bowl. Gently transfer the yolk back and forth between the two shells until the white is completely in the bowl. If you need more whites or yolks, use an additional bowl to keep the successful white or yolks while you continue separating the rest. Avoid separating an egg over the bowl of ingredients, just in case the yolk breaks and mixes with the white—that can mess up your recipe!

Tempering Eggs

When adding warm liquid to eggs, you'll need to "temper" the eggs. Tempering eggs means to raise the temperature of beaten eggs so they don't curdle (cook) when warm ingredients are added. You don't want pieces of scrambled eggs in your baked goods! To temper your eggs, slowly add the warm liquid to the beaten eggs in a bowl while stirring or whisking continuously.

LESSON 2 RECIPE TUTORIAL
little meringue clouds

PREP TIME: 15 minutes

COOK TIME: 2 hours (plus 2 hours left in oven)

YIELD: 24 clouds

TOOLS/EQUIPMENT

- 2 baking sheets
- Parchment paper
- Stand mixer (or hand mixer and a large bowl)

4 large egg whites, at room temperature

½ teaspoon cream of tartar

¼ teaspoon table salt

1 cup confectioners' sugar

TROUBLESHOOTING TIP:
If your meringues turned brown, use an oven thermometer to double-check that your oven temperature is correct. If it's off, you may need to reduce your cooking temperature next time and peek through with the oven light on to keep an eye on things.

Preheat the oven to 200°F.

But first, move one oven rack to the upper third of the oven, and the other to the lower third. Line 2 baking sheets with parchment paper.

Beat the egg whites.

In a bowl, add the egg whites, cream of tartar, and salt. With a mixer, blend on medium until the whites start getting foamy, 1 to 2 minutes. Increase the speed to medium-high and continue beating until the egg whites become thick and opaque, 1 to 2 additional minutes.

Add the sugar.

With the mixer on medium-high, slowly add the confectioners' sugar to the bowl, about 1 tablespoon at a time. Continue beating until the egg whites are shiny and stiff peaks form, 4 to 6 minutes.

Bake the meringues.

Using a small spoon, transfer little mounds of the egg white mixture onto the baking sheets, leaving about 2 inches between clouds. Using the back of a spoon, shape meringues into little clouds by making indentations and peaks into meringues. Bake for 2 hours. Turn the oven off and let the clouds remain in the oven for an additional 1 to 2 hours, or until dry and crispy.

MIXING AND FOLDING

There are many ways to combine ingredients, including mixing, beating, creaming, folding, and more. Does it really matter which you use? Well, sometimes it does and sometimes it doesn't. When in doubt, follow the recipe before experimenting with something different.

Following Mixing Instructions

When it comes to mixing, a good rule of thumb is to follow a recipe exactly the first time. The second time, you might choose to experiment a little so you can compare your results to the first time. Here are some basic mixing terms:

Beat: Combining the ingredients using a stand or electric hand mixer, or whisking by hand until well combined.

Cream: Some recipes will call for "creaming" the butter and sugar together. Creaming is combining a fat such as butter or shortening with sugar. It helps give structure to baked goods such as cakes, cookies, and pastries and helps them rise. It's easiest to do this with a stand mixer or electric hand mixer.

Fold: Folding is used for delicate ingredients, when you don't want to deflate air already whipped into the ingredients. See a detailed explanation of how to fold on the next page.

Stir: Stirring is a general term for hand-mixing ingredients, best done with a spoon or rubber spatula. It's a good and simple technique when you don't need to incorporate air into the ingredients.

Whip: Whipping is used for things such as cream and egg whites, when you want to add air into the ingredient(s). It's usually easiest to use a stand mixer or electric hand mixer, but you can also use a whisk for whipping. You may see the terms soft, medium, or stiff/firm peaks when whipping cream or egg whites. With whipping, when you stop beating and hold the beater upside down, soft peaks will flop over, medium peaks will hold their shape but curl a bit at the tip, and stiff/firm peaks will stand straight up.

Mixing Wet and Dry Ingredients Separately

For some baked goods, such as muffins and quick breads, you should mix the wet and dry ingredients separately before combining. In one bowl, mix together the wet ingredients until well combined. In another bowl, place the dry ingredients (see image A). Mix them until the ingredients are evenly spread out. Push the dry ingredients to the sides of the bowl to make a "well," and pour the wet ingredients into the middle (see image B). Mix the dry and wet ingredients together until just combined, being careful not to overmix (see image C).

Overmixing can cause:

- some baked goods, such as cookies, to over-aerate, which means they will rise then collapse when baked.

- too much gluten development. Too much gluten can cause cookies, muffins, cakes, and breads to be tough and chewier than you want.

- cold butter and shortening bits to become too small and warm, causing pastries, biscuits, scones, and pie dough to be less tender and flaky.

To avoid overmixing, combine ingredients until they are just mixed together and no streaks of ingredients remain, unless your recipe directs you otherwise. Do the minimum amount of mixing to blend ingredients, and don't continue mixing for long periods of time unless instructed to do so. For some baked goods such as muffins and quick breads, lumps in the batter are okay, even good.

Folding

Sometimes, delicate ingredients such as whipped egg whites or whipped cream must be "folded" into other ingredients. Folding is used to carefully combine ingredients without removing the air from the mixture. Rubber spatulas and large spoons are generally best for folding. With a gentle hand, add the lighter mixture (such as the whipped egg whites or cream) into the heavier mixture (such as cooled melted chocolate). Gently run the spatula or spoon around the side of the bowl, then along the bottom of the bowl, then fold the mixture onto itself. Rotate the bowl about 90 degrees, and repeat until the ingredients are just combined.

cinnamon buttermilk muffins

PREP TIME: 20 minutes

COOK TIME: 25 minutes

YIELD: 12 muffins

TOOLS/EQUIPMENT

- Muffin pan
- Paper liners (optional)
- 2 medium bowls
- Whisk
- Wire rack

FOR THE MUFFINS

Butter, for greasing the pan
  (optional)

Flour, for dusting the pan
  (optional)

2½ cups all-purpose flour

1 cup granulated sugar

2 teaspoons baking soda

1 teaspoon cinnamon plus
  ½ teaspoon cinnamon, divided

½ teaspoon table salt

¾ cup buttermilk

½ cup vegetable or canola oil

3 large eggs, at room temperature

2 teaspoons vanilla extract

FOR THE TOPPING

2 tablespoons granulated sugar

½ teaspoon cinnamon

Preheat the oven to 375˚F.
Grease and lightly flour a 12-cup muffin pan, or line with paper liners.

Mix the dry ingredients.
In a medium bowl, stir together the flour, 1 cup of granulated sugar, baking soda, 1 teaspoon cinnamon, and salt.

Mix the wet ingredients.
In another medium bowl, whisk together the buttermilk, oil, eggs, and vanilla until well blended.

Combine the ingredients.
Make a well in the dry mixture, and then pour the wet mixture into the middle. Mix until just combined. Some small lumps are okay.

Make the topping.
In a small bowl, mix together the 2 tablespoons granulated sugar and the remaining ½ teaspoon cinnamon until blended.

Bake the muffins.
Spoon the batter into the muffin cups about ⅔ full. Sprinkle the cinnamon sugar topping on top. Bake for 20 to 25 minutes, or until a toothpick inserted into the middle of a muffin comes out clean. Cool slightly, then remove the muffins from the pan and cool on a wire rack.

TRY INSTEAD: For a crunchier topping, substitute an equal amount of turbinado sugar in the topping for the granulated sugar.

CREAMING BUTTER AND SUGAR

Learning how to cream butter and sugar will help you produce delicious baked goods. Creaming is combining a fat (such as butter or shortening) with sugar. Creaming helps baked goods rise, resulting in a light, fluffy texture.

Using an Electric Mixer

The best way to cream butter (or shortening) and sugar is to use a stand mixer or electric hand mixer. Here's how: Place room-temperature butter in a bowl, and beat on low speed until the butter is smooth, 10 to 20 seconds. Slowly add the sugar, and beat on medium speed. Scrape the sides of the bowl with a rubber spatula as needed to make sure everything is well mixed. It should take 2 to 5 minutes of beating to get the right texture. The butter and sugar mixture should be a pale yellow color, fluffy and smooth.

Getting the Right Texture

When creaming butter and sugar, it's important to start with room-temperature butter to achieve the right texture. Butter should be left on the counter for at least a half hour or until soft before you start. You can tell it's ready if when you press a finger on the butter, it leaves a small indentation. Some microwaves also have a "soften" setting for butter, but be careful using it so you don't end up with melted butter and have to start over!

IS IT DONE YET? HOW TO TELL

You can check your baked goods for doneness by using some tests and even just looking. Your oven, altitude, and humidity can all affect baking time and results. Use your best judgment, but always check for doneness on the earlier side specified in the recipe, or even a few minutes before.

CAKES AND CUPCAKES

Insert a toothpick into the center of the cake. If it's done, the toothpick should come out clean or with a few crumbs. If there is liquid batter on the toothpick, continue baking a few minutes more.

A cooked cake usually has a golden-brown surface and edges, and the edges pull away from the sides of the pan. If you gently touch the cake in the center, the cake should spring back.

PIES AND TARTS

The crust should look golden brown and toasted.

Fruit pies should be bubbling in the center. I also like to use a toothpick and test the doneness of the fruit in pies like apple and pear. Fruit should be soft in the center.

Other pies, such as pumpkin, may appear slightly jiggly or undercooked in the center, but will firm up or "set" once cooled.

BREAD

Yeast breads should have a golden-brown crust and be pulling away from the sides of the pan. If you gently tap on it, it should make a hollow sound.

Quick breads (no yeast) should be golden brown and slightly darker around the edges, and be pulling away from the sides of the pan. If done, a toothpick or wooden skewer inserted into the middle will come out clean or with a few crumbs.

COOKIES

Fully baked cookies will be golden brown on the bottom when lifted gently with a spatula. Cookies actually continue cooking slightly after being removed from the oven, so try to remove them from the oven a bit on the earlier side, before they get overcooked.

LESSON 4 RECIPE TUTORIAL
vanilla cupcakes
WITH CHOCOLATE FUDGE FROSTING

PREP TIME: 30 minutes

COOK TIME: 25 minutes

YIELD: 12 cupcakes

TOOLS/EQUIPMENT

- Muffin pan
- Stand mixer (or hand mixer and large bowl)
- Medium bowl
- Paper liners (optional)

FOR THE CAKE

Butter, for greasing the pan (optional)

Flour, for dusting the pan (optional)

1 cup all-purpose flour

1 teaspoon baking powder

¼ teaspoon baking soda

¼ teaspoon table salt

⅓ cup unsalted butter, at room temperature

⅔ cup granulated sugar

1½ teaspoons vanilla extract

2 large eggs, at room temperature

⅓ cup milk (2 percent or whole)

FOR THE FROSTING

⅓ cup unsalted butter

⅔ cup unsweetened cocoa powder

3 cups confectioners' sugar

⅓ cup milk (2 percent or whole)

1 teaspoon vanilla extract

Preheat the oven to 350°F.
Grease and lightly flour a 12-cup muffin pan or line with paper liners.

Mix the dry ingredients.
In a medium bowl, stir together the flour, baking powder, baking soda, and salt.

Cream the butter and sugar.
In a large bowl, beat the ⅓ cup butter with an electric mixer on medium speed for about 10 seconds, or until smooth. Beat in the granulated sugar and 1½ teaspoons of vanilla until well blended and light and fluffy, about 2 minutes. Beat in the eggs, one at a time, beating after each egg is added.

Combine the cake ingredients.
Alternate adding the flour mixture and the ⅓ cup milk to the butter mixture, beating on low after adding each, until the batter is just combined.

Bake the cupcakes.
Spoon the batter into muffin cups about ½ full. Bake for 18 to 20 minutes, or until a toothpick inserted into the center comes out clean. Cool slightly, then transfer to a wire rack to finish cooling. »

Make the frosting.

In a small saucepan over medium heat, melt the remaining ⅓ cup butter. Add the cocoa powder and bring to a boil, stirring constantly. Pour the mixture into a medium bowl and cool completely. Beat in the confectioners' sugar with the electric mixer on medium speed. Beat in the ⅓ cup milk, a little at a time, until the frosting is a smooth, spreadable consistency, then beat in 1 teaspoon of vanilla.

Frost the cupcakes.

When cupcakes are completely cooled, frost with a spatula.

HELPFUL HINT: If the frosting seems too dry, add a little more milk and continue beating. If frosting appears too thin, stir in a little more confectioners' sugar.

DID YOU KNOW? Letting your eggs stand at room temperature for 30 minutes before using provides more volume to baked goods.

HOW TO FROST AND DECORATE

Frosting and decorating cakes and cupcakes can be a lot of fun, because you can use your imagination and be infinitely creative! But for starters, the easiest way to frost a cake or cupcake is with a butter knife. Scoop some frosting onto a cooled cake or cupcake and use your spatula or knife to cover the surface. Frosting a still-warm cake can result in excess crumbs or melted frosting.

Fondant—a thick paste resembling icing—as well as piping bags and tips are fun tools for decorating cakes and cupcakes. These techniques take some practice, but there are many great videos and tutorials on the Internet to help you get started with both methods.

You don't need to spend a lot of time decorating to get a wonderful result. You probably have some great toppings already sitting in your kitchen. Here are some fun items to use to decorate your cakes and cupcakes:

- Animal crackers
- Candy
- Cereal
- Chocolate chips
- Cookies
- Fruit
- Graham crackers, crushed
- Ice cream cones, crushed
- Mini marshmallows
- Melted chocolate
- Nuts, chopped
- Sprinkles

MAKING DOUGH

Pie and pastry dough can be very delicate to work with.
When I was younger, I had the hardest time getting my
pie crusts to taste good, look pretty, and not fall down the sides of the pan
when baked. It can take some time and practice to get the hang of it, but
once you get there, you'll be so proud of your masterpiece!

Cutting in Butter

For pie dough and other baked goods like biscuits and scones,
you'll first want to learn how to cut in the butter. "Cutting in" is
combining butter or another fat with flour. You can use a pastry
cutter, the back of a fork, or two knives for this process. Start
cutting cold butter into small cubes and place them over the
flour. Using one of the mentioned tools, crush or cut the butter
into the flour until the mixture is crumbly and reduced to small
pea-size bits. Having small bits of butter or other fat will create
small air pockets in the dough. This is what makes pastry light
and flaky. Be careful to not overmix and overwork the dough, or
you won't get those nice pockets of air and flaky crust.

You can also cut in butter using a food processor! Place a
steel blade in the food processor bowl. Add the flour, salt, butter,
and shortening, and pulse the food processor again and again
until pea-size crumbs form. With the food processor running, slowly add
the water, 1 tablespoon at a time, through the feed tube at the top until a
dough forms.

> **KID CHEF TIP:**
> Protect your
> oven from overflow!
> Even as an adult, I'm still
> learning and making
> mistakes. One time, I
> had a pie overflow so
> badly in the oven it
> made a huge mess! Now
> I always try to place my
> pies on rimmed baking
> sheets just in case.

Rolling Dough

Once your dough is combined, for pastry and pie crusts you'll want to
refrigerate the dough to allow the butter to get cold again, about 30 to
45 minutes. Form the dough into a thick disk and wrap it tightly in plastic
wrap before placing in the refrigerator.

After the dough has chilled, unwrap it and place it on a floured surface.
Use a heavy rolling pin to roll out the dough to fit the pan you're planning
to use, or to the thickness directed in the recipe. If the dough is sticky, it's
helpful to flour the rolling pin and your hands.

Gently roll dough from the inside out, without creating holes in the dough. If your dough gets too soft, place it back in the fridge for 10 to 20 minutes or until cold and firm.

Pie crusts should be thin and even in thickness throughout. When you have the dough rolled out enough, roll the dough around your rolling pin, then transfer the dough to the pan, unrolling it over the pan.

Tips for Baking Crusts

Pies can be single crust or double crust. Either way, it's best for the dough to be as cold as possible before filling and baking. The cold butter and/or shortening help form thin layers in the dough. When the fat melts in the oven, it helps create flakiness in the crust.

For single-crust pies that do not require the filling to be baked, you'll need to "blind bake" the crust. Once your crust is in the pan and your edges fluted (see Pie Fluting: How To, below), use a fork to prick the bottom and sides of the pie crust to keep it from bubbling up while baking. You can also use dried beans to keep the pie crust put while baking—they even sell "pie beads," which are weighted beads designed to hold crusts in place as they bake!

For double-crust pies with a filling, cut some slits in the top crust so steam can escape from the filling. You can also cut out decorative shapes, like hearts or apple shapes—use a cookie cutter if you wish!

PIE FLUTING: HOW TO

Fluting, which is the art of pressing a pattern around the top edge of a pie crust before it is baked, has good reason for being there. For single-crust pies, it helps prevent the crust from sliding down the side of the pan when baked. For double-crusted pies, it helps seal the filling inside.

To flute a crust, using a knife or kitchen scissors, trim the edge of the dough to about an inch over the edge of the pan. Take the edging and roll it under itself, which will give you a thicker edge to work with. Place a hand on either side of the dough. Use the pointer finger of your inside hand to push the dough between the thumb and pointer finger of your other hand to form a U or V shape. Continue your pattern all around the edge of the pie.

LESSON 5 RECIPE TUTORIAL
pie dough

PREP TIME: 10 minutes (plus 30 minutes chill time)

COOK TIME: None (until used in a recipe)

YIELD: 1 pie crust

TOOLS/EQUIPMENT

- Medium bowl
- Pastry cutter (or fork or two knives; see Cutting in Butter, page 42)
- Plastic wrap

1⅓ cups all-purpose flour

½ teaspoon table salt

4 tablespoons cold unsalted butter, cubed

¼ cup shortening

3 to 6 tablespoons ice cold water

Mix the dry ingredients.

In a medium bowl, stir together the flour and salt.

Cut in the fats.

Add the butter and shortening to the dry ingredients. Using a pastry cutter (or the back of a fork or two knives), cut in the butter and shortening until pea-size crumbs of dough form.

Add the water.

Add the water, 1 tablespoon at a time, to the dough. Stir and repeat just until a soft dough forms. Form the dough into a ball.

Refrigerate the dough.

Place the ball of dough on a large piece of plastic wrap. Flatten the dough into a thick disk, then cover with plastic wrap and refrigerate for at least 30 minutes before rolling out.

HELPFUL HINT: This dough can be used in a variety of recipes, including Homemade PB&J Breakfast Tarts (page 162), Mini Blueberry Peach Crostatas (page 168), and Southern Chocolate Walnut Pie (page 160).

TRY INSTEAD: Add a dash of your favorite spice like cinnamon or a little citrus zest for a fun-flavored pie crust.

YEAST DOUGH

Working with yeast can be a little intimidating—after all, it's a living organism, and like anything living, it has its preferences! But when you learn the art of working with yeast, you can create delicious pizza crusts, breads, and other treats. Don't worry if the first few times you work with yeast, things don't work. It may take a little experimenting with, just like other baking techniques.

Water Temperature

Using the correct temperature of water in yeast doughs is really important. The water should be warm, but not too hot and not too cold. If your water and resulting dough are too hot, you can kill the yeast and your dough will not rise. If your water is too cold, the yeast will not be activated and your dough will also not rise. Most bakers will recommend your water to be between 95°F and 130°F. I usually aim for about 110°F.

If you are unsure how warm your water is, you can buy an inexpensive thermometer and try it out until you get used to feeling the different temperatures of water before making your dough.

Kneading

Once you combine all your dough ingredients, kneading is generally necessary. Kneading, or massaging and squeezing, dough allows the protein gluten to form, which gives bread its texture. There are different methods of kneading:

- **By hand.** Place the dough on a floured surface. Press down firmly on the dough then stretch it with the heel of your hand. Fold the dough over, rotate the dough 90 degrees, and repeat. This is a good workout!

- **Stand mixer.** A stand mixer with a dough hook can make kneading easy and hands-free, since you can let the mixer do all the work.

- **Bread machine.** Some bread machines can mix the ingredients *and* knead the dough for you; or just have it do the kneading for another hands-free option.

YEAST: A LIVING ORGANISM!

Ever wonder what yeast is? Yeast is actually a single-celled organism. But don't worry, it's perfectly safe to bake with and eat! Yeast cells are so small that it takes about 20 billion yeast cells just to weigh one gram.

Yeast is needed in many doughs to make them rise and create a light airy texture. There are different types of yeast, such as compressed cake yeast (also known as fresh yeast), active dry yeast, quick-rise yeast, and instant yeast. We will be using active dry yeast in this book. Active dry yeast is found in small packets, usually in the baking aisle of the grocery store.

Yeast gets its energy from its favorite food source: sugar and other sweeteners. When the yeast eats sugar, it starts a process of fermentation, which converts the sugar to alcohol and carbon dioxide. This allows the dough to rise and create air pockets. The yeast eventually dies off when you bake the dough, and the alcohol evaporates.

YEAST CAN BE TRICKY!

I still sometimes have a hard time getting my water temperature exactly right when working with yeast. If the water is not warm enough, the yeast will not activate and you'll have flat bread. If the water is too hot, you'll kill the yeast and end up with a flat, tough dough. Even when testing recipes for this book, all my dough came out great except for the one for the Honey Oat Bread (page 80). I was in a hurry and since everything else turned out fine, I wasn't careful and used water that was too hot. The dough was tough and hard, so I had to start over!

Dough is typically kneaded until it is elastic and smooth. Then it is placed in an oiled bowl (see image A, page 48), covered, and allowed to rise and "proof." Read on to learn about rising and proofing, and why it's so important to the baking process.

Rising and Proofing

Dough needs the chance to rise, because the yeast ferments, creating carbon dioxide, which allows air to develop inside the dough. This is what gives breads and other baked goods their volume and airiness. In fact, you'll often see recipes that call for allowing the dough to rise twice.

A   B

The second rise helps you get a finer crumb and avoid giant air holes in your bread.

Most recipes will tell you to cover the dough with a towel or plastic wrap, and let it rise in a dark, warm place. The humidity and temperature of homes can vary, so results will vary. But generally, if you cover your dough with a towel and place it in a dark corner, perhaps in a cabinet, you'll get the results you want (see image "B").

After the dough has risen once, your recipe may direct you to "punch down" your dough, reshape it, and let it rise again. Punching down helps remove extra gas bubbles from the dough, and results in a finer grain. The process of punching down and reshaping also moves the yeast and moisture around, allowing it to ferment other areas of the dough.

Proofing is the final rise before baking. Professional bakers may use a proof box, which is a large cabinet that holds the air temperature between 80°F and 90°F and humidity at about 75 percent. But for the rest of us who don't have such equipment, here are a few popular home methods for proofing dough:

- **Boiling water.** Adjust the racks in your oven to a lower and middle position, but leave the oven turned off. Place a cake pan or 9-by-13-inch baking pan on the bottom rack. Carefully pour about 3 cups of boiling water into the pan—have an adult help if this is new or uncomfortable to you. Place your dough in the covered bowl on the middle rack, above the pan with the water. Close the oven door and let the dough rise as directed in the recipe.

STORING BAKED GOODS

If you're lucky enough to have any left-overs, let's talk about storage. For different baked goods, there are different ways to store them for freshness. If you want to store baked goods for longer than a few days, most can be wrapped tightly, then placed in an airtight bag or container and frozen.

Yeast breads. Store crusty breads made with yeast at room temperature in a bag with a little air. An airtight bag will make the crust soggy. This bread will usually stay good for about three to four days.

Cakes, cookies, and muffins. Baked goodies such as brownies, cookies, muffins, quick breads, cakes, and cupcakes can be covered and stored at room temperature. They may start to taste a little stale after about two days, but can usually be eaten for about a week.

Non-dairy pies. Non-dairy pies can be stored covered at room temperature. Although they're best if eaten within a few days, non-dairy pies are good for about a week. However, the crust may become soggy and the taste may diminish after a day or two.

Cheesecakes and dairy baked goods. Cheesecakes, cream pies, and other baked goods with dairy, such as dairy-based frostings with butter, cream cheese, or cream, should be stored in the fridge. These baked goods usually stay good for about a week, but for best taste and texture, bring them to room temperature before serving.

- **Oven.** Preheat your oven to 200°F. Once preheated, turn the oven off. Place your dough in a covered bowl on the middle rack of the oven and let it rise. The oven will remain warm for a while, allowing your dough to rise. However, if your oven is too warm, your dough may become crispy around the edges.

- **Countertop.** Some people simply like to leave their dough in a covered bowl right on the countertop, away from windows and drafts. Results can vary, depending on how warm and humid your home is.

Once your dough is ready for the oven, remember to remove the cover (plastic wrap, towel, etc.) before baking!

LESSON 6 RECIPE TUTORIAL
homemade pizza dough

PREP TIME: 20 minutes (plus 1 hour for dough to rise)

COOK TIME: None (until used in a recipe)

YIELD: About 1 large pizza

TOOLS/EQUIPMENT

- Large bowl
- Stand mixer with hook attachment (or wooden spoon)
- Plastic wrap

2¾ to 3¼ cups all-purpose flour
1 (¼-ounce) envelope active dry yeast
1 teaspoon sugar
1 teaspoon table salt
1 cup warm water (105°F to 115°F)
3 tablespoons olive oil, divided
Flour, for dusting the work surface

Combine the dry ingredients.
In a large bowl, add 2¾ cups of flour and the yeast, sugar, and salt.

Add the liquid.
Add the water and 2 tablespoons of olive oil to the bowl. Beat with a stand mixer with a hook attachment or a wooden spoon until the dough forms a soft ball. Mix in additional flour as needed.

Knead the dough.
Place the dough onto a lightly floured surface and knead until the dough is smooth and elastic, 6 to 8 minutes.

Let the dough rest.
Grease a large bowl with the remaining tablespoon of oil, add the dough, turn to coat, cover with plastic wrap and place in a warm, draft-free place to double in size, about 1 hour.

> **TROUBLESHOOTING TIP:** If the dough is sticky, add more flour, 1 tablespoon at a time. If the dough is too dry, add more warm water, 1 tablespoon at a time.

> **PRO TIP:** To transform this crust into a pizza, roll out the crust thinly on a floured surface, transfer to a nonstick baking sheet, then top with desired toppings. Bake at 400°F until the cheese is melted and the crust is golden brown, about 10 minutes.

MELTING CHOCOLATE

Mmm . . . just the idea of warm, gooey melted chocolate can make you hungry! Delicious by itself, melted
chocolate also comes in handy for many baking applications, including
brownies, frostings, drizzling over cookies, and more. The secret to
perfect melted chocolate is to take your time and use care in melting it.
The slightest bit of water or steam can cause chocolate to "seize," turning
it clumpy and dull. Chocolate can also burn easily. To melt chocolate,
you can either use a double boiler or make your own melting vessel. Both
methods will warm your chocolate to a smooth and creamy consistency.

Using a Double Boiler

A double boiler is a tool that consists of two pots: a large saucepan, and
a smaller saucepan, which fits snugly on top of the larger one. To use a
double boiler, fill the bottom pan with an inch or two of water, and set
the smaller pan on top. Place the pans on the stovetop over medium-high
heat. When the water begins to boil, reduce the heat to low. Place your

MICROWAVING CHOCOLATE: IT CAN BE DONE!

The safest way to melt chocolate is in a
double boiler. However, you might be in a
hurry or want to experiment a little more,
so you're probably curious about using
a microwave to melt chocolate. You can
melt chocolate in the microwave; however,
microwaves vary. You'll need to practice
and see what works the best with your
microwave.

To melt chocolate in the microwave,
place the chocolate in a wide, shallow,
microwave-safe bowl. It's best if the

chocolate pieces are all about the same
size, so cut large bars of chocolate into
small pieces.

Place the bowl in the microwave, and heat
the chocolate for 15 to 20 seconds on low
to medium power. Remove the chocolate
from the microwave, and stir. Repeat,
heating the chocolate for 15- to 20-second
intervals, stirring well after each cook time,
until the chocolate is smooth. The heat in
the bowl will help melt the chocolate more
as you're stirring.

chocolate in the top pan and stir constantly until the chocolate is melted and smooth (see image A).

The steam from the water below will slowly heat the upper saucepan, letting the chocolate melt slowly, consistently, and smoothly. Too high of heat can cause the chocolate to burn or seize, so a double boiler offers a safe way to melt chocolate without complications.

If your pan is starting to cool down, check to make sure the water hasn't all evaporated from the bottom pan, and add more water if necessary. Be careful not to get any steam or water into the chocolate.

Make Your Own Double Boiler

You can easily make your own double boiler using a saucepan and a heat-proof bowl.

Fill a small to medium saucepan with an inch or two of water. Heat the water to a boil, then reduce the heat to low. Gently place a heat-proof bowl on top of the saucepan. Stainless steel bowls work well for this. The bowl should be completely dry. Make sure the bowl fits snugly over the bottom pan so that steam doesn't escape from the pan below and cause your chocolate to seize. The bowl should not be touching the water.

Just like with a double boiler, fill the bowl with your chocolate, and stir continuously until the chocolate is melted and smooth (see image B). Now it's ready to use for spreading or dipping!

Bars of Chocolate

Bars and blocks of chocolate work well for melting; often better than chocolate chips. If using a bar or block, first cut the chocolate into uniform-size chunks. A serrated (jagged-edged) knife works well for cutting chocolate. High-quality semisweet, bittersweet, and unsweetened chocolate are common types of chocolate that often come in bars or blocks.

LESSON 7 RECIPE TUTORIAL
brownie bites

PREP TIME: 30 minutes

COOK TIME: 20 minutes

YIELD: 24 brownie bites

TOOLS/EQUIPMENT

- Mini muffin pan
- Hand mixer
- Mini paper liners (optional)
- Small bowl
- Medium bowl

Butter, for greasing the pan
(optional)

½ cup (1 stick) unsalted butter

1 cup semisweet chocolate chips

¼ cup plus 2 tablespoons
all-purpose flour

¾ teaspoon baking powder

¼ teaspoon table salt

2 large eggs, at room temperature

½ cup granulated sugar

1 teaspoon vanilla extract

Preheat the oven to 350°F.
Grease a mini muffin pan or line with mini paper liners.

Melt the chocolate.
In the top of a double boiler, add the butter and chocolate chips. Place over boiling water, then reduce the heat to low. Stir constantly, until the chocolate and butter are melted and smooth. Remove from heat and cool completely.

Mix the dry ingredients.
In a small bowl, mix together the flour, baking powder, and salt until blended.

Mix the eggs and sugar.
In a medium bowl, mix together the eggs and sugar with a whisk or an electric mixer on medium speed until well blended. Beat in the vanilla. Beat in the cooled melted chocolate, then mix in the dry ingredients until just combined.

Bake the brownies.
Spoon the brownie batter into mini muffin cups, about ¾ full. Bake for 15 to 20 minutes, or until a toothpick inserted into the middle comes out clean. Cool brownies completely, then remove from the pan.

TRY INSTEAD: For a deeper chocolate flavor, you can substitute dark chocolate chips for the semisweet chocolate chips.

PART TWO
recipes

3

muffins & breads

mini triple chocolate muffins

PREP TIME: 20 minutes

COOK TIME: 12 minutes

YIELD: 24 mini muffins

TOOLS/EQUIPMENT

- Mini muffin pan
- Paper liners (optional)
- 2 medium bowls
- Wire rack

Butter, for greasing the pan (optional)

Flour, for dusting the pan (optional)

1¼ cups all-purpose flour

½ cup brown sugar

½ cup unsweetened cocoa powder

½ teaspoon table salt

½ teaspoon baking powder

½ teaspoon baking soda

¾ cup milk (2 percent or whole)

⅓ cup vegetable or canola oil

2 large eggs, at room temperature

2 teaspoons vanilla extract

¼ cup finely chopped semisweet chocolate

¼ cup finely chopped white chocolate

Preheat the oven to 375°F.
Grease and lightly flour a 24-cup mini muffin pan or line with paper liners.

Mix the dry ingredients.
In a medium bowl, stir together the flour, brown sugar, cocoa powder, salt, baking powder, and baking soda.

Mix the wet ingredients.
In another bowl, stir together the milk, oil, eggs, and vanilla until well blended.

Blend the ingredients.
Make a well in the middle of the dry ingredients, then pour the wet ingredients in the middle and stir to mix. When almost blended, add the semisweet and white chocolate, and mix until just combined. Some small lumps are okay.

Bake the muffins.
Spoon the batter into the muffin cups about ⅔ full. Bake for 8 to 12 minutes, or until a toothpick inserted into the middle of a muffin comes out clean. Cool slightly, then transfer the muffins to a wire rack to cool.

TRY INSTEAD: Instead of chopped semisweet chocolate and white chocolate, you can use chopped nuts, toffee chips, or your favorite baking chips.

cherry orange scones

PREP TIME: 20 minutes

COOK TIME: 20 minutes

YIELD: 8 scones

TOOLS/EQUIPMENT

- Baking sheet
- Parchment paper (optional)
- Large bowl
- Zester
- Pastry cutter (or fork or two knives; see Cutting in Butter, page 42)
- Pastry brush
- Small bowl
- Whisk (or fork)

FOR THE SCONES

Butter, for greasing the baking sheet (optional)

Flour, for the work surface

2 cups all-purpose flour

2 tablespoons granulated sugar

1 tablespoon baking powder

1 teaspoon table salt

1 teaspoon freshly grated orange zest

5 tablespoons cold unsalted butter, cut into cubes

¾ cup dried cherries, chopped

1 cup plus 2 tablespoons heavy whipping cream, divided

FOR THE GLAZE

½ cup confectioners' sugar

2 tablespoons freshly squeezed orange juice

Preheat the oven to 400°F.

Grease a baking sheet or line with parchment paper.

Mix the dry ingredients.

In a large bowl, mix together the flour, granulated sugar, baking powder, salt, and orange zest.

Cut in the butter.

Using a pastry cutter, cut in the butter until the flour mixture is coarse pea-size crumbs. Stir in the dried cherries.

Combine the ingredients.

Make a well in the center of the dry ingredients. Pour 1 cup of cream into the middle and stir until just combined.

Form the scones.

Divide the dough in half. Place each half on a lightly floured surface and form each half into a circle about 1¼ inch thick. Cut each circle in half, and then in half again, forming 8 triangles between the two rounds.

Bake the scones.

Place the scones on the prepared baking sheet. Brush the tops of the scones with the remaining 2 tablespoons of cream. Bake for 15 to 20 minutes or until golden brown around the edges. Cool slightly.

Make the glaze.

In a small bowl, whisk together the confectioners' sugar and orange juice until thin and smooth. Brush over the scones.

blueberry muffin tops
WITH CHEESECAKE DRIZZLE

PREP TIME: 15 minutes

COOK TIME: 14 minutes

YIELD: 24 muffin tops

TOOLS/EQUIPMENT

- 2 baking sheets
- Parchment paper (optional)
- 2 medium bowls
- Whisk
- Small bowl
- Wire rack

FOR THE MUFFIN TOPS

Butter, for greasing the baking
   sheets (optional)

1½ cups all-purpose flour

¾ cup granulated sugar

1½ teaspoons baking powder

½ teaspoon table salt

⅓ cup milk (2 percent or whole)

⅓ cup vegetable or canola oil

1 large egg plus 1 large egg yolk

1 teaspoon vanilla extract

2 cups fresh blueberries

FOR THE CHEESECAKE DRIZZLE

4 ounces cream cheese,
   at room temperature

½ cup confectioners' sugar

¼ teaspoon vanilla extract

3 to 5 tablespoons milk (2 percent
   or whole)

Preheat the oven to 375°F.
Grease 2 large baking sheets, or line with parchment paper.

Mix the dry ingredients.
In a medium bowl, stir together the flour, granulated sugar, baking powder, and salt.

Mix the wet ingredients.
In another medium bowl, whisk together the ⅓ cup of milk, oil, egg and egg yolk, and 1 teaspoon vanilla until well combined.

Combine the ingredients.
Make a well in the center of the dry ingredients. Add the wet ingredients to the middle of the dry ingredients, and stir until nearly blended. Some lumps are okay. Gently fold in the blueberries until everything is just combined.

Bake the muffins.
Using a large ice cream scoop or spoon, spoon about 3 tablespoons of the batter onto the prepared pans for each top, leaving about 2 inches of room between each. Bake for 10 to 14 minutes, or until a toothpick inserted into the middle comes out clean and muffins are slightly browned around edges. Cool slightly, then remove muffins from the pans and cool on a wire rack. »

Make the drizzle.

Meanwhile, in a small bowl, mix together the cream cheese, confectioners' sugar, and ¼ teaspoon of vanilla. Slowly stir in the milk, a little at a time, until well blended and a thin consistency. With a fork, drizzle over the cooled muffins.

TRY INSTEAD: For a crunchy muffin topping, sprinkle the tops of the muffins with turbinado sugar.

TROUBLESHOOTING TIP: If your muffins stick to the pan, run a butter knife around the edges to loosen.

HELPFUL HINT: I tested making these muffin tops three ways: on baking sheets, in greased and floured muffin tins, and in muffins tins with paper liners. All three methods worked well but had slightly different results. I liked the large muffin tops that the baking sheets made, but the lightly greased and floured muffin tins made great golden-brown tops, and of course using a pan with paper liners is an easy option with less cleanup!

cornbread muffins
WITH ORANGE HONEY BUTTER

PREP TIME: 10 minutes

COOK TIME: 17 minutes

YIELD: 18 muffins

TOOLS/EQUIPMENT

- 2 muffin pans
- Paper liners (optional)
- Large bowl
- Medium bowl
- Zester
- Small bowl

FOR THE MUFFINS

Butter, for greasing the pans (optional)

Flour, for dusting the pans (optional)

1 cup all-purpose flour

1 cup yellow cornmeal

½ cup granulated sugar

1 tablespoon baking powder

1 teaspoon table salt

1 cup milk (2 percent or whole)

½ cup (1 stick) unsalted butter, melted and cooled

¼ cup honey

2 large eggs, at room temperature

FOR THE ORANGE HONEY BUTTER

½ cup (1 stick) unsalted butter, at room temperature

¼ teaspoon table salt

2 tablespoons honey

1 teaspoon freshly grated orange zest

1 teaspoon freshly squeezed orange juice

Preheat the oven to 400°F.

Generously grease and lightly flour 18 cups of 2 (12-cup) muffin pans, or line the pans with paper liners.

Mix the dry ingredients.

In a large bowl, mix together the flour, cornmeal, sugar, baking powder, and 1 teaspoon of salt.

Mix the wet ingredients.

In a medium bowl, mix together the milk, ½ cup of melted butter, ¼ cup of honey, and the eggs until well combined.

Blend the ingredients.

Make a well in the middle of the dry ingredients, and pour the wet ingredients into the middle. Mix until just combined.

Bake the muffins.

Spoon the batter into the prepared pans. Bake for 14 to 17 minutes or until a toothpick inserted into the middle of a muffin comes out clean.

Make the orange honey butter.

Meanwhile, in a small bowl, mix together the ½ cup of room-temperature butter, ¼ teaspoon of salt, 2 tablespoons of honey, orange zest, and orange juice until well combined. Serve with the warm muffins.

> TRY INSTEAD: Instead of orange zest and orange juice, you can mix in a little of your favorite jam or jelly.

sticky monkey bread bites

PREP TIME: 40 minutes (plus 2 hours for dough to rise)

COOK TIME: 20 minutes

YIELD: 18 bites

TOOLS/EQUIPMENT

- 2 muffin pans
- Paper liners (optional)
- Stand mixer or large bowl
- 2 small bowls

FOR THE DOUGH

1 cup warm milk (2 percent or whole, 105 to 115°F)

2 tablespoons granulated sugar

1 (¼-ounce) envelope active dry yeast

2 tablespoons butter, at room temperature, plus additional for greasing the pans

3 to 4 cups all-purpose flour

½ teaspoon table salt

1 large egg

1 tablespoon vegetable or canola oil

FOR THE TOPPING

½ cup (1 stick) unsalted butter, melted

1 cup brown sugar

1 tablespoon cinnamon

Prepare the yeast.

In the bowl of a stand mixer with the hook attachment on, stir together the warm milk, granulated sugar, and yeast, then let it sit for about 5 minutes. Meanwhile, grease the muffin pans or line them with paper liners.

Combine the ingredients.

Add 2 tablespoons of room-temperature butter, 2½ cups of flour, the salt, and egg to the bowl. Mix on low with the hook attachment until well combined. Add more flour as needed, a little at a time, until a dough forms. Raise the speed to medium, and continue kneading for 4 to 6 minutes, or until dough is smooth and elastic.

Let the dough rise.

Grease a large bowl with oil. Add the dough, turn to coat, cover with plastic wrap and place in a warm, dark, draft-free place to double in size, about 1 hour.

Make the topping.

Meanwhile, place the melted butter in a small bowl. In another small bowl, mix together the brown sugar and cinnamon.

Form the dough.

Punch down the dough and divide it evenly into 18 pieces. Divide each piece into 4, and roll each into a ball in the palms of your hands. Dip the dough balls in the melted butter, then roll in the cinnamon sugar. Place 4 balls in each muffin cup, repeating until all dough is dipped and rolled. Discard any leftover butter or sugar. Lightly cover the dough, and place in a warm, dark, draft-free place for another hour or until risen again.

Preheat the oven to 350°F.

Bake for 15 to 20 minutes, or until golden brown. Cool slightly before removing from pan.

TRY INSTEAD: Instead of cinnamon, you can use another spice combination such as nutmeg or allspice.

HELPFUL HINT: These treats can be a little sticky, so I recommend using a nonstick pan or paper liners.

DID YOU KNOW? If you don't have a stand mixer, you can make the dough by hand with a large spoon.

soft pretzel sticks
WITH HONEY MUSTARD DIP

PREP TIME: 30 minutes (plus
1 hour for dough to rise)

COOK TIME: 17 minutes

YIELD: 24 pretzels

TOOLS/EQUIPMENT

- Stand mixer or large bowl
- Large gowl
- 2 baking sheets
- Parchment paper (optional)
- Large saucepan
- Slotted spoon
- Pastry brush
- Wire rack
- Small bowl

FOR THE PRETZELS

1½ cups warm water (105 to 115°F)

1 tablespoon granulated sugar

1 (¼-ounce) envelope active
  dry yeast

4 to 4½ cups all-purpose flour,
  plus more to flour the work
  surface

2 teaspoons table salt

4 tablespoons unsalted butter,
  melted

1 tablespoon vegetable or
  canola oil

Butter, for greasing the baking
  sheets (optional)

Prepare the yeast.
In the bowl of a stand mixer with the hook attachment on, stir together 1½ cups of warm water, sugar, and yeast until blended, then let it sit for about 5 minutes.

Blend the ingredients.
Add about 3½ cups of flour, the salt, and melted butter to the bowl. Mix on low with the hook attachment until well blended. Add more flour as needed for the dough to come together. Raise the speed to medium, and continue kneading for 4 to 6 minutes or until dough is smooth and elastic.

Let the dough rise.
Grease a large bowl with the oil, add the dough, turn it to coat, cover with plastic wrap and place in a warm, draft-free place to double in size, about 1 hour.

Preheat the oven to 450°F.
Generously grease 2 baking sheets or line with parchment paper.

Prepare the water bath.
In a large saucepan over high heat, add the 8 cups of water and baking soda. Bring to a boil, and stir to blend.

Form the pretzel sticks.
While waiting for the water to boil, place the risen dough on a lightly floured surface. Divide the dough in half, then divide each half into 12 balls, for a total of 24 balls. Roll out each ball into a rope 4 to 5 inches long. Dust off any excess flour from the pretzels. ›

**FOR THE WATER BATH
AND TOPPING**

8 cups water

½ cup baking soda

1 egg yolk

1 to 2 teaspoons pretzel salt or
coarse salt

FOR THE HONEY MUSTARD DIP

½ cup mayonnaise

¼ cup honey

¼ cup yellow mustard

Put the pretzels in the water bath.

Gently lower each pretzel into the boiling water, 2 or 3 at a time, and cook for 20 to 30 seconds. Remove the pretzels with a large slotted spoon or spatula, gently shaking off any excess water, then place the pretzels on the baking sheets. Mix the egg yolk with a little water to thin in a small bowl. With a pastry brush, lightly brush the egg yolk on top of the pretzels, then sprinkle with the pretzel or coarse salt.

Bake the pretzels.

Bake for 12 to 17 minutes, or until dark golden brown. Cool slightly, then transfer the pretzels to a wire rack to finish cooling before serving.

Make the honey mustard dip.

In a small bowl, mix together the mayonnaise, honey, and mustard, and serve alongside the pretzels.

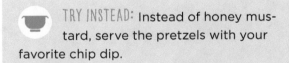 TRY INSTEAD: Instead of honey mustard, serve the pretzels with your favorite chip dip.

quick and easy drop biscuits

PREP TIME: 15 minutes

COOK TIME: 12 minutes

YIELD: 18 biscuits

TOOLS/EQUIPMENT

- Medium bowl
- Pastry cutter (or fork or two knives; see Cutting in Butter, page 42)
- 2 baking sheets
- Parchment paper (optional)

2 cups all-purpose flour

2 teaspoons baking powder

½ teaspoon table salt

½ cup (1 stick) cold unsalted butter, cut into small cubes

¾ cup cold milk (2 percent or whole)

Preheat the oven to 425°F.

Mix the dry ingredients.

In a medium bowl, mix together the flour, baking powder, and salt until blended.

Cut in the butter.

Using a pastry cutter or the back of a fork, cut the butter into the flour mixture until the mixture is even and crumbly.

Add the wet ingredients.

Mix the milk into the flour mixture, and stir until the dough is just combined (don't overmix) and a soft moist dough forms.

Bake the biscuits.

Using a spoon, drop the biscuit dough onto 2 nonstick baking sheets or baking sheets lined with parchment paper to make 18 biscuits. Bake for 9 to 12 minutes, or until browned on the bottom.

TRY INSTEAD: Make garlic cheddar biscuits by adding 1 cup shredded Cheddar cheese and ½ teaspoon garlic powder to the dough.

TROUBLESHOOTING TIP: The dough should be soft and moist. If your dough is a little crumbly or dry, add a little more milk.

fluffy buttermilk chive biscuits

PREP TIME: 20 minutes

COOK TIME: 17 minutes

YIELD: 16 biscuits

TOOLS/EQUIPMENT

- Cast-iron pan or skillet (about 10½-inch diameter)
- Large bowl
- Pastry cutter
- 2-inch round cookie or biscuit cutter
- Pastry brush

Butter, for greasing the pan

2¾ cups plus 2 tablespoons all-purpose flour

4½ teaspoons baking powder

1 teaspoon table salt

6 tablespoons cold, cubed unsalted butter

½ cup chopped fresh chives

1 to 1½ cups cold buttermilk

Flour, for the work surface

3 tablespoons melted unsalted butter

Preheat the oven to 425°F.

Set the oven rack at the lowest level. Grease a cast-iron pan.

Mix the dry ingredients.

In a large bowl, mix together the flour, baking powder, and salt until combined.

Cut in the butter.

With a pastry cutter or back of a fork, cut in the 6 tablespoons of cold butter, until the mixture resembles coarse crumbs. Stir in the chives.

Add the wet ingredients.

Add 1 cup buttermilk to the flour mixture. Stir to combine, and add more milk as necessary until the dough just comes together but is still moist. Be careful not to overwork the dough or the biscuits may come out dry.

Form the biscuits.

Place the dough on a floured surface. Gently press the dough until 1 inch thick. With a 2-inch round cutter, cut the dough into 16 biscuits.

Bake the biscuits.

Place the biscuits next to each other in the prepared pan. Bake on the bottom rack for 12 to 17 minutes or until golden brown. Brush with the 3 tablespoons of melted butter. Cool slightly before serving.

TRY INSTEAD: Instead of chives, you can use chopped cooked bacon, shredded cheese, or even chopped precooked onion.

homemade mini cheese bagels

PREP TIME: 45 minutes (plus 1½ hours for dough to rise)

COOK TIME: 25 minutes

YIELD: 12 mini bagels

TOOLS/EQUIPMENT

- Stand mixer (optional) or large bowl
- Large bowl
- 2 baking sheets
- Large saucepan
- Slotted spoon

FOR THE BAGELS

1 cup warm water (105 to 115°F)

1 tablespoon granulated sugar

1 (¼-ounce) envelope active dry yeast

2½ to 3 cups all-purpose flour

1 teaspoon table salt

1 teaspoon olive oil, plus 1 to 2 tablespoons olive oil, divided

FOR THE WATER BATH

8 cups water

1 tablespoon granulated sugar

FOR THE TOPPING

½ cup shredded Parmesan or Asiago cheese

Prepare the yeast.

In the bowl of a stand mixer with the hook attachment on, stir together the 1 cup of water, 1 tablespoon of sugar, and the yeast, then let it sit for about 5 minutes.

Make the dough.

Add 2 cups of flour and the salt to the bowl. Mix on low with the hook attachment until well combined, adding more flour, a little at a time, until a dough forms. Increase the speed to medium, and continue kneading for 4 to 6 minutes or until the dough is smooth and elastic.

Let it rise.

Grease a large bowl with oil. Add the dough, turn it to coat, then cover with plastic wrap and place in a warm, dark, draft-free place to double in size, about 1 hour.

Prepare the baking sheet.

Generously grease the baking sheet with 1 or 2 tablespoons of olive oil, or line with parchment paper.

Form the bagels.

When the dough has doubled, punch it down. Divide the dough into 12 balls. Roll each ball into a log 5 to 6 inches long. Join the ends together, place fingers through the hole and roll the ends together until smooth. Place the bagels on the prepared baking sheet. Cover the bagels with a clean, light towel, and place in a warm, dark, draft-free place for about 30 minutes or until dough has risen a bit more.

Preheat the oven to 400°F.
Grease another baking sheet or line with parchment paper.

Prepare the water bath.
In a large saucepan over high heat, add the 8 cups of water and 1 tablespoon sugar. Bring to a boil, stirring to combine.

Dip the bagels in the water bath.
In batches, add a few bagels at a time to the boiling water for 20 seconds, then with a slotted spoon, turn the bagels over and cook an additional 20 seconds. Remove the bagels from the water, gently shaking off excess water, and place on the prepared baking sheet.

Bake the bagels.
Bake for 15 to 25 minutes or until golden brown. In the last 5 minutes of baking, sprinkle the bagels with the cheese and continue baking.

rosemary onion focaccia

PREP TIME: 30 minutes (plus 1 hour 20 minutes for dough to rise)

COOK TIME: 20 minutes

YIELD: 1 flat loaf (serves 12)

TOOLS/EQUIPMENT

- Stand mixer or large bowl
- Large bowl
- Plastic wrap
- Baking sheet
- Pastry brush

FOR THE BREAD

1 cup warm water (105 to 115°F)

2 tablespoons granulated sugar

1 (¼-ounce) envelope active dry yeast

3½ to 4 cups all-purpose flour

¼ cup plus 2 to 3 tablespoons olive oil, divided

1 teaspoon table salt

FOR THE TOPPING

2 tablespoons olive oil

½ small red onion, very thinly sliced

¼ cup shredded Parmesan cheese

2 garlic cloves, minced

½ teaspoon table salt

⅛ teaspoon freshly ground black pepper

2 tablespoons fresh rosemary

Prepare the yeast.
In the bowl of a stand mixer with the hook attachment on, stir together the warm water, sugar, and yeast, then let it sit for about 5 minutes.

Combine the ingredients.
Add 3 cups of flour, ¼ cup of olive oil, and 1 teaspoon of salt to the bowl. Mix on low with the hook attachment until well blended. Add more flour as needed, a little at a time, until a dough forms. Raise the speed to medium, and continue kneading for 4 to 6 minutes, or until the dough is smooth and elastic.

Let the dough rise.
Grease a large bowl with 1 tablespoon of olive oil. Add the dough, turn to coat, cover with plastic wrap and place in a warm, dark, draft-free place to double in size, about 1 hour.

Prepare the baking sheet.
Generously grease the baking sheet with 1 or 2 tablespoons of olive oil.

Form the bread.
Transfer the dough to the prepared baking sheet. Spread the dough out into a long oblong shape, about ½ inch thick. Cover loosely with plastic wrap and return to a warm, dark, draft-free place for 15 to 20 minutes to rest and rise slightly.

Preheat the oven to 400°F.
But first, place the oven rack at the lowest level.

Top the bread.
Remove the plastic wrap from the dough, and using your fingertips, gently push down on the dough to leave slight dimples. Brush 2 table-spoons of olive oil over the top of the dough. Lay the onion slices on top. Sprinkle the cheese, garlic, ½ teaspoon of salt, black pepper, and rosemary on top.

Bake the bread.
Bake on the lowest oven rack for 15 to 20 minutes, or until golden brown.

> **TRY INSTEAD:** Instead of fresh rose-mary, you can use other fresh herbs, such as chopped basil or oregano.

> **DID YOU KNOW?** If you don't have a stand mixer, you can make the dough by hand with a large spoon.

> **TROUBLESHOOTING TIP:** Check on your bread now and then. If the bread or the toppings appear to be getting too brown or burnt, simply cover the entire bread lightly with aluminum foil to protect it while it finishes baking.

old-fashioned white sandwich bread

PREP TIME: 30 minutes (plus 1½ hours for dough to rise)

COOK TIME: 40 minutes

YIELD: 2 loaves (serves 24)

TOOLS/EQUIPMENT

- Stand mixer or large bowl
- Large bowl
- Plastic wrap
- 2 loaf pans (8½ by 4½ by 2½ inches)
- Pastry brush
- Wire rack

FOR THE BREAD

2 cups warm milk (2 percent or whole, 105-115°F)

2 tablespoons granulated sugar

1 (¼-ounce) envelope active dry yeast

2 tablespoons butter, at room temperature

5 to 6 cups all-purpose flour

2 teaspoons table salt

1 tablespoon vegetable or canola oil

Butter, for greasing the pans

FOR THE TOPPING

2 tablespoons butter, melted

Prepare the yeast.
In the bowl of a stand mixer with the hook attachment on, stir together the warm milk, sugar, and yeast, then let it sit for about 5 minutes.

Combine the ingredients.
Add the 2 tablespoons room-temperature butter, 4 cups of flour, and salt to the yeast mixture. Mix on low with the hook attachment until well blended. Add more flour as needed, a little at a time, until a dough forms. Raise the speed to medium, and continue kneading for 4 to 6 minutes, or until the dough is smooth and elastic.

Let it rise.
Grease a large bowl with oil. Add the dough, turn it to coat, cover with plastic wrap and place in a warm, dark, draft-free place to double in size, about 1 hour. Punch down the dough, form it into 2 loaves, and place each in a greased loaf pan. Lightly brush the tops of the loaves with the melted butter. Cover with plastic wrap, and place in a warm, dark, draft-free place to rise again, about 30 minutes.

Preheat the oven to 350°F.

Bake the bread.

Bake for 30 to 40 minutes or until browned and hollow-sounding when lightly tapped. Cool slightly, then remove and place on a wire rack to finish cooling.

DID YOU KNOW? If you don't have a stand mixer, you can make the dough by hand with a large spoon.

HELPFUL HINT: To help the bread maintain its shape, cool bread completely before slicing with a serrated (jagged-edge) knife.

honey oat bread

PREP TIME: 20 minutes (plus 1 hour for dough to rise)

COOK TIME: 55 minutes

YIELD: 2 loaves (serves 24)

TOOLS/EQUIPMENT

- Large bowl
- Small saucepan
- Whisk or spoon
- 2 loaf pans (approximately 8½ by 4½ by 2½ inches)
- Aluminum foil
- Pastry brush
- Wire rack

1 (¼-ounce) envelope active dry yeast

¼ cup warm water (105 to 115°F)

2 cups milk (2 percent or whole)

4 tablespoons unsalted butter, divided

2 tablespoons honey

1 teaspoon table salt

1¼ cups old-fashioned rolled oats

4 to 5 cups all-purpose flour, plus more to flour the work surface

Butter, for greasing the pans

Prepare the yeast.
In a large bowl, stir together the yeast and warm water. Let sit for about 5 minutes.

Heat the milk.
In a small saucepan over medium heat, add the milk, 3 tablespoons of butter, the honey, and salt. Whisk until the butter has melted and the mixture is blended. Let this mixture cool a bit, then pour into the yeast mixture.

Blend the ingredients.
Add the oats and 4 cups of flour to the yeast mixture, and stir until well blended. Add more flour as needed until a sticky dough forms.

Knead the dough.
Place the dough on a well-floured surface. Knead the dough 6 to 8 minutes, adding flour as necessary, until smooth and elastic.

Let it rise.
Divide the dough in half, form into two loaves, and place each in a well-greased loaf pan. Cover lightly with plastic wrap and place in a dark, warm, draft-free place to double in size, about 1 hour.

TROUBLESHOOTING TIP: Make sure your water and your milk mixture aren't too hot when combined with the yeast, or you'll kill the yeast and your dough won't rise.

Preheat the oven to 350°F.

Bake the bread.

Bake the bread for about 25 minutes, then cover with aluminum foil to prevent further browning. Continue baking for an additional 20 to 30 minutes or until the loaves sound hollow when lightly tapped. Melt the remaining tablespoon of butter and brush it on the tops of the loaves. Cool slightly, then transfer to a wire rack to finish cooling.

yogurt banana bread

PREP TIME: 20 minutes
COOK TIME: 60 minutes
YIELD: 1 loaf (serves 12)

TOOLS/EQUIPMENT
- Loaf pan (8½ by 4½ by 2½ inches)
- 2 medium bowls

Butter, for greasing the pan
Flour, for dusting the pan
1⅔ cups all-purpose flour
1 teaspoon baking soda
½ teaspoon cinnamon
½ teaspoon table salt
2 large eggs, at room temperature
¾ cup granulated sugar
1½ cups mashed, very ripe
   bananas (3 to 5 bananas)
½ cup vegetable or canola oil
2 tablespoons plain Greek yogurt
1 teaspoon vanilla extract

Preheat the oven to 350°F.
Lightly grease and flour a loaf pan.

Mix the dry ingredients.
In a medium bowl, mix together the flour, baking soda, cinnamon, and salt until well combined.

Mix remaining ingredients.
In another medium bowl, beat together the eggs and sugar for 3 to 5 minutes, or until light and fluffy. Stir in the banana, oil, yogurt, and vanilla until just combined.

Combine the ingredients.
Make a well in the center of the dry ingredients. Pour the wet ingredients into the well. Stir until just combined.

Bake the bread.
Pour the batter into the prepared loaf pan. Bake at 350°F for 45 to 60 minutes, or until a toothpick inserted in the center comes out clean.

> TRY INSTEAD: For a different flavor, try adding ⅔ cup chopped nuts or mini chocolate chips to the batter.

> TROUBLESHOOTING TIP: Make sure the inside of your oven is clean before baking. Leftover food that has fallen to the bottom of the oven can catch on fire, but it can also smoke, which can give your baked goods a smoky and funny smell and flavor!

4

cakes & cupcakes

sprinkle cake pops

PREP TIME: 60 minutes
(plus 1 hour chill time)

COOK TIME: 25 minutes

YIELD: 24 cake pops

TOOLS/EQUIPMENT

- 9-inch round cake pan
- Medium bowl
- Large bowl
- Electric stand or hand mixer
- Wire rack
- Baking sheet
- Wax or parchment paper
- Double boiler (or see Make Your Own Double Boiler, page 53)
- Spatula
- White lollipop sticks
- Cake pop stand, box, or foam (see Pro Tip, page 88)

FOR THE CAKE

Butter, for greasing the pan
Flour, for dusting the pan
1 cup all-purpose flour
1 teaspoon baking powder
¼ teaspoon baking soda
¼ teaspoon table salt
⅓ cup unsalted butter,
    at room temperature
⅔ cup granulated sugar
2 large eggs, at room temperature
1½ teaspoons vanilla extract
⅓ cup milk (2 percent or whole)

Preheat the oven to 350°F.

Grease and lightly flour a 9-inch round cake pan.

Mix the dry ingredients.

In a medium bowl, stir together the flour, baking powder, baking soda, and salt.

Cream the butter and sugar.

In a large bowl, beat ⅓ cup of room-temperature butter with an electric mixer on medium speed for about 10 seconds or until smooth. Beat in the granulated sugar until well combined and light and fluffy, about 2 minutes. Beat in the eggs, one at a time, beating after each egg is added. Beat in the vanilla.

Combine the ingredients.

Alternate adding some of the flour mixture and ⅓ cup of milk to the butter mixture, beating on low after each addition, until the batter is just combined.

Bake the cake.

Pour the cake batter into the prepared pan. Bake for 20 to 25 minutes, or until a toothpick inserted into the middle comes out clean. Cool slightly, then remove the cake from the pan to finish cooling on a wire rack.

FOR THE FROSTING

4 tablespoons unsalted butter,
   at room temperature

2 cups confectioners' sugar

2 to 4 tablespoons milk (2 percent
   or whole)

FOR THE CANDY COATING

White candy melts, about
   2 (10-ounce) bags

Sprinkles

Make the frosting.

When the cake is completely cooled, prepare the frosting. In a medium bowl, add 4 tablespoons of room-temperature butter and beat with an electric mixer for about 10 seconds, or until smooth. Gradually beat in the confectioners' sugar. Add 2 tablespoons of milk and beat until smooth, adding a little more milk at a time as needed. The frosting should be a little on the thicker side.

Stir together the cake and frosting.

In a large bowl, crumble the cooled cake into pieces. Add ¼ cup of frosting. Using a sturdy spatula or large spoon, mix together the cake and frosting. Add a little more frosting at a time until the cake is fully crumbled and the mixture starts to clump together.

Form the cake balls.

Scoop the cake mixture out into 1-inch balls, roll in your hands if necessary to form a ball, and place on a baking sheet lined with wax or parchment paper. Refrigerate for about 1 hour, or until the cake balls are firm. ≫

TRY INSTEAD: Instead of sprinkles, substitute your favorite chopped candy, mini chocolate chips, or chopped nuts!

HELPFUL HINT: Make sure the cake is completely cooled before mixing with the frosting, otherwise, the frosting will melt and the cake will not mold into balls.

PRO TIP: You can buy a cake pop stand, which makes it easier to stand pops straight up after dipping. A stand also makes a festive display for serving. You can also poke holes in a box or use a block of foam to hold cake pops up.

Dip the cake balls.

Place the candy melts in the top of a double boiler. Place over boiling water, then reduce the heat to low. Stir constantly, until the candy melts are melted and smooth. Dip about ¼ inch of the tip of a lollipop stick into the melted candy melt, then insert the stick into the cake ball. Dip the cake balls, one at a time, in the candy melts, covering the entire cake ball and just below to the stick. You can pour the melted candy melts into a tall narrow container or glass for easier dipping. Before the candy melt hardens, sprinkle the sprinkles on top of the cake balls. Place the cake pops on a cake pop stand or in foam (see Pro Tip) to stand upright. Repeat with the remaining cake balls.

angel food cake

PREP TIME: 50 minutes

COOK TIME: 45 minutes

YIELD: 1 cake (serves 12)

TOOLS/EQUIPMENT

- Medium bowl
- Large bowl
- Stand mixer with whisk attachment or electric hand mixer
- Sifter (or mesh strainer)
- 10-inch tube pan (with removable bottom)
- Wire rack or sturdy glass bottle

1½ cups confectioners' sugar, sifted

1 cup all-purpose flour, sifted

1½ cups egg whites (from 10 to 12 large eggs)

1½ teaspoons cream of tartar

1 teaspoon vanilla extract

1 cup granulated sugar

Preheat the oven to 350˚F.

But first, make sure the oven rack is in the lowest position.

Combine the sugar and flour.

In a medium bowl, mix together the confectioners' sugar and flour until well blended with no lumps.

Whip up the egg whites.

In a large bowl, add the egg whites (see Separating Eggs, page 29), cream of tartar, and vanilla. Beat on medium until the whites start getting foamy, 1 to 2 minutes. Increase the speed to medium-high, and continue beating until the egg whites become thick and opaque, 1 to 2 minutes.

Add the granulated sugar.

With the mixer on medium-high speed, slowly add the granulated sugar, 1 to 2 tablespoons at a time. Continue beating until the egg whites are shiny and stiff peaks form, 4 to 6 minutes.

TRY INSTEAD: Instead of vanilla extract, try another extract, such as lemon, coconut, or almond.

HELPFUL HINT: When baking angel food cake in a tube pan, the pan is never greased, because the batter clings to the sides of the pan, which helps it rise.

TROUBLESHOOTING TIP: Sifting your dry ingredients will prevent heavy lumps in this delicate cake. Also, bring your egg whites to room temperature for the best volume when beating. You can quickly warm cold eggs by covering the eggs in a bowl of warm tap water for 5 to 10 minutes.

Fold in the dry ingredients.

Gently sift about a quarter of the flour and confectioners' sugar mixture over the egg whites. Very gently fold in the flour mixture with a large rubber spatula, being careful to not deflate the egg whites. Repeat with the remaining flour and confectioners' sugar until just folded in.

Bake the cake.

Pour the batter into an ungreased 10-inch tube pan. Lightly run a butter knife through the batter to remove any air bubbles. Bake for 35 to 45 minutes, or until the top is lightly browned and springs back when lightly touched. Set the cake upside down over a wire rack or sturdy glass bottle to cool. When cooled, run a butter knife around the edge to loosen before inverting onto a plate.

lemon loaf cake

PREP TIME: 20 minutes

COOK TIME: 60 minutes

YIELD: 1 cake (serves 12)

TOOLS/EQUIPMENT

- Loaf pan (approximately 8½ by 4½ by 2½ inches)
- Small bowl
- Medium bowl
- Large bowl
- Electric hand mixer or stand mixer
- Zester
- Wire rack
- Whisk (or fork)

FOR THE CAKE

Butter, for greasing the pan

Flour, for dusting the pan

⅓ cup milk (2 percent or whole)

2 tablespoons freshly squeezed lemon juice

1½ cups all-purpose flour

¼ teaspoon baking powder

¼ teaspoon baking soda

¼ teaspoon table salt

½ cup (1 stick) unsalted butter, at room temperature

1 cup granulated sugar

2 large eggs, at room temperature

½ teaspoon vanilla extract

1 tablespoon freshly grated lemon zest

Preheat the oven to 350°F.

Grease and lightly flour a loaf pan.

Make the sour milk.

In a small bowl, add ⅓ cup of milk and 2 table-spoons of lemon juice, and stir to combine. Let sit about 10 minutes.

Mix the dry ingredients.

In a medium bowl, stir together the flour, baking powder, baking soda, and salt.

Cream the butter and sugar.

In a large bowl, beat the butter with an electric mixer on medium speed for about 10 seconds, or until smooth. Beat in the granulated sugar until well blended and light and fluffy, about 2 min-utes. Beat in the eggs, one at a time, beating after each egg is added. Beat in the vanilla and lemon zest.

Combine all ingredients.

Alternate adding the flour mixture and the milk mixture to the butter mixture, beating on low after each addition, until the batter is just combined.

Bake the cake.

Pour the cake batter into the prepared pan. Bake for 45 to 60 minutes, or until a toothpick inserted into the middle comes out clean. Cool slightly, then remove the cake from the pan to finish cool-ing on a wire rack.

FOR THE GLAZE

¾ cup confectioners' sugar

2 teaspoons freshly squeezed lemon juice

1 to 3 tablespoons milk (2 percent or whole)

Make the glaze.

In a medium bowl, whisk together the confectioners' sugar, 2 teaspoons of lemon juice, and 1 tablespoon of milk. Whisk in more milk as needed until thick but spreadable. Spoon the glaze over the top of the cake, so it can drizzle down the sides.

TROUBLESHOOTING TIP: If you aren't getting much juice from your citrus fruit, use the palm of your hand to firmly roll the fruit on the counter, or microwave the fruit for 10 to 20 seconds before juicing.

TRY INSTEAD: For a stronger lemon flavor, use 1 teaspoon lemon extract instead of the vanilla extract.

HELPFUL HINT: Resist the urge to open the oven door while the cake is baking. The temperature of the oven will change quickly. Instead, use the oven light to check on things.

orange vanilla pound cake

PREP TIME: 30 minutes

COOK TIME: 90 minutes

YIELD: 1 cake (serves 16)

TOOLS/EQUIPMENT
- 1 (10-inch) tube pan
- Large bowl
- Electric hand mixer or stand mixer
- Zester
- Small saucepan
- Pastry brush

FOR THE CAKE

Butter, for greasing the pan

Flour, for dusting the pan

3 cups all-purpose flour

½ teaspoon baking powder

½ teaspoon table salt

1½ cups (3 sticks) unsalted butter, at room temperature

3 cups granulated sugar

5 large eggs, at room temperature

2 tablespoons freshly grated orange zest

2 teaspoons vanilla extract

1 cup milk (2 percent or whole)

FOR THE ORANGE GLAZE

½ cup granulated sugar

½ cup freshly squeezed orange juice (from 2 or 3 oranges)

Preheat the oven to 350°F.

Grease and flour a 10-inch tube pan.

Combine the dry ingredients.

In a large bowl, combine the flour, baking powder, and salt until well combined.

Cream the butter and sugar.

In a separate large bowl, beat the butter with an electric mixer on medium speed until smooth, about 10 seconds. Beat in 3 cups of sugar until well blended and light and fluffy, about 2 minutes. Beat in the eggs, one at a time, then beat in the orange zest and vanilla until blended.

Combine the ingredients.

Alternate beating in the dry ingredients and the milk into the butter mixture until just combined.

Bake the cake.

Pour the batter into the tube pan. Bake for 60 to 90 minutes, or until a toothpick inserted into the middle comes out clean.

Prepare the glaze.

In a small saucepan over medium heat, heat ½ cup of sugar and orange juice, stirring until slightly thickened, about 5 minutes. Brush the glaze over the top and sides of the warm cake.

 HELPFUL HINT: For best results, don't substitute margarine for butter in this recipe.

cinnamon nut coffee cake

PREP TIME: 30 minutes

COOK TIME: 60 minutes

YIELD: 1 cake (serves 16)

TOOLS/EQUIPMENT

- 10-inch tube pan (with removable bottom)
- Small bowl
- 2 large bowls
- Electric hand mixer or stand mixer
- Wire rack

Butter, for greasing the pan
Flour, for dusting the pan

FOR THE FILLING

½ cup granulated sugar
1 cup chopped walnuts or pecans
1½ teaspoons cinnamon

FOR THE CAKE

2¼ cups all-purpose flour
2 teaspoons baking powder
½ teaspoon baking soda
¼ teaspoon table salt
⅓ cup unsalted butter, at room temperature
1 cup granulated sugar
⅓ cup vegetable or canola oil
2 large eggs, at room temperature
2 teaspoons vanilla extract
1 cup sour cream or plain Greek yogurt

Preheat the oven to 350˚F.
Grease and flour a 10-inch tube pan.

Make the filling.
In a small bowl, mix together ½ cup of sugar, the walnuts or pecans, and cinnamon until well combined.

Blend the dry ingredients.
In a large bowl, mix the flour, baking powder, baking soda, and salt until well blended.

Cream the butter and sugar.
In a separate large bowl, beat the butter with an electric mixer on medium speed for about 10 seconds, or until smooth. Beat in 1 cup of sugar and the oil, until well blended and light and fluffy, about 2 minutes. Beat in the eggs, one at a time, beating after each egg is added. Beat in the vanilla, then beat in the sour cream.

Combine the ingredients.
Slowly beat the butter mixture into the dry ingredients until just blended.

Assemble the cake.
Spoon half of the cake batter into the tube pan. Spread with a spoon to form an even layer across the bottom of the pan. Sprinkle half of the nut filling over the batter, then top with the remaining batter.

Bake the cake.
Bake for 45 to 60 minutes, or until a toothpick inserted into the middle comes out clean. Cool slightly, then remove from the pan to cool completely on a wire rack.

pick-your-flavor ice cream cake

PREP TIME: 30 minutes (plus 1 to 2 hours freezing time)

COOK TIME: 25 minutes

YIELD: 1 cake (serves 16)

TOOLS/EQUIPMENT

- 2 (9-inch) cake pans
- Medium bowl
- Large bowl
- Wire rack
- Small saucepan

FOR THE CAKE

Butter, for greasing the pans

Flour, for dusting the pans

1½ cups all-purpose flour

½ cup unsweetened cocoa powder

1 teaspoon baking powder

¼ teaspoon baking soda

¾ cup granulated sugar

½ cup brown sugar

¾ cup (1½ sticks) unsalted butter, melted and cooled

2 large eggs, at room temperature

1 teaspoon vanilla extract

1 cup milk (2 percent or whole)

4 cups ice cream, any flavor

FOR THE CHOCOLATE TOPPING

1 cup semisweet chocolate chips

2 teaspoons corn syrup

½ cup heavy whipping cream

Preheat the oven to 350°F.
Grease and lightly flour 2 (9-inch) round cake pans.

Blend the flour mixture.
In a medium bowl, mix together the flour, cocoa powder, baking powder, and baking soda until well blended.

Blend the sugar and butter.
In a large bowl, mix the granulated sugar, brown sugar, and butter until well blended, about 2 minutes. Add the eggs one at time, beating after each addition, then beat in the vanilla.

Combine the ingredients.
Alternate beating in the dry ingredients and the milk to the wet ingredients until just combined.

Bake the cakes.
Pour the batter evenly into the 2 prepared pans. Bake for 20 to 25 minutes, or until a toothpick inserted into the middle comes out clean. Cool slightly, then remove from pans and place on a wire rack to cool completely.

Assemble the cake.
Let the ice cream sit on the counter for 5 to 10 minutes, until soft but not soupy. Place the bottom cake layer, flat side up, on a serving plate. Spoon the ice cream on top of the bottom cake layer, and spread the ice cream to the edge of the cake with a spoon. Top with the other cake layer, flat side down, and press gently on the cake to help spread the ice cream to the edges. Place the cake in the freezer for 1 to 2 hours, or until firm.

Prepare the topping.

In a medium bowl, add the chocolate chips and corn syrup. In a small saucepan over low heat, heat the heavy cream, whisking continuously, until it just starts to boil. Pour the hot cream over the chocolate chips. Let sit about 1 minute, then stir to combine until smooth. Let cool.

Top the cake.

Spoon the cooled chocolate over the top of the cake and let it drip down the sides of the cake. Return the cake to the freezer until ready to serve, at least a half hour. Let the cake sit at room temperature for 10 to 20 minutes to soften before slicing and serving.

zebra marble cake
WITH VANILLA FROSTING

PREP TIME: 30 minutes

COOK TIME: 45 minutes

YIELD: 1 cake (serves 8)

TOOLS/EQUIPMENT

- 1 (9-inch) round cake pan
- Medium bowl
- Large bowl
- Electric hand mixer or stand mixer
- Whisk or fork
- Wire rack

FOR THE CAKE

Butter, for greasing the pan

Flour, for dusting the pan

2 cups all-purpose flour

2 teaspoons baking powder

¼ teaspoon table salt

1 cup granulated sugar

4 large eggs, at room temperature

1 cup vegetable or canola oil

1 cup milk (2 percent or whole)

1 teaspoon vanilla extract

3 tablespoons sifted unsweetened cocoa powder

FOR THE FROSTING

½ cup (1 stick) butter, at room temperature

1¾ cups confectioners' sugar

½ teaspoon vanilla extract

⅛ teaspoon table salt

3 to 5 tablespoons milk (2 percent or whole)

Preheat the oven to 350°F.

Grease and flour a 9-inch round cake pan.

Mix the dry ingredients.

In a medium bowl, stir together the flour, baking powder, and ¼ teaspoon of salt.

Blend the sugar and eggs.

In a large bowl, beat together the granulated sugar and eggs with an electric mixer on medium until well blended, about 2 minutes. Add the oil, 1 cup of milk, and 1 teaspoon of vanilla, beating until well blended.

Combine the ingredients.

Add the flour mixture to the egg mixture, beating on medium until just blended.

Make the chocolate batter.

Spoon half of the batter into a separate bowl. Whisk the cocoa powder into one of the bowls, stirring to blend.

Assemble the cake.

To make stripes, alternate adding the two batters to the pan. Spoon about 3 tablespoons of vanilla batter into the center of the pan. Then spoon about 3 tablespoons of chocolate batter in the middle of the pan on top of the vanilla batter. Repeat until all the batter is in the pan. The cake batter will spread to the edge of the pan as you add more. »

TRY INSTEAD: Instead of chocolate and vanilla, try dyeing the 2 bowls of cake batter with your favorite colors using food coloring!

TROUBLESHOOTING TIP: If stripes don't appear when you cut into the cake, you may have shaken the pan too much while adding the cake batter, or perhaps you varied the amount of batter you added to the pan each time (too much or too little at once). The good news is, it will still taste great!

Bake the cake.

Bake for 30 to 45 minutes, or until a toothpick inserted into the middle comes out clean. Let the cake cool slightly in the pan, then remove from the pan and place on a wire rack to finish cooling.

Make the frosting.

In a medium bowl, beat together the butter and confectioners' sugar with an electric mixer on medium speed. Beat in ½ teaspoon of vanilla and ⅛ teaspoon of salt. Add a little milk if necessary to thin the frosting. Spread the frosting over the cooled cake.

mini almond flourless chocolate cakes

PREP TIME: 10 minutes

COOK TIME: 30 minutes

YIELD: 4 cakes

TOOLS/EQUIPMENT

- 4 (4-ounce) ramekins
- Baking sheet
- Double boiler (or see Make Your Own Double Boiler, page 53)
- Medium bowl
- Whisk or fork

Butter, for greasing the ramekins

6 tablespoons unsalted butter

¼ cup honey

⅔ cup dark chocolate chips

1 cup finely ground almonds (or almond flour)

2 large eggs, at room temperature, beaten

1 teaspoon vanilla extract

½ teaspoon table salt

Preheat the oven to 350°F.

Lightly grease 4 small ramekins and place them on a baking sheet.

Melt the chocolate.

Add the butter, honey, and chocolate chips to the top of a double boiler over boiling water, then reduce the heat to low, mixing until smooth. Set aside to cool completely, about 30 to 45 minutes.

Whisk the ingredients.

In a medium bowl, whisk together the almonds, eggs, vanilla, and salt until well blended. Slowly whisk in the cooled chocolate mixture.

Bake the cakes.

Bake for 20 to 30 minutes, or until a toothpick inserted into the middle comes out clean.

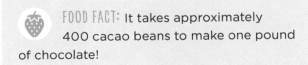

TRY INSTEAD: Instead of dark chocolate chips, substitute semisweet or bittersweet for a different flavor. You can also top this with fresh berries and whipped cream!

HELPFUL HINT: If you don't have 4-ounce ramekins, you can use 6- or 8-ounce ones, but they may cook more quickly, so you may need to adjust the baking time.

FOOD FACT: It takes approximately 400 cacao beans to make one pound of chocolate!

chocolate fudge layer cake
WITH PEANUT BUTTER FROSTING

PREP TIME: 30 minutes

COOK TIME: 35 minutes

YIELD: 1 (2-layer) cake (serves 16)

TOOLS/EQUIPMENT
- 2 (9-inch) round cake pans
- Medium bowl
- Large bowl
- Electric hand mixer or stand mixer
- Wire rack
- Offset spatula or butter knife

FOR THE CAKE
Butter, for greasing the pans

Flour, for dusting the pans

2 cups all-purpose flour

¾ cup unsweetened cocoa powder

1 teaspoon baking soda

¾ teaspoon baking powder

½ teaspoon table salt

¾ cup (1½ sticks) unsalted butter, at room temperature

2 cups granulated sugar

3 large eggs, at room temperature

2 teaspoons vanilla extract

1½ cups milk (2 percent or whole)

1 cup mini chocolate chips

FOR THE FROSTING
1 cup (2 sticks) unsalted butter, at room temperature

1¼ cups creamy peanut butter

3 cups confectioners' sugar

1 to 2 tablespoons milk (2 percent or whole)

Preheat the oven to 350°F.
Grease and lightly flour 2 (9-inch) round cake pans.

Mix the dry ingredients.
In a medium bowl, stir together the flour, cocoa powder, baking soda, baking powder, and salt.

Cream the butter and sugar.
In a large bowl, beat ¾ cup of butter with an electric mixer on medium speed for about 10 seconds, or until smooth. Beat in the granulated sugar until well blended and light and fluffy, about 2 minutes. Beat in the eggs, one at a time, beating after each egg is added. Beat in the vanilla.

Combine the ingredients.
Alternate adding the flour mixture and 1½ cups of milk to the butter mixture, beating on low after each addition until batter is just combined. Fold in the chocolate chips.

Bake the cake.
Spoon the batter evenly among the 2 prepared cake pans. Bake for 30 to 35 minutes, or until a toothpick inserted into the center comes out clean. Cool slightly, then remove the cakes from the pans to finish cooling on a wire rack.

Make the frosting.

In a large bowl, blend 1 cup of butter and the peanut butter with an electric mixer on low speed. Beat in the confectioners' sugar. Slowly add 1 to 2 tablespoons of milk, beating until the frosting is a spreading consistency.

Frost the cake.

When the cakes are completely cool, place one layer, flat side up, on a serving plate. Spread the frosting over the top with an offset spatula or butter knife. Place the second cake layer on top, flat side down. Spread more frosting on the top and sides of cake as desired.

grasshopper cake stacks

PREP TIME: 30 minutes

COOK TIME: 25 minutes

YIELD: 15 cakes

TOOLS/EQUIPMENT

- 2 (9-inch) round cake pans
- Medium bowl
- Large bowl
- Electric hand mixer or stand mixer
- Wire rack
- 2-inch round cookie or biscuit cutter

FOR THE CAKES

Butter, for greasing the pans

Flour, for dusting the pans

1⅓ cups all-purpose flour

½ cup unsweetened cocoa powder

¾ teaspoon baking soda

½ teaspoon baking powder

¼ teaspoon table salt

½ cup (1 stick) unsalted butter, at room temperature

1⅓ cups granulated sugar

2 large eggs, at room temperature

1 teaspoon vanilla extract

1 cup milk (2 percent or whole)

Preheat the oven to 350°F.

Grease and lightly flour 2 (9-inch) round cake pans.

Mix the dry ingredients.

In a medium bowl, stir together the flour, cocoa powder, baking soda, baking powder, and salt.

Cream the butter and sugar.

In a large bowl, beat ½ cup of butter with an electric mixer on medium speed for about 10 seconds, or until smooth. Beat in the granulated sugar until well blended and light and fluffy, about 2 minutes. Add the eggs, one at a time, beating after each egg is added. Beat in the vanilla.

Blend the ingredients.

In batches, alternate adding the flour mixture and 1 cup of milk to the butter mixture, beating on low after each addition until the batter is just combined.

Bake the cake.

Spoon the batter evenly between two prepared cake pans. Bake for 20 to 25 minutes, or until a toothpick inserted into the center comes out clean. Cool slightly, then remove the cakes from pans to finish cooling on a wire rack.

Make the cake rounds.

Using a 2-inch round cookie cutter, cut cake into small rounds. You should get about 15 per pan for a total of 30. Save the cake scraps for other uses (see Did You Know?).

FOR THE MINT CHOCOLATE CHIP FROSTING

¾ cup (1½ sticks) unsalted butter, at room temperature

1 (16-ounce) bag (3¾ cups) confectioners' sugar

2 to 4 tablespoons milk (2 percent or whole)

1 teaspoon mint extract

Green food coloring

1 cup finely chopped semisweet chocolate, plus more for garnish (optional)

Prepare the frosting.

Beat together ¾ cup of butter and the confectioners' sugar with an electric mixer on medium speed. Slowly add the milk, 1 tablespoon at a time, until it has a frosting consistency. Beat in the mint extract and a few drops of green food coloring until well blended. Add a little more green food coloring as needed to achieve the desired color. Stir in the chopped chocolate.

Assemble the cakes.

Spread about 1 tablespoon of frosting over each cake round. Then place one frosted cake round on another to make 15 cakes in total. Garnish with chopped chocolate, if desired.

 TRY INSTEAD: You can use your favorite frosting instead of the mint chocolate chip.

 DID YOU KNOW? Cake crumbs are great on top of ice cream!

HELPFUL HINT: To flour the pan, combine a little flour and unsweetened cocoa powder in a small bowl, mix, then dust over the pan. Flip the pan over a sink, and tap lightly to remove excess. Save a little of the mixture. Then, when cutting the cake rounds, dip your cookie cutter in a little flour to make cutting easier.

dark chocolate fudge lava cakes

PREP TIME: 20 minutes

COOK TIME: 12 minutes

YIELD: 4 cakes

TOOLS/EQUIPMENT

- 4 (6-ounce) ramekins
- Baking sheet
- Double boiler (or see Make Your Own Double Boiler, page 53)
- Medium bowl
- Electric hand mixer
- Spatula

Butter, for greasing the ramekins
Flour, for dusting the ramekins
½ cup (1 stick) unsalted butter
6 ounces dark chocolate, chopped
¼ cup granulated sugar
2 large eggs, at room temperature
2 large egg yolks
⅛ teaspoon table salt
2 tablespoons all-purpose flour

Preheat the oven to 350°F.
Grease and lightly flour 4 (6-ounce) ramekins. Set the ramekins on a baking sheet.

Melt the chocolate.
Place the butter and the chocolate in the top of a double boiler over boiling water, reduce the heat to low, and mix until smooth. Remove from heat, and cool completely.

Blend the ingredients.
In a medium bowl, beat the sugar, eggs, egg yolks, and salt with an electric mixer on medium speed until frothy. With a spatula, fold in the cooled chocolate, along with the flour, until just combined.

Bake the cakes.
Spoon the batter into the prepared ramekins. Bake for 10 to 12 minutes or until the sides of the cakes look firm but the center still looks a little soft. Cool the cakes for 1 to 2 minutes, then using oven mitts, gently flip them over onto serving plates. Let them sit a few seconds, then wiggle the ramekins slightly to allow the cakes to come out. If the cakes are stuck, gently loosen the edges with a butter knife. Serve immediately.

TRY INSTEAD: Instead of dark chocolate, you can use bittersweet or semisweet chocolate.

DID YOU KNOW? These cakes are great served with ice cream, whipped cream, and/or fresh berries!

upside-down apple cupcakes

PREP TIME: 30 minutes

COOK TIME: 20 minutes

YIELD: 18 cupcakes

TOOLS/EQUIPMENT

- 2 muffin pans
- Medium skillet
- Medium bowl
- Large bowl
- Electric mixer

Butter, for greasing the pans

FOR THE APPLES

4 tablespoons unsalted butter

⅔ cup brown sugar

2 large apples, cored, peeled, and very thinly sliced

FOR THE CAKES

1 cup all-purpose flour

1¼ teaspoons baking powder

½ teaspoon cinnamon

¼ teaspoon table salt

½ cup (1 stick) unsalted butter, at room temperature

1 cup granulated sugar

1 large egg

1 teaspoon vanilla extract

¼ cup buttermilk

Preheat the oven to 350˚F.
Generously grease 18 cups of 2 (12-cup) muffin pans.

Cook the apples.
In a medium skillet over medium heat, heat 4 tablespoons of butter and the brown sugar, stirring until combined and melted. Add the apples, stirring to combine, and cook for 4 to 5 minutes or until the apples are soft, stirring occasionally. Spoon 2 or 3 apple slices and a little sauce into the bottom of each muffin cup.

Mix the dry ingredients.
In a medium bowl, stir together the flour, baking powder, cinnamon, and salt.

Cream the butter and sugar.
In a large bowl, beat ½ cup of room-temperature butter with an electric mixer on medium speed for about 10 seconds, or until smooth. Beat in the granulated sugar until well blended and light and fluffy, about 2 minutes. Add the eggs, one at a time, beating after each egg is added, then beat in the vanilla. »

TRY INSTEAD: Instead of apple, you could try pear, peach, or chopped pineapple.

DID YOU KNOW? These mini cakes are great served with vanilla ice cream or whipped cream!

HELPFUL HINT: When alternating flour and liquid in a cake recipe, generally it's best to add the dry and wet ingredients in two or three batches, starting with and ending with the dry ingredients. Adding too much wet mixture at once can cause the batter to separate, while adding too much dry mixture at once can lead to overmixing and a tougher cake.

Combine the ingredients.

In batches, alternate adding the flour mixture and the buttermilk to the butter mixture, beating on low after each addition until the batter is just combined.

Bake the cupcakes.

Spoon the batter over the apples in the muffin cups until half to ⅔ full. Bake for 18 to 20 minutes, or until a toothpick inserted into the center comes out clean. Cool slightly, then gently flip the cakes over onto a platter or serving plate.

coconut explosion cupcakes

PREP TIME: 30 minutes

COOK TIME: 20 minutes

YIELD: 12 cupcakes

TOOLS/EQUIPMENT

- Muffin pan
- Paper liners (optional)
- Medium bowl
- Large bowl
- Electric hand mixer or stand mixer
- Wire rack
- Spatula

FOR THE CUPCAKES

Butter, for greasing the pan (optional)

Flour, for dusting the pan (optional)

1 cup all-purpose flour

½ teaspoon baking powder

½ teaspoon baking soda

⅛ teaspoon table salt

¼ cup shortening, at room temperature

¾ cup granulated sugar

2 large egg whites

½ teaspoon vanilla extract

½ teaspoon coconut extract

¾ cup sweetened flaked coconut

⅔ cup buttermilk

FOR THE FROSTING

1 (8-ounce brick) cream cheese, at room temperature

6 tablespoons shortening, softened

½ teaspoon coconut extract

3 to 4 cups confectioners' sugar

½ cup sweetened flaked coconut

Milk (2 percent or whole, optional)

Preheat the oven to 350°F.

Grease and lightly flour a 12-cup muffin pan or line with paper liners.

Mix the dry ingredients.

In a medium bowl, stir together the flour, baking powder, baking soda, and salt.

Cream the shortening and sugar.

In a large bowl, beat ¼ cup of shortening with an electric mixer on medium speed for about 10 seconds, or until smooth. Beat in the granulated sugar until well blended and light and fluffy, about 2 minutes. Beat in the egg whites, one at a time, beating after each is added. Beat in the vanilla and ½ teaspoon of coconut extract. Fold in ¾ cup of flaked coconut.

Combine the ingredients.

Alternate adding the flour mixture and the buttermilk to the shortening mixture, beating on low after each addition until batter is just blended.

Bake the cupcakes.

Spoon the batter into muffin cups about ⅔ full. Bake for 18 to 20 minutes, or until a toothpick inserted into the center comes out clean. Cool slightly, then remove the cupcakes to finish cooling on a wire rack. »

TRY INSTEAD: If you can't find coconut extract, you can substitute vanilla extract or even almond extract.

DID YOU KNOW? Using egg whites instead of whole eggs, and shortening instead of butter, gives these cupcakes a nice white color. If desired, you can substitute one whole egg for the two egg whites, and butter for the shortening.

HELPFUL HINT: Garnish the tops of cupcakes with toasted coconut if desired. To make toasted coconut, spread sweetened flaked coconut in a single layer on a baking sheet. Bake in a preheated 350°F oven for 5 to 10 minutes, stirring occasionally, until crispy and golden brown. Keep an eye on it because it can burn quickly!

Make the frosting.

In a large bowl, beat together the cream cheese and 6 tablespoons of shortening until smooth. Beat in ½ teaspoon of coconut extract. Beat in 2 cups of confectioners' sugar, adding more as needed while beating until a spreading consistency. Fold in ½ cup of flaked coconut. If the frosting is too thick, you can stir in a little milk, a few teaspoons at a time.

Frost the cupcakes.

When the cupcakes are completely cooled, frost the cupcakes with a spatula.

roasted strawberry shortcakes

PREP TIME: 25 minutes

COOK TIME: 25 minutes

YIELD: 6 shortcakes

TOOLS/EQUIPMENT

- Baking sheet
- Parchment paper (optional)
- Medium bowl
- Small bowl
- Whisk (or fork)
- Pastry cutter (see Cutting in Butter, page 42)
- Large spoon
- Pastry brush
- Wire rack
- Large bowl
- Electric hand mixer or stand mixer

FOR THE BISCUITS

Butter, for greasing the baking sheet (optional)

2 cups all-purpose flour

2 tablespoons granulated sugar

1 tablespoon baking powder

½ teaspoon table salt

⅓ cup plus 1 tablespoon cold heavy whipping cream, divided

⅓ cup water

1 large egg

4 tablespoons cold unsalted butter, cubed

Preheat the oven to 375°F.

Lightly grease a baking sheet or line with parchment paper.

Mix the dry ingredients.

In a medium bowl, mix together the flour, 2 tablespoons of sugar, baking powder, and salt.

Mix the wet ingredients.

In a small bowl, whisk together ⅓ cup of heavy cream, the water, and egg until well blended.

Cut in the butter.

Using a pastry cutter or the back of a fork, cut the butter into the flour mixture until the mixture is crumbly. Stir in the wet ingredients until just combined.

Bake the biscuits.

Using a large spoon, drop the biscuit dough onto the prepared baking sheet to make 6 biscuits, leaving about 2 inches of space in between. Brush 1 tablespoon of heavy cream over the top of the biscuits. Bake for 20 to 25 minutes, or until golden brown. Cool slightly, then transfer the biscuits to a wire rack to finish cooling. Keep the oven on for the strawberries.

FOR THE STRAWBERRIES

1½ pounds fresh strawberries, tops removed and thinly sliced
¼ cup granulated sugar
½ teaspoon vanilla extract

FOR THE WHIPPED CREAM

1½ cups cold heavy whipping cream
2 tablespoons granulated sugar

TRY INSTEAD: Instead of making your own whipped cream, you can use store-bought whipped cream or whipped topping.

DID YOU KNOW? If you don't want to get out an electric mixer, you can make whipped cream with a whisk. Simply whip the whipped cream until soft peaks form. Be forewarned, it takes a while and your arm may get tired!

Make the strawberries.

Lightly grease another baking sheet or line with parchment paper. Place the strawberry slices on the pan and toss gently with ¼ cup of sugar. Bake for 10 to 15 minutes, or until soft. Spoon the berries into a small bowl, and stir in the vanilla. Set aside to cool.

Make the whipped cream.

In a large, cold bowl, add 1½ cups of heavy cream and 2 tablespoons of sugar. Whip with an electric mixer on medium-high until soft peaks form.

Assemble the shortcakes.

Cut the biscuits in half to make a top and a bottom. Place the bottom half on serving plates, then spoon the strawberries and whipped cream on top. Cover with the top half of the biscuit. Serve immediately.

5

cookies & bars

snickerdoodle bites

PREP TIME: 20 minutes
(plus 1 hour chill time)

COOK TIME: 12 minutes

YIELD: 30 cookies

TOOLS/EQUIPMENT

- Small bowl
- Large bowl
- Electric hand mixer
- Plastic wrap
- 2 baking sheets
- Parchment paper (optional)
- Wire rack

FOR THE COOKIES

1¼ cups plus 2 tablespoons
    all-purpose flour

1 teaspoon cream of tartar

½ teaspoon baking soda

⅛ teaspoon table salt

½ cup (1 stick) unsalted butter,
    at room temperature

¾ cup granulated sugar

1 large egg

½ teaspoon vanilla extract

FOR THE TOPPING

3 tablespoons granulated sugar

1 teaspoon cinnamon

Mix the dry ingredients.

In a small bowl, stir together the flour, cream of tartar, baking soda, and salt.

Cream the butter and sugar.

In a large bowl, beat the butter with an electric mixer on medium speed for about 10 seconds, or until smooth. Beat in ¾ cup of sugar until well blended and light and fluffy, about 2 minutes. Beat in the egg, then beat in the vanilla until well blended.

Beat the ingredients.

Add the flour mixture to the butter and sugar mixture, beating with an electric mixer on medium speed until blended.

Refrigerate the dough.

Cover the bowl with plastic wrap and refrigerate to chill for about an hour, or until dough is firm and cold.

Preheat the oven to 350°F.

Prepare the topping.

In a small bowl, mix together 3 tablespoons of sugar and the cinnamon in a small bowl until well blended.

Make the cookies.

Form the dough into 30 balls, about 2 teaspoons each. Roll each ball lightly in the cinnamon sugar mixture. Place the dough on 2 ungreased baking sheets, or baking sheets lined with parchment paper, leaving about 2 inches between cookies.

Bake the cookies.

Bake for 7 to 12 minutes or until lightly browned around the edges, rotating the pans halfway through cooking. Cool slightly, then transfer the cookies to a wire rack to cool completely.

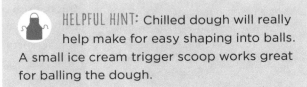 **TRY INSTEAD:** Instead of cinnamon, you can experiment with other spices. Try nutmeg or allspice, or skip the spices and sugar and dip into rainbow sprinkles!

HELPFUL HINT: Chilled dough will really help make for easy shaping into balls. A small ice cream trigger scoop works great for balling the dough.

shortbread dippin' sticks

PREP TIME: 20 minutes (plus 30 minutes chill time)

COOK TIME: 20 minutes

YIELD: 36 cookies

TOOLS/EQUIPMENT

- Small bowl
- Large bowl
- Electric hand mixer
- Plastic wrap
- Rolling pin
- Cookie cutter (optional)
- 2 baking sheets
- Parchment paper (optional)
- Wire rack

3½ cups all-purpose flour

¼ teaspoon table salt

1½ cups (3 sticks) unsalted butter, at room temperature

1 cup granulated sugar

1 teaspoon vanilla extract

Flour, for dusting the work surface

Ice cream toppings like chocolate sauce, caramel, and strawberry sauce for dipping (optional)

Preheat the oven to 350˚F.

Mix the dry ingredients.
In a small bowl, stir together the flour and salt.

Cream the butter and sugar.
In a large bowl, beat the butter with an electric mixer on medium speed for about 10 seconds, or until smooth. Beat in the sugar until light and fluffy, about 2 minutes. Beat in the vanilla.

Beat the ingredients.
Add the flour mixture to the butter and sugar mixture, and beat with an electric mixer on medium speed until blended.

Refrigerate the dough.
Wrap dough completely in plastic wrap. Flatten to form a large, flat disk. Refrigerate dough for 30 minutes to one hour, or until cold and firm.

Cut out the cookies.
Unwrap the dough and place on a lightly floured surface. Roll out dough to about a ½-inch thickness. Using a knife or cookie cutter, cut the dough into rectangles, about 1 inch by 2 inches.

Bake the cookies.
Place the cookies on 2 ungreased baking sheets or baking sheets lined with parchment paper, leaving about 2 inches between cookies. Bake for 15 to 20 minutes, or until lightly browned around the edges, rotating the pans halfway through cooking. Cool slightly, then transfer the cookies to a wire rack to cool completely. Serve with sauces for dipping.

spiced oatmeal raisin cookies

PREP TIME: 20 minutes
(plus 2 hours chill time)

COOK TIME: 17 minutes

YIELD: 12 cookies

TOOLS/EQUIPMENT

- Medium bowl
- Large bowl
- Electric mixer
- Plastic wrap
- Baking sheets
- Parchment paper (optional)
- Wire rack

1¼ cups old-fashioned rolled oats

¾ cup all-purpose flour

¾ teaspoon cinnamon

½ teaspoon table salt

½ teaspoon baking powder

⅛ teaspoon ground cloves

⅛ teaspoon ground nutmeg

⅛ teaspoon ground ginger

½ cup (1 stick) unsalted butter,
    at room temperature

¾ cup granulated sugar

2 tablespoons molasses

1 large egg

1 teaspoon vanilla extract

1 cup raisins

Mix the dry ingredients.

In a medium bowl, stir together the oats, flour, cinnamon, salt, baking powder, cloves, nutmeg, and ginger.

Cream the butter and sugar.

In a large bowl, beat the butter with an electric mixer on medium speed for about 10 seconds or until smooth. Beat in the sugar and molasses until well blended and light and fluffy, about 2 minutes. Beat in the egg, then beat in vanilla until well blended.

Beat the ingredients.

Add the flour mixture to the butter and sugar mixture, and beat with an electric mixer on medium speed until blended. With a spoon, stir in the raisins.

Refrigerate the dough.

Cover the dough with plastic wrap and refrigerate for at least 2 hours or overnight to firm up.

Preheat the oven to 350˚F. »

TRY INSTEAD: Instead of raisins, you can substitute another chewy dried fruit, like chopped dried cherries.

HELPFUL HINT: You don't have to refrigerate the dough, but doing so does seem to improve the taste and texture of the cookies!

FOOD FACT: Half of the world's raisin supply is grown in California!

Bake the cookies.

Drop the cookie dough in big (3-tablespoon) lumps onto ungreased baking sheets or baking sheets lined with parchment paper, leaving about 2 inches between cookies. Bake for 13 to 17 minutes, or until golden brown around the edges, rotating the pans halfway through cooking. Cool slightly, then transfer the cookies to a wire rack to cool completely.

bite-size coconut macaroons

PREP TIME: 20 minutes
COOK TIME: 15 minutes
YIELD: 12 cookies

TOOLS/EQUIPMENT

- Baking sheet
- Parchment paper (optional)
- Food processor
- Large bowl
- Whisk or fork
- Wire rack

Butter, for greasing the baking sheet (optional)
2 cups sweetened flaked coconut
2 large egg whites
¼ cup granulated sugar
½ teaspoon vanilla extract
⅛ teaspoon table salt

Preheat the oven to 350°F.
Lightly grease a baking sheet or line with parchment paper.

Chop the coconut.
Place the coconut in a food processor, and pulse until finely chopped.

Whisk the ingredients.
In a large bowl, whisk together the egg whites, sugar, vanilla, and salt until well blended. Stir in the coconut.

Bake the macaroons.
Drop the coconut mixture, about 2 teaspoons each, onto the prepared baking sheet, leaving about 2 inches between cookies. Bake for 10 to 15 minutes, or until golden brown around the edges. Cool for a few minutes, then transfer the cookies to a wire rack to finish cooling.

 TRY INSTEAD: Instead of vanilla extract, try a different extract like almond or orange.

HELPFUL HINT: You don't have to chop the coconut, but I prefer smaller pieces. You can also chop the coconut with a knife on a cutting board.

 FOOD FACT: The white, fleshy part of the coconut seed is called coconut meat.

vanilla tuiles

PREP TIME: 20 minutes
(plus 2 hours chill time)

COOK TIME: 10 minutes

YIELD: 24 cookies

TOOLS/EQUIPMENT

- Large bowl
- Whisk or fork
- Plastic wrap
- Baking sheets
- Parchment paper (optional)
- Offset spatula or butter knife

¾ cup granulated sugar

3 large egg whites

½ cup (1 stick) unsalted butter, melted and cooled

1 teaspoon vanilla extract

½ cup all-purpose flour

⅛ teaspoon table salt

Butter, for greasing the baking sheets (optional)

Mix all the ingredients.
In a large bowl, whisk together the sugar and egg whites until well blended. Whisk in the melted butter and vanilla until well blended, then beat in the flour and salt until just combined.

Refrigerate the batter.
Cover the bowl with plastic wrap and refrigerate at least 2 to 3 hours or overnight.

Preheat the oven to 350˚F.
But first, position an oven rack in the middle of the oven. Grease baking sheets or line them with lightly greased parchment paper.

Form the cookies.
Spoon about 2 teaspoons of batter onto prepared baking sheets. With an offset spatula or the back of a spoon, spread the batter into a very thin circle, 3 to 4 inches wide. Repeat, leaving about an inch of space between cookies.

Bake the cookies.
Bake for 7 to 10 minutes, or until golden brown around the edges. Cool for a few seconds, then remove from the pan and quickly roll the cookies into tubes before they cool (see Helpful Hint). Cool completely.

> **HELPFUL HINT:** The cookies harden quickly so only bake a few cookies at a time, and make sure your pan is completely cool before placing a new batch on the pan.

honey roasted peanut butter cookies

PREP TIME: 20 minutes (plus 30 minutes chill time)

COOK TIME: 17 minutes

YIELD: 24 cookies

TOOLS/EQUIPMENT

- Medium bowl
- Large bowl
- Electric hand mixer
- Plastic wrap
- 2 baking sheets
- Parchment paper (optional)
- Fork
- Wire rack

2¾ cups all-purpose flour

1¼ teaspoons baking soda

¼ teaspoon table salt

¾ cup (1½ sticks) unsalted butter, at room temperature

¼ cup shortening

1¼ cups brown sugar

½ cup plus 1 tablespoon granulated sugar, divided

1 cup creamy peanut butter

2 large eggs, at room temperature

2 teaspoons vanilla extract

1 cup chopped honey roasted peanuts

Mix the dry ingredients.

In a medium bowl, stir together the flour, baking soda, and salt.

Cream the butter and sugar.

In a large bowl, beat the butter and shortening with an electric mixer on medium speed for about 10 seconds, or until smooth. Beat in the brown sugar and ½ cup of granulated sugar until well blended and light and fluffy, about 2 minutes. Beat in the peanut butter, then beat in the eggs one at a time, beating after each addition. Beat in the vanilla until well blended.

Mix the ingredients.

Beat the flour mixture into the butter and sugar mixture until just combined. With a spoon, stir in the nuts.

Refrigerate the dough.

Cover the dough with plastic wrap and refrigerate for a half-hour or more, until firm.

Preheat the oven to 375°F.

Bake the cookies.

Drop the cookie dough in big (3-tablespoon) lumps onto ungreased baking sheets or baking sheets lined with parchment paper, leaving about 2 inches between cookies. Gently press down on the cookies with a fork (up and down, and side to side) to make a crisscross pattern. Sprinkle lightly with the remaining tablespoon of sugar. Bake for 13 to 17 minutes, or until golden brown around the edges, rotating the pans halfway through baking. Cool slightly, then transfer the cookies to a wire rack to cool completely.

TRY INSTEAD: Instead of chopped peanuts, substitute your favorite chocolate chip!

DID YOU KNOW? Peanut allergies can be very serious—even life threatening. Be sure to check with people if they have a nut allergy before serving.

thick and chewy chocolate chip cookies

PREP TIME: 30 minutes
(plus 2 hours chill time)

COOK TIME: 18 minutes

YIELD: 30 cookies

TOOLS/EQUIPMENT

- Medium bowl
- Large bowl
- Electric hand mixer
- Plastic wrap
- 2 baking sheets
- Parchment paper (optional)
- Wire rack

3⅓ cups all-purpose flour
1 tablespoon cornstarch
1 teaspoon baking powder
1 teaspoon baking soda
1 teaspoon table salt
1 cup (2 sticks) unsalted butter, melted and cooled slightly
1 cup brown sugar
1 cup granulated sugar
1 large egg
2 large egg yolks
1 teaspoon vanilla extract
1 (12-ounce) bag mini chocolate chips

Mix the dry ingredients.
In a medium bowl, stir together the flour, cornstarch, baking powder, baking soda, and salt.

Cream the butter and sugar.
In a large bowl, beat the melted butter, brown sugar, and granulated sugar with an electric mixer on medium speed until well blended and light and fluffy, about 2 minutes. Beat in the egg and egg yolks, then beat in vanilla until well blended.

Beat the ingredients.
Add the flour mixture to the butter and sugar mixture, and beat with an electric mixer on medium speed until blended. With a spoon, stir in the chocolate chips.

Refrigerate the dough.
Drop the dough in large (3-tablespoon) lumps on a large baking sheet or 2 baking sheets, leaving about 2 inches between cookies. Cover the dough with plastic wrap and refrigerate at least 2 hours or overnight. >>

TRY INSTEAD: Instead of mini chocolate chips, use another favorite—white chocolate, butterscotch, or peanut butter chips all work!

HELPFUL HINT: A large trigger ice cream scoop helps make cookies the same size. Flatten the cookies slightly before baking if using an ice cream scoop.

TROUBLESHOOTING TIP: The melted butter should be slightly warm when adding it to other ingredients, but make sure it's not hot. If it's too hot, it may cook the eggs before you bake the cookies!

Preheat the oven to 325°F.

Bake the cookies.
Bake for 15 to 18 minutes on ungreased baking sheets or baking sheets lined with parchment paper, or until lightly browned around the edges, rotating the pans halfway through cooking. Cool slightly, then transfer the cookies to a wire rack to cool completely.

chocolate pecan tassie cookie cups

PREP TIME: 30 minutes

COOK TIME: 30 minutes

YIELD: 24 cookies

TOOLS/EQUIPMENT

- 2 medium bowls
- Electric mixer
- Mini muffin pan (24-cup)
- Wire rack

FOR THE COOKIES

½ cup (1 stick) unsalted butter, at room temperature

⅓ cup (3 ounces) plain cream cheese, at room temperature

1 cup all-purpose flour

FOR THE FILLING

1 large egg

¾ cup brown sugar

1 tablespoon unsalted butter, melted

⅓ cup chopped pecans

⅓ cup mini chocolate chips

Preheat the oven to 325°F.

Make the cookie dough.
In a medium bowl, beat together ½ cup of room-temperature butter and the cream cheese with an electric mixer on medium speed until well blended. Beat in the flour until just blended.

Prepare the filling.
In another medium bowl, whisk together the egg, brown sugar, and melted butter until well blended. Stir in the pecans and chocolate chips.

Form the cookies.
Press a rounded teaspoon of cookie dough in each cup of an ungreased 24-cup mini muffin pan. Press the dough in the middle so it goes up the sides to form a little cookie cup. Spoon the filling into each cookie cup about ¾ full.

Bake the cookies.
Bake for 25 to 30 minutes, or until golden brown and slightly puffed. Cool slightly in the pan, then transfer the cookies to a wire rack to finish cooling.

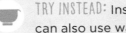 TRY INSTEAD: Instead of pecans, you can also use walnuts or another favorite nut.

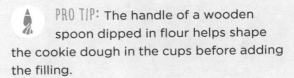 PRO TIP: The handle of a wooden spoon dipped in flour helps shape the cookie dough in the cups before adding the filling.

frosted sugar cookie pops

PREP TIME: 45 minutes
(plus 2 hours chill time)

COOK TIME: 14 minutes

YIELD: 24 cookie pops

TOOLS/EQUIPMENT

- Medium bowl
- Large bowl
- Electric mixer
- Plastic wrap
- 2 baking sheets
- Parchment paper (optional)
- Rolling pin
- Round cookie cutter
- White lollipop sticks
- Wire rack

FOR THE COOKIES

3 cups all-purpose flour

¾ teaspoon baking powder

¼ teaspoon table salt

1 cup (2 sticks) unsalted butter,
    at room temperature

1 cup granulated sugar

1 large egg

1 tablespoon milk (2 percent
    or whole)

1 teaspoon vanilla extract

Butter, for greasing the baking
    sheets (optional)

Mix the dry ingredients.

In a medium bowl, stir together the flour, baking powder, and salt.

Cream the butter and sugar.

In a large bowl, beat 1 cup of butter with an electric mixer on medium speed for about 10 seconds or until smooth. Beat in the granulated sugar until well blended and light and fluffy, about 2 minutes. Beat in the egg, 1 tablespoon of milk, and 1 teaspoon of vanilla until well blended.

Blend the ingredients.

Add the flour mixture to the butter and sugar mixture, and beat with an electric mixer on medium speed until blended.

Refrigerate the dough.

Divide the dough in half, and place each half on a large piece of plastic wrap. Flatten each piece to form a large disk, then wrap tightly with plastic wrap. Refrigerate for at least 2 hours or until firm.

Preheat the oven to 375°F.

Lightly grease 2 baking sheets or line with parchment paper.

Create the pops.

Roll out one piece of dough on a lightly floured surface to ¼-inch thick. Using a 3-inch round cookie cutter, cut out circles. Place the circles on the prepared baking sheets. Gently press a lollipop stick about a half-inch into each cookie from the side. Use cookie dough scraps to cover the stick if it pops through.

FOR THE FROSTING

½ cup (1 stick) unsalted butter,
    at room temperature
4 cups confectioners' sugar
½ teaspoon vanilla extract
3 to 6 tablespoons whole milk
Food coloring (optional)
Sprinkles (optional)

Bake the cookies.

Bake for 9 to 14 minutes, or until golden brown around the edges, rotating the pans halfway through baking. Cool slightly, then transfer the cookies to a wire rack to finish cooling.

Make the frosting.

In a medium bowl, beat ½ cup of butter with an electric mixer for about 10 seconds or until smooth. Gradually beat in the confectioners' sugar and ½ teaspoon vanilla. Add 2 tablespoons of milk and beat until smooth, adding a little more milk, one tablespoon at a time, as needed. Add a few drops of food coloring, if desired. Once cookies are completely cooled, frost them and decorate with sprinkles, if desired.

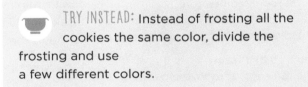

TRY INSTEAD: Instead of frosting all the cookies the same color, divide the frosting and use a few different colors.

PRO TIP: If you don't have a 3-inch cookie cutter, use a small bowl or glass and cut with a knife around the rim.

classic lemon bars

PREP TIME: 30 minutes
(plus 2 hours chill time)

COOK TIME: 50 minutes

YIELD: 16 bars

TOOLS/EQUIPMENT

- 8-inch square baking pan
- Small bowl
- Large bowl
- Electric mixer
- Whisk or fork
- Zester

FOR THE CRUST

Butter, for greasing the pan
1 cup all-purpose flour
⅛ teaspoon table salt
¾ cup (1½ sticks) unsalted butter, at room temperature
¼ cup confectioners' sugar
2 tablespoons brown sugar

FOR THE FILLING

2 large eggs, at room temperature
1 large egg yolk
1 cup granulated sugar
3 tablespoons all-purpose flour
½ teaspoon freshly grated lemon zest
½ cup freshly squeezed lemon juice (3 or 4 lemons)

FOR THE GARNISH

2 tablespoons confectioners' sugar

Preheat the oven to 350°F.
Lightly grease an 8-inch square baking pan.

Mix the dry ingredients.
In a small bowl, stir together 1 cup of flour and the salt.

Cream the butter and sugar.
In a large bowl, beat the butter with an electric mixer on medium speed for about 10 seconds, or until smooth. Beat in ¼ cup of confectioners' sugar and the brown sugar until well blended and light and fluffy, about 2 minutes. Add the flour mixture to the butter mixture until just combined. Press the dough evenly onto the bottom of the pan and about ½ inch up the sides of the pan to form the crust.

Bake the crust.
Bake for 15 to 20 minutes, or until golden brown around the edges.

Prepare the filling.
Meanwhile, in a large bowl whisk together the eggs, egg yolk, granulated sugar, 3 tablespoons of flour, lemon zest, and lemon juice until well blended.

Bake the bars.
Remove the crust from the oven and reduce the oven temperature to 300°F. Pour the filling over the cooked crust. Bake for 25 to 30 minutes, or until the filling appears set (firm). Cool the bars, then refrigerate for at least 2 to 3 hours, or until firm enough to cut into bars. Dust with 2 table-spoons of confectioners' sugar before serving.

strawberry cheesecake bars

PREP TIME: 15 minutes
(plus 3 hours chill time)
COOK TIME: 40 minutes
YIELD: 16 bars

TOOLS/EQUIPMENT
- 8-inch square baking pan
- 2 medium bowls
- Electric mixer
- Blender

FOR THE CRUST
Butter, for greasing the pan
1½ cups graham cracker crumbs
    (10 to 12 whole graham
    crackers)
4 tablespoons unsalted butter,
    melted

FOR THE CHEESECAKE
2 (8-ounce) bricks cream cheese,
    at room temperature
½ cup granulated sugar
2 large eggs, at room temperature
½ teaspoon vanilla extract

FOR THE STRAWBERRY SAUCE
1 pound frozen strawberries,
    thawed
¼ cup granulated sugar
1 teaspoon vanilla extract

Preheat the oven to 350°F.
Lightly grease an 8-inch square baking pan.

Prepare the crust.
In a medium bowl, mix together the graham cracker crumbs and melted butter. Press the mixture evenly into the bottom of the pan.

Make the cheesecake.
In another medium bowl, beat the cream cheese with an electric mixer on medium speed until smooth. Beat in ½ cup of sugar until well blended. Beat in the eggs one at a time, beating after each addition, then beat in ½ teaspoon of vanilla. Pour the mixture over the crust.

Bake the cheesecake.
Bake for 30 to 40 minutes, or until center is almost set (firm). Let cool, then refrigerate at least 3 hours, or overnight, until fully chilled.

Make the strawberry sauce.
Meanwhile, in a blender, add the thawed strawberries, ¼ cup of granulated sugar, and 1 teaspoon of vanilla. Pulse repeatedly until smooth.

Serve the treat.
Once the cheesecake is fully chilled, cut it into bars, and drizzle with a little strawberry sauce before serving.

HELPFUL HINT: You can use a food processor instead of a blender to make the strawberry sauce. If you like your sauce really smooth, pour the sauce through a fine mesh strainer to get any seeds out.

PRO TIP: Thawed frozen berries work well for making quick sauces, because they are soft and full of liquid.

TROUBLESHOOTING TIP: Cheesecake is best served the next day. So, if you're having a hard time cutting it into bars, make sure it is fully chilled.

no campfire s'mores bars

PREP TIME: 20 minutes

COOK TIME: 30 minutes

YIELD: 16 bars

TOOLS/EQUIPMENT

- 8-inch square baking pan
- Medium bowl
- Large bowl
- Electric hand mixer
- Spatula
- Wax or parchment paper

Butter, for greasing the pan

1¼ cups all-purpose flour

¾ cup graham cracker crumbs
(5 or 6 whole graham crackers)

½ teaspoon baking soda

½ teaspoon table salt

1 cup (2 sticks) unsalted butter,
at room temperature

¾ cup granulated sugar

¾ cup brown sugar

1 large egg

1 teaspoon vanilla extract

4 (1½-ounce) milk chocolate
candy bars

1 (7½-ounce) jar marshmallow
crème (Marshmallow Fluff)

Preheat the oven to 350°F.

Lightly grease an 8-inch square baking pan.

Mix the dry ingredients.

In a medium bowl, stir together the flour, graham cracker crumbs, baking soda, and salt.

Cream the butter and sugar.

In a large bowl, beat the butter with an electric mixer on medium speed for about 10 seconds, or until smooth. Beat in the granulated sugar and brown sugar on medium speed until well blended and light and fluffy, about 2 minutes. Beat in the egg, then add the vanilla, beating until well blended.

Beat the ingredients.

Add the flour mixture to the butter and sugar mixture, and beat on medium speed until blended.

Form the cookies.

Spread half of the cookie batter on the bottom of the pan, using your fingers or the back of a fork to evenly cover the pan. Place the chocolate bars on top of the dough in a single layer, breaking the bars into pieces as necessary to fit. Using a spatula, spread the marshmallow crème on top of the chocolate in an even layer. Press the remaining cookie dough on a large sheet of wax or parchment paper to form an 8-inch square. Flip the cookie dough over on top of the marshmallow crème, and remove the paper. »

Bake the cookies.

Bake for 25 to 30 minutes, or until golden brown around the edges. Cool completely before cutting into bars.

TRY INSTEAD: Instead of plain chocolate bars, you can use a 12-ounce bag of milk chocolate chips or other kinds of chocolate bars.

HELPFUL HINT: To make graham cracker crumbs, place graham crackers into a resealable plastic bag. Roll over the bag with a rolling pin a few times until the crackers are crushed into crumbs. You can also use a food processor.

TROUBLESHOOTING TIPS: Marshmallow crème can be difficult to spread over chocolate. Spoon small scoops of the fluff all over the chocolate, then gently spread in each little area.

oat pear bars

PREP TIME: 30 minutes

COOK TIME: 40 minutes

YIELD: 16 bars

TOOLS/EQUIPMENT

- 8-inch square baking pan
- Medium bowl
- Large bowl
- Electric mixer
- Small saucepan
- Slotted spoon

Butter, for greasing the pan

¾ cup all-purpose flour

¾ cup old-fashioned rolled oats

½ teaspoon baking powder

½ teaspoon table salt

3 tablespoons unsalted butter, melted and cooled

½ cup brown sugar

1 large egg yolk

½ teaspoon vanilla extract

2 cups peeled, cored, and finely chopped pear (2 or 3 pears)

3 tablespoons maple syrup

Preheat the oven to 350°F.

Lightly grease an 8-inch square baking pan.

Mix the dry ingredients.

In a medium bowl, stir together the flour, oats, baking powder, and salt.

Cream the butter and sugar.

In a large bowl, beat together the melted butter and brown sugar with an electric mixer on medium speed until well blended and light and fluffy, about 2 minutes. Beat in the egg yolk, then beat in the vanilla.

Combine the ingredients.

Beat the flour mixture into the butter and sugar mixture until just combined.

Bake the crust.

Spread about ⅔ of the cookie batter evenly over the bottom of the prepared pan. Using your fingers or the back of a fork, press down to make an even layer. Bake the crust for 10 to 15 minutes, or until slightly puffed and golden brown around the edges.

Cook the pears.

Meanwhile, in a small saucepan over medium heat, heat the chopped pears and maple syrup. Cook for 5 to 7 minutes, or until the pears begin to soften.

Bake the bars.

Remove the crust from the oven. With a slotted spoon, spoon the pears over the top of the crust. Sprinkle the remaining cookie batter on top. Bake for 15 to 20 minutes, or until the edges are slightly browned. Cool completely before cutting into bars.

chocolate chunk brownies

PREP TIME: 20 minutes
COOK TIME: 30 minutes
YIELD: 16 brownies

TOOLS/EQUIPMENT

- 8-inch square baking pan
- Double boiler (or Make Your Own Double Boiler, page 53)
- Small bowl
- Large bowl
- Whisk

Butter, for greasing the pan

1 (12-ounce) bag semisweet chocolate chips, divided

½ cup (1 stick) unsalted butter

⅓ cup all-purpose flour

¾ teaspoon baking powder

¼ teaspoon table salt

½ cup granulated sugar

2 large eggs, at room temperature

1 teaspoon vanilla extract

1 cup chopped pecans or walnuts

Preheat the oven to 350°F.
Lightly grease an 8-inch square baking pan.

Melt the chocolate.
In the top of a double boiler, combine 1 cup of chocolate chips and the butter. Place over boiling water, then reduce the heat to low. Stir constantly until the chocolate and butter are melted and smooth. Remove from heat and let cool completely, 30 to 45 minutes.

Mix the dry ingredients.
In a small bowl, stir together the flour, baking powder, and salt.

Whisk additional ingredients.
In a large bowl, whisk together the sugar, eggs, and vanilla until well blended.

Combine the ingredients.
Slowly whisk the cooled chocolate mixture into the egg mixture until well blended, then stir in the flour mixture until just combined. Stir in the remaining chocolate chips and nuts.

Bake the brownies.
Pour the batter into the baking pan, spreading evenly. Bake 25 to 30 minutes, or until almost set in middle. Cool completely before cutting into bars.

TROUBLESHOOTING TIP: Underbake these fudgy brownies just slightly, because they can burn around the edges quickly!

white chocolate blondies

PREP TIME: 20 minutes

COOK TIME: 30 minutes

YIELD: 16 blondies

TOOLS/EQUIPMENT
- 8-inch square baking pan
- Medium bowl
- Large bowl
- Electric mixer

Butter, for greasing the pan
1 cup all-purpose flour
½ teaspoon baking powder
¼ teaspoon baking soda
½ teaspoon table salt
5 tablespoons unsalted butter, at room temperature
¾ cup light brown sugar
1 large egg
1 large egg yolk
1 teaspoon vanilla extract
1 cup white chocolate chips

Preheat the oven to 350°F.
Lightly grease an 8-inch square baking pan.

Mix the dry ingredients.
In a medium bowl, stir together the flour, baking powder, baking soda, and salt.

Cream the butter and sugar.
In a large bowl, beat the butter with an electric mixer on medium speed for about 10 seconds, or until smooth. Beat in the brown sugar until well blended and light and fluffy, about 2 minutes. Beat in the egg and egg yolk, then beat in the vanilla until well blended.

Beat the ingredients.
Add the flour mixture to the butter and sugar mixture, and beat with an electric mixer on medium speed until blended. With a spoon, stir in the white chocolate chips.

Bake the blondies.
Pour the batter into the prepared pan. Bake for 25 to 30 minutes, or until light golden brown around the edges. Cool completely before cutting into bars.

TRY INSTEAD: Instead of white chocolate chips, you could use your favorite chip and/or chopped nuts!

DID YOU KNOW? Toss the chips in a little flour before adding them to the batter to prevent them from sinking.

6

pies, tarts & pastries

baked peach hand pies

PREP TIME: 45 minutes (plus 30 minutes chill time)

COOK TIME: 30 minutes

YIELD: 16 pies

TOOLS/EQUIPMENT

- 2 baking sheets
- Parchment paper
- Small saucepan
- Plastic wrap
- Rolling pin
- 4-inch round cookie cutter (optional)
- Pastry brush
- Slotted spoon
- Wire rack

FOR THE PIE

1 Pie Dough (page 45)
3½ cups peeled, finely chopped fresh ripe peaches (3 or 4 peaches)
¼ cup granulated sugar
½ teaspoon vanilla extract
¼ teaspoon cinnamon
⅛ teaspoon table salt
Flour, for dusting the work surface

FOR THE EGG WASH

1 large egg, beaten
1 teaspoon granulated sugar

Chill the pie dough.
Refrigerate the pie dough while preparing the other ingredients, so it will be easier to handle.

Preheat the oven to 450°F.
Line 2 baking sheets with parchment paper.

Prepare the peach filling.
In a small saucepan over medium heat, heat the chopped peaches, ¼ cup of sugar, vanilla, cinnamon, and salt. Cook for 7 to 10 minutes, stirring occasionally, until the mixture is thickened and the peaches are soft. Spoon into a small bowl, cover with plastic wrap, and refrigerate until completely cool, about 30 minutes.

Form the crust.
Meanwhile, roll out half of the chilled pie dough on a lightly floured surface, to about ⅛ inch thick. Cut out 4-inch circles. Gather the dough scraps, roll out again, and cut out more rounds. Repeat with the remaining dough. Place the rounds on prepared baking sheets.

Assemble the pies.
Lightly brush the outside rim of each crust round with a little beaten egg. With a slotted spoon, spoon about 2 teaspoons of cooled peach filling in the center of each round. Fold the rounds over into half-circles, and press the seams together to seal. Brush the tops with a little more beaten egg, and sprinkle the remaining teaspoon of sugar on top of the pies.

Bake the pies.

Bake for 16 to 20 minutes or until puffed and golden brown, rotating the pans halfway through baking. Cool slightly, then transfer the pies to a wire rack to finish cooling.

TRY INSTEAD: What's in season? Instead of peach, try other fruit such as apricots, nectarines, or plums.

HELPFUL HINT: Rolling out the dough on a nonstick mat makes it easy to pick up the rounds after they're cut.

DID YOU KNOW? You can use the back of a fork to seal the seams together—and make a fun pattern doing so!

key lime pie bites

PREP TIME: 20 minutes
(plus 3 hours chill time)

COOK TIME: 20 minutes

YIELD: 16 bars

TOOLS/EQUIPMENT

- 8-inch square baking pan
- 2 medium bowls
- Zester
- Electric mixer

FOR THE CRUST

Butter, for greasing the pan

1 cup graham cracker crumbs
(7 or 8 whole graham crackers)

3 tablespoons unsalted butter,
melted

FOR THE FILLING

3 large egg yolks

1 teaspoon freshly grated key
lime zest

1 (14-ounce) can sweetened
condensed milk

½ cup freshly squeezed key lime
juice

Preheat the oven to 350°F.

Lightly grease an 8-inch square baking pan.

Make the crust.

In a medium bowl, mix together the graham cracker crumbs and melted butter. Press the mixture evenly into the bottom of the pan.

Make the filling.

In a medium bowl, beat the egg yolks and lime zest with an electric mixer about 2 minutes, or until frothy. Beat in the condensed milk, and then the lime juice, until well blended and thickened.

Bake the bars.

Pour the filling over the crust. Bake for 15 to 20 minutes, or until set. Cool completely, then refrigerate for 3 to 4 hours, or until completely chilled.

TRY INSTEAD: If you can't find key limes, you can substitute limes or bottled key lime juice. You can also freeze this pie for a nice frozen dessert!

HELPFUL HINT: These Key Lime Pie Bites can be pretty tart, depending on your limes. Sweeten the deal with a garnish of confectioners' sugar, whipped cream and/or quartered key lime slices.

old-fashioned strawberry pie

PREP TIME: 45 minutes (plus 2 hours and 20 minutes chill time)

COOK TIME: 20 minutes

YIELD: 1 pie (serves 8)

TOOLS/EQUIPMENT

- Rolling pin
- 9-inch pie pan
- Parchment paper and/or aluminum foil
- Pie weights or dried beans (optional)
- Blender
- Large saucepan
- Whisk or fork

Flour, for dusting the work surface

1 chilled Pie Dough (page 45)

7 cups fresh strawberries, stems removed and sliced, divided

⅔ to 1 cup water

¾ cup granulated sugar

3 tablespoons cornstarch

Prepare the pie crust.

Roll out the chilled pie dough on a lightly floured surface to about ¼ inch thick. Transfer the dough to a 9-inch pie pan. Trim the extra dough around the edges, and crimp or flute the edges as desired (see Pie Fluting: How To, page 43). Refrigerate for at least 20 to 30 minutes, or until cold.

Preheat the oven to 375˚F.

Blind bake the crust.

Line the crust with parchment paper or aluminum foil. Top with pie weights or dried beans, if using. Lightly cover the outer rim of the crust with aluminum foil to prevent over-browning. Bake for 15 to 20 minutes, or until very light golden brown. Remove the pie weights or beans and paper or foil from the crust. Lightly poke any air bubbles that may have formed around the crust to flatten the dough. Set aside to cool.

Blend some berries.

Place 1 cup of strawberries and ⅔ cup of water in a blender, and process until smooth. Add more water as needed so you have 1½ cups of berry mixture. »

HELPFUL HINT: Garnish this pie with whipped cream before serving!

TROUBLESHOOTING TIP: Be sure to chill the pie completely before slicing so the glaze and pie can set.

Make the glaze.

In a large saucepan, whisk together the sugar and cornstarch. Whisk in the blended berry mixture. Place the saucepan over medium-high heat. Cook for 5 to 7 minutes, stirring, until bubbly and thickened. Remove from the heat to cool.

Assemble the pie.

Spread about ¼ cup of glaze over the bottom and sides of the pie crust. Add the remaining whole strawberries into the pan with the glaze, stir to mix, then spoon the blended strawberries over the glaze in the pie crust into an even layer. Place the pie in the refrigerator for 2 to 3 hours, or until completely chilled.

double-crust blueberry pie

PREP TIME: 20 minutes

COOK TIME: 60 minutes

YIELD: 1 pie (serves 8)

TOOLS/EQUIPMENT

- Large bowl
- Zester
- 9-inch pie pan
- Rolling pin
- Pastry brush
- Baking sheet

4 cups fresh blueberries

½ cup granulated sugar, plus
1 tablespoon for the topping

½ cup all-purpose flour

1 teaspoon freshly grated
lemon zest

2 tablespoons freshly squeezed
lemon juice (about 1 lemon)

Flour, for dusting the work surface

2 chilled Pie Doughs (page 45)

1 egg, lightly beaten

Preheat the oven to 400°F.

Prepare the filling.
In a large bowl, gently stir together the blueberries, ½ cup of sugar, the flour, lemon zest, and lemon juice until blended.

Form the crusts.
Roll out each prepared chilled pie dough crust on a lightly floured surface to about ¼-inch thick. Gently transfer one to a 9-inch pie pan. Cut off any excess dough around edges.

Assemble the pie.
Spoon the blueberry mixture over the dough in the pie pan. Gently place the second dough on top. Press the edges together with a fork or crimp or flute as desired to form a nice seal (see Pie Fluting: How To, page 43). With a pastry brush, brush a little beaten egg over the crust, then cut 3 to 5 slits in the top pie crust with a sharp knife. Sprinkle 1 tablespoon of sugar on top.

Bake the pie.
Place the pie on a baking sheet. Bake for 45 to 60 minutes, or until the pie is golden brown and the filling is bubbly. Cool completely before slicing and serving.

> PRO TIP: The slits in the top pie crust allow the steam to escape while the pie is baking. You can also cut out small shapes instead of slits—use a fun-shaped small cookie cutter if you like!

caramel apple streusel pie

PREP TIME: 30 minutes

COOK TIME: 60 minutes

YIELD: 1 pie (serves 8)

TOOLS/EQUIPMENT

- Small bowl
- Pastry cutter (see Cutting in Butter, page 42)
- Large bowl
- Rolling pin
- 9-inch pie pan
- Aluminum foil
- Baking sheet

FOR THE STREUSEL CRUMB TOPPING

½ cup all-purpose flour

¼ cup brown sugar

½ teaspoon cinnamon

⅛ teaspoon table salt

4 tablespoons cold unsalted butter, cubed

FOR THE PIE

½ cup thick caramel ice cream topping

3 tablespoons all-purpose flour

¼ teaspoon cinnamon

¼ teaspoon table salt

6 cups peeled, thinly sliced cooking apples such as Granny Smith (about 2¼ pounds or 4 to 5 large apples)

1 chilled Pie Dough (page 45)

Flour, for dusting the work surface

Preheat the oven to 375°F.

Make the streusel.

In a small bowl, mix together ½ cup of flour, brown sugar, ½ teaspoon of cinnamon, and ⅛ teaspoon of salt until well blended. With a pastry cutter or the back of a fork, cut in the cold butter cubes until it forms coarse crumbs.

Prepare the apple filling.

In a large bowl, whisk together the caramel topping, 3 tablespoons of flour, ¼ teaspoon of cinnamon, and ¼ teaspoon of salt until well blended. Gently stir in the apples until blended.

Form the crust.

Roll out the chilled pie dough on a lightly floured surface to about ¼-inch thick. Transfer to a 9-inch pie pan. Cut off the excess dough around the edges of the pan.

Make the pie.

Spoon the apples into the pie crust. Sprinkle streusel over the top. Flute or crimp the pie crust as desired (see Pie Fluting: How To, page 43). Cover the edges of the pie crust with aluminum foil.

Bake the pie.

Place the pie on a baking sheet. Bake for about 40 minutes. Remove the foil from edges, then bake for an additional 20 minutes, or until the apples are soft. Cool before slicing and serving.

TRY INSTEAD: Instead of caramel ice cream topping, you can substitute butterscotch.

DID YOU KNOW? Some apples are better for baking than others. Some good baking apple varieties include Cortland, Fuji, Granny Smith, Jonagold, and Golden Delicious. Try one, or even a combination of varieties, in the pie.

TROUBLESHOOTING TIP: Be sure to slice the apples very thin so they cook all the way through. You can also precook the apples a little in a large skillet with a little butter beforehand to ensure they cook through and get nice and soft.

apple tarte tatin

PREP TIME: 30 minutes
(plus 1 hour chill time)

COOK TIME: 50 minutes

YIELD: 1 tarte Tatin (serves 10)

TOOLS/EQUIPMENT

- Medium bowl
- Pastry cutter (see Cutting in Butter, page 42)
- 10½-inch cast-iron pan or oven-safe skillet
- Plastic wrap
- Spoon or tongs
- Rolling pin
- Sharp knife

FOR THE CRUST

1 cup all-purpose flour

¼ cup granulated sugar

⅛ teaspoon table salt

½ cup (1 stick) cold unsalted butter, cubed

1 large egg yolk

2 to 4 tablespoons ice cold water

Flour, for dusting the work surface

FOR THE FILLING

6 tablespoons unsalted butter

1 cup granulated sugar

1 tablespoon freshly squeezed lemon juice

¼ teaspoon table salt

5 large (or 6 small) baking apples (such as Granny Smith), peeled, cored, and quartered

Make the crust.

In a medium bowl, stir together the flour, ¼ cup of sugar, and ⅛ teaspoon of salt until well blended. With a pastry cutter or the back of a fork, cut in ½ cup of cold butter. Stir in the egg yolk. Stir in the cold water, a little at a time, until the dough comes together. Form the dough into a disk, cover completely with plastic wrap, and refrigerate about 1 hour, or until cold and firm.

Preheat the oven to 425°F.

Prepare the filling.

In a cast-iron pan or oven-safe skillet over medium high-heat, add 6 tablespoons of butter, 1 cup of sugar, lemon juice, and ¼ teaspoon of salt. Stir occasionally until blended and butter has melted. Add the apple quarters. Cook 15 to 20 minutes, stirring and turning the apples occasionally, until the liquid has thickened and darkened in color and the apples are a little soft. Remove from heat. With a spoon or tongs, arrange the apples in a single layer in the pan.

Roll out the dough.

On a lightly floured surface, roll out the dough to a circle 11 or 12 inches across. Place the dough over the apples in the pan, and cut off the excess around the edges. With a sharp knife, cut 3 to 5 slits in the crust. »

Bake the tarte.

Bake for 20 to 30 minutes, or until golden brown. Gently turn the pan upside down onto a serving plate, and release the tarte. Serve tarte warm (as it is traditionally served) or cool before serving.

HELPFUL HINT: The skillet will be hot, so use oven mitts when handling. Also, cast-iron pans are really heavy, so don't hesitate to ask a grown-up for help.

TROUBLESHOOTING TIP: If your apple tarte Tatin sticks to the pan while trying to flip it over, run a butter knife around the edges to loosen.

DID YOU KNOW? The tarte Tatin was said to be created by two French sisters, Caroline and Stephanie Tatin, who owned the Hotel Tatin in a rural town outside of Paris.

chocolate pecan pie squares

PREP TIME: 25 minutes

COOK TIME: 40 minutes

YIELD: 16 bars

TOOLS/EQUIPMENT
- 8-inch square baking pan
- Medium bowl
- Electric mixer
- Large bowl

FOR THE CRUST
Butter, for greasing the pan

¾ cup all-purpose flour

⅛ teaspoon table salt

4 tablespoons unsalted butter, at room temperature

2 tablespoons brown sugar

FOR THE FILLING
1 large egg

1 large egg yolk

⅓ cup corn syrup

⅓ cup granulated sugar

1 tablespoon unsweetened cocoa powder

1 tablespoon unsalted butter, melted

½ teaspoon vanilla extract

⅛ teaspoon table salt

¾ cup chocolate chips

¾ cup coarsely chopped pecans

Preheat the oven to 350°F.

Lightly grease an 8-inch square baking pan.

Make the crust.

In a medium bowl, add the flour, ⅛ teaspoon of salt, 4 tablespoons of room-temperature butter, and brown sugar. Beat with an electric mixer on medium speed until blended and crumbly. Press the crust in an even layer over the bottom of the prepared pan. Bake for 10 to 15 minutes, or until golden brown around the edges.

Make the filling.

Meanwhile, in a large bowl, beat the egg, egg yolk, corn syrup, granulated sugar, cocoa powder, 1 tablespoon of melted butter, vanilla, and ⅛ teaspoon of salt with an electric mixer on medium speed until well blended. With a spoon, stir in the chocolate chips and pecans.

Bake the pie squares.

Remove the crust from the oven, and pour the filling evenly over the top of the crust. Bake for 20 to 25 minutes, or until the middle appears set. Cool completely before cutting into bars.

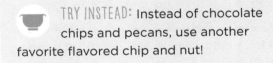

TRY INSTEAD: Instead of chocolate chips and pecans, use another favorite flavored chip and nut!

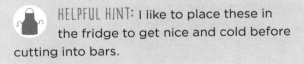

HELPFUL HINT: I like to place these in the fridge to get nice and cold before cutting into bars.

coconut custard pie
WITH QUICK STRAWBERRY SAUCE

PREP TIME: 30 minutes (plus 20 minutes chill time)

COOK TIME: 80 minutes

YIELD: 1 pie (serves 8)

TOOLS/EQUIPMENT

- Rolling pin
- 9-inch pie pan
- Parchment paper and/or aluminum foil
- Pie weights or dried beans (optional)
- Large bowl
- Whisk or fork
- Baking sheet
- Blender

FOR THE PIE

Flour, for dusting the work surface

1 chilled Pie Dough (page 45)

¾ cup granulated sugar

1 cup half-and-half

4 tablespoons unsalted butter, melted and cooled

6 large eggs, at room temperature

1 teaspoon vanilla extract

¼ teaspoon table salt

2 cups shredded sweetened coconut

FOR THE STRAWBERRY SAUCE

1 pound frozen strawberries, thawed

¼ cup granulated sugar

1 teaspoon vanilla extract

Prepare the pie crust.

Roll out the chilled prepared pie dough on a lightly floured surface to about ¼-inch thick. Transfer the dough to a 9-inch pie pan. Trim the extra dough around the edges and crimp or flute the edges as desired (see Pie Fluting: How To, page 43). Refrigerate the crust for at least 20 to 30 minutes, or until cold.

Preheat the oven to 375°F.

Blind bake the crust.

Line the cold crust with parchment paper or aluminum foil. Top with pie weights or dried beans to prevent bubbles from forming, if desired. Lightly cover the outside rim of the crust with aluminum foil to prevent over-browning. Bake for 15 to 20 minutes, or until very light golden brown. Leave the foil in place around the pie crust, but remove the paper or foil from the bottom of the crust, and also remove the weights or beans. Lightly poke any air bubbles that may have formed on the crust to flatten them.

Lower the oven temperature to 350°F.

Prepare the pie filling.

In a large bowl, whisk together ¾ cup of sugar, half-and-half, melted butter, eggs, 1 teaspoon of vanilla, and salt until well blended. Stir in the coconut.

Bake the pie.

Place the pie pan on a baking sheet, then pour the filling over the crust. Bake for 45 to 60 minutes, or until the filling appears set and golden brown on top. Remove the pie from the oven, and the foil from the crust. Cool completely.

Make the strawberry sauce.

Meanwhile, in a blender, add the thawed strawberries, ¼ cup of sugar, and 1 teaspoon of vanilla. Pulse repeatedly until smooth.

Drizzle and serve.

Drizzle the sauce over the pie right before serving.

banana cream pie

PREP TIME: 30 minutes
(plus 5 hours chill time)

COOK TIME: 45 minutes

YIELD: 1 pie (serves 8)

TOOLS/EQUIPMENT

- Rolling pin
- 9-inch pie pan
- Parchment paper or aluminum foil
- Pie weights or dried beans (optional)
- Small bowl
- Large saucepan
- Whisk or spoon
- Large bowl

FOR THE PIE

Flour, for dusting the work surface
1 chilled Pie Dough (page 45)
2 large egg yolks
¾ cup granulated sugar
¼ cup cornstarch
¼ teaspoon table salt
3 cups milk (2 percent or whole)
3 tablespoons unsalted butter
1 teaspoon vanilla extract
2 large firm, ripe bananas, thinly sliced

FOR THE WHIPPED CREAM

1½ cups cold heavy whipping cream
2 tablespoons granulated sugar

Prepare the crust.

Roll out the prepared chilled pie dough on a lightly floured surface to about ¼ inch thick. Transfer the dough into a 9-inch pie pan. Trim the extra dough around the edges, and crimp or flute the edges as desired (see Pie Fluting: How To, page 43). Refrigerate for at least 20 to 30 minutes, or until cold.

Preheat the oven to 375°F.

Blind bake the crust.

Line the crust with parchment paper or aluminum foil. Top with pie weights or dried beans, if desired. Lightly cover the outer rim of the crust with foil to prevent over-browning. Bake for 15 to 20 minutes, or until very light golden brown. Remove the pie weights or beans and paper and foil from the crust. Lightly poke any air bubbles that may have formed in the crust to flatten the dough. Set aside to cool.

Prepare the filling.

In a small bowl, beat the egg yolks, then set aside. In a large saucepan over medium-high heat, whisk together ¾ cup of sugar, the cornstarch, salt, and milk. Whisking frequently, cook until very thick, 10 to 20 minutes. While whisking, spoon a little of the hot milk mixture into the bowl with the eggs. Slowly spoon in more milk until the eggs are warm. Pour the remaining milk mixture and the egg mixture into the saucepan. Bring the mixture to a gentle boil and cook 2 to 3 minutes

TRY INSTEAD: You can substitute a prepared graham cracker crust for the pie crust.

TROUBLESHOOTING: Be sure to cook the filling for a long time on the stovetop—until very thick. Otherwise, the filling won't thicken nicely and may be quite soupy.

FOOD FACT: A cluster of bananas is known as a "hand," and a single banana is known as a "finger."

longer, whisking constantly. Remove the pan from heat, and stir in the butter and vanilla until the butter has melted.

Refrigerate the filling.
Pour the filling into a large bowl, cover with plastic wrap, and refrigerate for at least 30 minutes, or until cold.

Add the banana.
Arrange the banana slices evenly over the bottom of the pan. Pour the custard filling over the bananas.

Make whipped cream.
In a large cold bowl, whip the heavy cream and 2 tablespoons of sugar with an electric mixer on medium-high speed until soft peaks form.

Assemble the pie.
Spread the whipped cream on top of the pie. Refrigerate for 4 to 6 hours or overnight. Serve cold.

southern chocolate walnut pie

PREP TIME: 30 minutes (20 minutes chill time, plus cooling time)

COOK TIME: 65 minutes

YIELD: 1 pie (serves 8)

TOOLS/EQUIPMENT

- Rolling pin
- 9-inch pie pan
- Parchment paper and/or aluminum foil
- Pie weights or dried beans (optional)
- Large bowl
- Whisk or fork
- Baking sheet

Flour, for dusting the work surface
1 chilled Pie Dough (page 45)
¾ cup granulated sugar
½ cup all-purpose flour
¼ cup brown sugar
¼ teaspoon table salt
2 large eggs, at room temperature
½ cup (1 stick) unsalted butter, melted and cooled
1 teaspoon vanilla extract
1¼ cups chopped walnuts
1 cup semisweet chocolate chips

Prepare the pie crust.

Roll out the chilled pie dough on a lightly floured surface to about ¼-inch thick. Transfer the dough to a 9-inch pie pan. Trim the extra dough around the edges, and crimp or flute the edges as desired (see Pie Fluting: How To, page 43). Return to the refrigerator for at least 20 to 30 minutes, or until cold.

Preheat the oven to 375°F.

Blind bake the crust.

Line the crust with parchment paper or aluminum foil. Top with pie weights or dried beans, if using. Lightly cover the outer rim of the crust with aluminum foil to prevent over-browning. Bake for 15 to 20 minutes, or until very light golden brown. Leave the foil in place around the edge of the pie crust, but remove the weights or beans and paper or foil from the bottom of the crust. Lightly poke any air bubbles that may have formed around crust to flatten the dough.

Lower the oven temperature to 325°F.

Prepare the filling.

In a large bowl, whisk together the granulated sugar, flour, brown sugar, and salt until well blended. Whisk in the eggs, melted butter, and vanilla until blended. Stir in the walnuts and chocolate chips.

Bake the pie.

Place the pie pan on a baking sheet, then pour the filling over the crust, spreading the walnuts and chocolate chips to evenly distribute. Bake for about 25 minutes, remove the foil from the crust, then bake an additional 10 to 20 minutes, or until the filling appears set (firm). Cool completely before slicing.

TRY INSTEAD: Instead of semisweet chocolate chips, you can use bitter-sweet or dark chocolate chips.

HELPFUL HINT: To add extra flavor to this pie, toast and cool the walnuts beforehand.

FOOD FACT: This dish is a little different than traditional pecan pie and tastes a little like cookie dough.

homemade pb&j breakfast tarts

PREP TIME: 45 minutes
COOK TIME: 25 minutes
YIELD: 4 tarts

TOOLS/EQUIPMENT
- Rolling pin
- Sharp knife
- Parchment paper (optional)
- Baking sheet
- Pastry brush
- Fork
- Plastic wrap

Flour, for dusting the work surface
Butter, for greasing the pan (optional)
1 chilled Pie Dough (page 45)
¼ cup peanut butter
¼ cup jelly
1 large egg, beaten
1 teaspoon granulated sugar

Roll out the dough.
On a lightly floured surface, roll out the chilled pie dough to a 10-by-14-inch rectangle, about ⅛-inch thick.

Cut the dough.
Using a sharp knife, cut out 8 (4-by-3-inch) rectangles. Re-roll the scraps if necessary to get 8 rectangles. Place 4 rectangles on a lightly greased baking sheet or a baking sheet lined with parchment paper, leaving an inch or so between each rectangle.

Fill the dough.
Spread a little peanut butter over the middle of the dough on the baking sheet, leaving about a half-inch border around the edges. Top the peanut butter with the jelly.

Make the tarts.
Lightly brush a little beaten egg around the half-inch dough border. Place the remaining rectangles of dough over the rectangles on the baking sheet. Using the back of a fork, press down around the edges to seal.

Refrigerate the tarts.
Cover lightly with plastic wrap and refrigerate for about 30 minutes, or until chilled.

Preheat the oven to 400°F.

Bake the tarts.
Brush a little of the remaining egg wash over top of the tarts. Sprinkle with sugar. Bake for 20 to 25 minutes, or until golden brown.

 TRY INSTEAD: Use your favorite flavor of jelly or jam in these tarts!

HELPFUL HINT: If the dough gets too warm and sticky to work with, cover and refrigerate for 20 to 30 minutes.

TROUBLESHOOTING TIP: If you have a hard time cutting the dough into rectangles, cut a piece of 4-by-3-inch paper and use that as your pattern to cut around.

cinnamon sugar palmiers

PREP TIME: 20 minutes (plus 30 minutes chill time)

COOK TIME: 18 minutes

YIELD: 30 palmiers

TOOLS/EQUIPMENT

- 2 baking sheets
- Parchment paper (optional)
- Small bowl
- Rolling pin
- Plastic wrap
- Wire rack

Butter, for greasing the baking sheets (optional)

½ cup granulated sugar

2 teaspoons cinnamon

1 frozen puff pastry sheet (half of a 17-ounce package), thawed according to package directions

Preheat the oven to 400°F.

Lightly grease 2 baking sheets or line them with parchment paper.

Make the cinnamon sugar.

In a small bowl, mix together the sugar and cinnamon until blended.

Roll out the pastry.

Sprinkle half of the cinnamon-sugar mixture evenly on a large, clean, dry surface. Place the puff pastry on top of the mixture. Sprinkle the rest of the cinnamon-sugar evenly on top of the puff pastry. Using a rolling pin, roll the puff pastry into a 9-by-15-inch rectangle, about ⅛-inch thick.

Form the palmiers.

Starting at the long end of the rectangle, tightly roll up both sides of the dough to meet in the middle. Gently press dough together to stick. Cover the pastry with plastic wrap, and refrigerate 30 to 60 minutes, or until firm.

Slice the palmiers.

Unwrap the chilled pastry. Slice into about ½-inch-thick slices. Place the slices on the prepared baking sheets. »

Bake the palmiers.

Bake for 8 minutes. Remove the palmiers from the oven, flip them over, rotate the pans, then bake an additional 6 to 10 minutes, or until golden brown. Cool slightly, then transfer to a wire rack to finish cooling.

HELPFUL HINT: Puff pastry is a light flaky pastry dough. You can make a homemade version, or it can be found, already made, in the freezer section of your grocery store. Most packages contain 2 sheets. Thaw the puff pastry according to the directions on the package before starting the recipe.

TROUBLESHOOTING TIP: Check on these regularly while they bake. Since the pastry is so thin, it can burn quickly.

FOOD FACT: Palmiers are a French pastry. Palmier is French for "palm" or "palm tree," reflecting their shape.

skillet-baked peach cobbler

PREP TIME: 30 minutes

COOK TIME: 50 minutes

YIELD: 1 cobbler (serves 10)

TOOLS/EQUIPMENT

- 10½-inch cast-iron pan or ovenproof skillet
- Medium bowl
- Large bowl

FOR THE CRUST

6 tablespoons unsalted butter

1 cup all-purpose flour

¾ cup granulated sugar

2 teaspoons baking powder

¼ teaspoon table salt

¾ cup milk (2 percent or whole)

FOR THE FILLING

½ cup brown sugar

1 tablespoon all-purpose flour

1 teaspoon cinnamon

1 tablespoon freshly squeezed orange juice

1 teaspoon vanilla extract

4 cups peeled and sliced fresh ripe peaches (6 to 8 peaches)

Preheat the oven to 375˚F.

Melt the butter.
Place the butter in a 10½-inch cast-iron pan or ovenproof skillet. Place the pan in the oven for 3 to 5 minutes, or until the butter is melted. Remove from the oven, and swirl the pan around to form an even layer of melted butter.

Make the crust batter.
Meanwhile, in a medium bowl, mix together 1 cup of flour, the granulated sugar, baking powder, and salt until blended. Stir in the milk.

Create the filling.
In a large bowl, gently stir together the brown sugar, 1 tablespoon of flour, and cinnamon until blended. Stir in the orange juice and vanilla. Gently mix in the peach slices.

Build the cobbler.
Spoon the crust batter over the melted butter in the pan. Spoon the peaches on top.

Bake the cobbler.
Bake for 30 to 45 minutes, or until the crust is golden brown.

mini blueberry peach crostatas

PREP TIME: 30 minutes

COOK TIME: 35 minutes

YIELD: 4 crostatas

TOOLS/EQUIPMENT

- Baking sheets
- Parchment paper (optional)
- Rolling pin
- Large bowl
- Pastry brush

Butter, for greasing the baking
  sheets (optional)

1 chilled Pie Dough (page 45)

Flour, for dusting the work surface

2 cups peeled, coarsely chopped
  fresh ripe peaches
  (3 or 4 peaches)

1 cup fresh blueberries

3 tablespoons granulated sugar,
  divided

2 teaspoons all-purpose flour

1 teaspoon freshly squeezed lemon
  juice

1 large egg, beaten

Preheat the oven to 375°F.

Lightly grease baking sheets or line with parchment paper.

Form the crusts.

Divide prepared chilled pie dough into 4 equal balls. Roll out each ball on a lightly floured surface to about ¼-inch thick to form a circle 6 or 7 inches wide. Place the crusts on the baking sheets. Refrigerate the crusts while you make the filling.

Prepare the filling.

In a large bowl, gently stir together the peaches, blueberries, 2 tablespoons of sugar, flour, and lemon juice until blended.

Assemble the crostatas.

With a pastry brush, lightly brush a little beaten egg around the edge of each pie crust. Spoon the peach and blueberry filling into the center of each pie crust, leaving about a half-inch border around the edge. Lift and overlap the edges of the crust just over the edge of the filling so the filling in the center is not completely covered. Lightly brush the crust of the dough with a little more egg, and sprinkle the crust with the remaining tablespoon of sugar. »

Bake the crostatas.

Bake for 25 to 35 minutes, or until golden brown around the edges. Serve warm or at room temperature.

TRY INSTEAD: Instead of peaches, you could substitute other fruit, such as plums, nectarines, or apricots.

HELPFUL HINT: These crostatas are extra delightful with a little ice cream or whipped cream on top!

DID YOU KNOW? Crostatas are a great way to practice handling pie dough, since they are supposed to look rustic and not-so-perfect!

maple pear crisp

PREP TIME: 30 minutes

COOK TIME: 55 minutes

YIELD: serves 8

TOOLS/EQUIPMENT

- Large bowl
- 9-inch pie pan
- Pastry cutter or fork (see Cutting in Butter, page 42)

FOR THE FILLING

5 cups ripe pears, peeled, cored, and thinly sliced (4 or 5 pears)

3 tablespoons maple syrup

1 teaspoon vanilla extract

FOR THE TOPPING

¾ cup old-fashioned rolled oats

¾ cup all-purpose flour

¾ cup brown sugar

1 teaspoon cinnamon

¼ teaspoon table salt

½ cup (1 stick) cold unsalted butter, cubed

Preheat the oven to 350°F.

Make the filling.
In a large bowl, gently stir the pears, maple syrup, and vanilla. Pour into a 9-inch pie pan.

Make the topping.
In a large bowl, stir together the oats, flour, brown sugar, cinnamon, and salt until well blended. Cut in the butter with a pastry cutter or the back of a fork until the mixture resembles coarse crumbs. Crumble the topping over the pears.

Bake the crisp.
Bake for 40 to 55 minutes, or until the pears are soft and the topping is crisp and browned.

 TRY INSTEAD: Instead of pears, you can use apples.

 HELPFUL HINT: Be sure the pears are thinly sliced so the pear can cook through.

chocolate dipped cream puffs
(PROFITEROLES)

PREP TIME: 35 minutes

COOK TIME: 32 minutes

YIELD: 12 cream puffs

TOOLS/EQUIPMENT

- Baking sheet
- Parchment paper (optional)
- Small saucepan
- Wooden spoon
- Medium bowl
- Pastry brush
- Double boiler (or see Make Your Own Double Boiler, page 53)
- Wire rack

Butter, for greasing the baking sheet (optional)

¾ cup water

6 tablespoons unsalted butter

1 teaspoon granulated sugar

¼ teaspoon table salt

¾ cup all-purpose flour

4 large eggs, at room temperature, divided

1½ cups chopped semisweet chocolate or chocolate chips

Whipped cream or ice cream, for serving

Preheat the oven to 400°F.

Lightly grease a baking sheet or line with parchment paper.

Make the dough.

In a small saucepan over medium-high heat, add the water, butter, sugar, and salt. Bring to a boil, stirring occasionally with a sturdy large wooden spoon. Stir in the flour. Stir the dough for 1 to 2 minutes, or until the dough comes together and forms a ball. Remove from heat. Transfer the dough to a medium bowl and cool for 5 to 10 minutes.

Add the eggs.

Add 3 eggs, one at a time, to the dough in the bowl, stirring after each addition. Keep stirring until the eggs are well blended and the dough comes together.

Form the cream puffs.

Spoon the dough (about 1½ tablespoons each) onto the prepared baking sheet. Beat the remaining egg in a small bowl, and brush lightly over tops of cream puffs.

Bake the cream puffs.

Bake for 25 to 30 minutes, or until golden brown and puffed. Cool slightly, then transfer to a wire rack to finish cooling.

Melt the chocolate.
Place the chocolate in the top of a double boiler over boiling water, then reduce the heat to low. Stir constantly until chocolate is melted and smooth. Dip the tops of the cream puffs in the melted chocolate, then place them on the wire rack to cool until the chocolate sets.

Fill the cream puffs.
Before serving, cut the cream puffs in half, stuff them with whipped cream or ice cream, then reassemble and serve immediately.

HELPFUL HINT: Instead of spooning the dough onto the baking sheets, you can use a pastry bag with a large plain tip. A large resealable plastic bag with a corner cut off, or even a trigger ice cream scoop, also works well!

TROUBLESHOOTING TIP: If the egg is too thick to brush, you can add a little water or milk to the beaten egg before brushing over the puffs.

cranberry clafoutis

PREP TIME: 15 minutes

COOK TIME: 60 minutes

YIELD: 1 clafoutis (serves 8)

TOOLS/EQUIPMENT

- 1 deep 9-inch pie pan
- Large bowl
- Electric mixer

Butter, for greasing the pan
1 tablespoon unsalted butter
⅔ cup granulated sugar
3 large eggs, at room temperature
1¼ cup milk (2 percent or whole)
⅛ teaspoon table salt
1 teaspoon vanilla extract
½ cup all-purpose flour
2 cups fresh cranberries

Preheat the oven to 350°F.
Grease a deep 9-inch pie pan with butter.

Combine the ingredients.
In a large bowl, beat the sugar and eggs with an electric mixer on medium speed until well blended and pale yellow, about 2 minutes. Beat in the milk, salt, and vanilla until well blended, then beat in the flour until just combined. The batter will be thin.

Bake the clafoutis.
Pour the batter into the prepared pan. Spoon the cranberries on top. Bake for 45 to 60 minutes, or until golden brown. A toothpick inserted into the middle should come out clean.

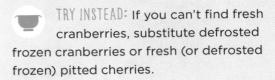

TRY INSTEAD: If you can't find fresh cranberries, substitute defrosted frozen cranberries or fresh (or defrosted frozen) pitted cherries.

HELPFUL HING: For a nice presentation, serve warm or at room temperature with a little sifted confectioners' sugar on top.

PRO TIP: While the clafoutis cools, the center may fall—this is okay.

chocolate raspberry turnovers

PREP TIME: 30 minutes

COOK TIME: 20 minutes

YIELD: 9 turnovers

TOOLS/EQUIPMENT

- 2 baking sheets
- Parchment paper (optional)
- Small bowl
- Sharp knife
- Pastry brush
- Fork
- Wire rack
- Double boiler (or Make Your Own Double Boiler, page 53)

Butter, for greasing the baking sheets (optional)

¼ cup chopped fresh raspberries

1 tablespoon raspberry jam

¼ teaspoon vanilla extract

1 frozen puff pastry sheet (half of a 17-ounce package), thawed according to package directions

1 large egg, beaten

¾ cup chopped semisweet chocolate or chocolate chips

Preheat the oven to 400°F.

Lightly grease 2 baking sheets or line with parchment paper.

Make the filling.

In a small bowl, stir together the raspberries, jam, and vanilla until blended.

Cut the pastry.

Unfold the puff pastry. With a sharp knife, cut the pastry along the two folds, then cut each piece into 3 equal parts to get 9 pieces in total. Lightly brush the edges with the beaten egg.

Assemble the turnovers.

Spoon about a heaping teaspoon of raspberry filling in the center of each puff pastry. From one corner to the opposite corner, fold the dough over the filling to form a triangle. Using the back of a fork, press down edges of the turnovers to seal.

Bake the turnovers.

Place the turnovers on the prepared baking sheets. Brush the tops of the turnovers lightly with the beaten egg. Bake for 15 to 20 minutes, until puffed and golden brown. Cool slightly, then transfer to a wire rack to finish cooling.

Melt the chocolate.

Place the chocolate in the top of a double boiler over boiling water, then reduce the heat to low. Stir constantly, until the chocolate is melted and smooth. Remove from the heat. With a fork, drizzle the chocolate over the turnovers. Cool until the chocolate sets.

TROUBLESHOOTING TIP: It's okay if a little filling leaks out while the turnovers are baking. With practice, you'll get better at sealing pastry, and besides, these will still taste great!

DID YOU KNOW? An egg wash gives a nice shine and color to baked dough and pastries.

PRO TIP: If you have leftover melted chocolate, spread it on a piece of wax paper. Let the chocolate cool to harden. Then you can break it into pieces and store it in an airtight bag or container for another recipe.

luscious layered chocolate chip bread pudding

PREP TIME: 10 minutes

COOK TIME: 45 minutes

YIELD: 2 (8-ounce) ramekins (serves 2)

TOOLS/EQUIPMENT

- 2 (8-ounce) ramekins
- Baking sheet
- Small bowl
- Whisk or fork

Butter, for greasing the ramekins

2 large eggs, at room temperature

1 cup milk (2 percent or whole)

2 tablespoons granulated sugar

½ teaspoon vanilla extract

⅛ teaspoon table salt

1½ cups cubed day-old fresh bread (about 2 bread slices)

2 tablespoons mini chocolate chips

Preheat the oven to 350°F.

Grease 2 (8-ounce) ramekins with butter and place the ramekins on a baking sheet.

Make the batter.

In a small bowl, whisk together the eggs, milk, sugar, vanilla, and salt until well blended.

Layer the bread pudding.

Place a quarter of the bread cubes into the bottom of each ramekin. Top each with a quarter of the chocolate chips. Top with the remaining bread cubes then the remaining chocolate chips. Slowly pour some of the milk mixture over the bread until the ramekin is about ¾ full. With the back of a fork, gently press down on the bread to soak up some of the liquid. Depending on your bread, you may have extra liquid left; discard any leftovers.

Bake the bread puddings.

Bake for 35 to 45 minutes, or until the puddings appear set (firm) and a toothpick inserted into the middle comes out clean. Serve warm.

TRY INSTEAD: Instead of mini chocolate chips, you can use your favorite chopped chocolate. You can also use 1 cup chocolate milk instead of the milk and sugar.

HELPFUL HINT: Be sure the bread you use is a good-quality day-old bread (or two-day old). Fresh soft bread is already moist so it won't soak up the liquid as well.

mini orange cookie tarts

PREP TIME: 30 minutes (plus 30 minutes chill time)

COOK TIME: 25 minutes

YIELD: 20 tarts

TOOLS/EQUIPMENT

- 2 medium bowls
- Electric hand mixer
- Whisk or fork
- Zester
- Mini muffin pan

FOR THE CRUST

½ cup (1 stick) unsalted butter, at room temperature

½ cup confectioners' sugar

1 cup all-purpose flour

⅛ teaspoon table salt

FOR THE FILLING

½ cup plus 2 tablespoons sweetened condensed milk

¼ cup freshly squeezed orange juice (1 or 2 oranges)

2 tablespoons orange zest

2 large egg yolks

½ teaspoon orange extract

¼ teaspoon vanilla extract

Preheat the oven to 325°F.

Make the cookie crust.

In a medium bowl, beat the butter with an electric mixer on medium speed for about 10 seconds, or until smooth. Add the sugar, beating until well blended and light and fluffy, about 2 minutes. Beat in the flour and salt until just combined.

Make the filling.

In another medium bowl, whisk together the milk, orange juice, zest, yolks, orange extract, and vanilla until well blended.

Form the cookies.

Press a rounded teaspoon of cookie dough in about 20 cups of an ungreased 24-cup mini muffin pan. Press in the center to push the dough up the sides of each pan cup to form a little cookie cup. Spoon about 2 teaspoons of the filling into each cookie cup, or until each cup is about ¾ full.

Bake the cookies.

Bake for 20 to 25 minutes, or until filling is set and cookies are golden brown. Cool slightly in pan, then finish cooling in refrigerator for about 30 minutes, or until chilled.

TRY INSTEAD: The orange extract gives a more intense orange flavor to the tart. If you can't find it, you can substitute an equal amount of vanilla extract instead.

savory baked goods

ham and cheese quiche

PREP TIME: 30 minutes (plus 20 minutes chill time)

COOK TIME: 50 minutes

YIELD: 1 quiche (serves 8)

TOOLS/EQUIPMENT

- Rolling pin
- 9-inch pie pan
- Parchment paper and/or aluminum foil
- Pie weights or dried beans (optional)
- Small bowl
- Large bowl

Flour, for dusting the work surface
1 chilled Pie Dough (page 45)
1 cup chopped ham
½ cup shredded Cheddar cheese
½ cup shredded Swiss cheese
2 tablespoons chopped scallion
4 large eggs
1¼ cups half-and-half or whole milk
1 teaspoon Dijon mustard
½ teaspoon table salt
⅛ teaspoon freshly ground black pepper

Prepare the pie crust.

On a lightly floured surface, roll out the chilled pie dough to about ¼-inch thick. Transfer the dough to a 9-inch pie pan. Trim the extra dough around the edges, and crimp or flute the edges as desired (see Pie Fluting: How To, page 43). Refrigerate for at least 20 to 30 minutes, or until cold.

Preheat the oven to 375°F.

Blind bake the crust.

Line the crust with parchment paper or aluminum foil. Top with pie weights or dried beans, if using. Lightly cover the outer rim of the crust with aluminum foil to prevent over-browning. Bake for 15 to 20 minutes, or until very light golden brown. Remove the pie weights or beans and paper or foil from crust. Lightly poke any air bubbles that may have formed around the crust to flatten the dough. Set aside to cool.

Reduce the oven temperature to 350°F.

Mix the ham and cheese.

In a small bowl, mix together the ham, Cheddar cheese, Swiss cheese, and scallion. Spoon evenly over the pie crust.

Blend remaining ingredients.

In a large bowl, whisk the eggs until well beaten. Beat in the half-and-half or milk, mustard, salt, and black pepper until well blended. Pour the mixture over the ham and cheese in the pie crust.

Bake the quiche.

Bake for 35 to 50 minutes, or until a toothpick or knife inserted near the center comes out clean. Cool about 10 minutes before slicing and serving.

TRY INSTEAD: Quiche is a fun dish to test your creativity. Instead of ham and Swiss and Cheddar cheeses, use any favorite precooked meats and cheeses. You can also substitute or add in finely chopped vegetables such as peppers and onions.

HELPFUL HINT: You can use a store-bought pie crust for quiche. They often come in packages of two, so if you'd like, double the filling recipe.

DID YOU KNOW? Half-and-half can be found in the refrigerated section of your grocery store. It's made of half heavy cream and half milk.

breakfast strata

PREP TIME: 25 minutes
(plus 4 hours chill time)

COOK TIME: 65 minutes

YIELD: serves 8

TOOLS/EQUIPMENT

- 8-inch square baking pan
- Large bowl
- Fork or spatula

Butter, for greasing the pan

4 cups cubed day-old good-quality bread (4 or 5 slices)

1 cup precooked, crumbled or chopped breakfast sausage

1 cup shredded cheese (such as Cheddar or Swiss)

4 large eggs

1 cup milk (2 percent or whole)

1 teaspoon Dijon mustard

¼ teaspoon table salt

⅛ teaspoon freshly ground black pepper

Prepare the pan.
Lightly grease an 8-inch square baking pan.

Build the layers.
Add half the bread cubes to the pan. Sprinkle half the sausage and half the cheese on top. Repeat with another layer of bread, sausage, and cheese.

Make the filling.
In a large bowl, whisk the eggs until beaten. Whisk in the milk, mustard, salt, and black pepper until well blended. Pour the mixture in the pan over the bread. Gently press down on the bread with the back of a fork or a spatula to help the bread absorb the liquid.

Refrigerate the strata.
Lightly cover the strata, and refrigerate for at least 4 hours or overnight. Remove the strata from the refrigerator about 30 minutes before baking. (Putting the strata right in the oven can be risky—the sudden change of temperature can cause some pans to crack or break.)

Preheat the oven to 325°F.

Bake the strata.

Bake for 50 to 65 minutes, or until the center appears set and a knife inserted into the center comes out clean. Cool 10 to 15 minutes before cutting and serving.

TRY INSTEAD: Instead of store-bought bread, try the Old-Fashioned White Sandwich Bread (page 78).

PRO TIP: Use a full-fat cheese for best melting. And use any kind of sausage you like, such as pork, turkey, or chicken. I like to use chicken sausage and a shredded Italian cheese blend. You can also add a cup of chopped precooked vegetables.

FOOD FACT: A strata is similar to a bread pudding. It's a dish generally made up of layers of bread, cheese, and meat or vegetables, with a mixture of egg and milk poured over top. It's usually refrigerated for a while before it's baked.

rosemary french cheese puffs
(GOUGÈRES)

PREP TIME: 35 minutes

COOK TIME: 37 minutes

YIELD: 30 puffs

TOOLS/EQUIPMENT

- 2 baking sheets
- Parchment paper (optional)
- Small saucepan
- Wooden spoon
- Medium bowl
- Small bowl
- Pastry brush
- Wire rack

Butter, for greasing the baking sheets (optional)

¾ cup water

6 tablespoons unsalted butter

¼ teaspoon table salt

⅛ teaspoon freshly ground black pepper

¾ cup all-purpose flour

4 large eggs, at room temperature, divided

1 cup grated Gruyère or Swiss cheese

2 tablespoons chopped fresh rosemary

½ teaspoon Dijon mustard

Preheat the oven to 400°F.

Lightly grease 2 baking sheets or line with parchment paper.

Make the dough.

In a small saucepan over medium-high heat, heat the water, butter, salt, and black pepper. Bring to a boil, stirring occasionally with a large, sturdy wooden spoon. Stir in the flour. Stir the dough 1 to 2 minutes, or until the dough comes together and forms a ball. Remove from the heat. Place the dough in a medium bowl and cool 5 to 10 minutes.

Add eggs.

Add 3 eggs, one at a time, to the dough in bowl, stirring after each egg. Keep stirring until eggs are well incorporated and the dough comes together.

Add other ingredients.

Stir in the cheese, rosemary, and mustard until well blended.

Make the puffs.

Spoon the dough (about 2 teaspoons each) onto the prepared baking sheets. In a small bowl, beat the remaining egg, and brush lightly over the tops of the puffs.

Bake the puffs.

Bake for 20 to 25 minutes, or until golden brown and puffed. Cool slightly, then transfer to a wire rack to finish cooling.

TRY INSTEAD: Instead of rosemary, add another favorite fresh herb!

DID YOU KNOW? You can cut these in half and make mini sandwiches with them. Try with your favorite meats or salad, like egg salad or ham salad.

FOOD FACT: This dough is also known as choux pastry, or *pâte à choux*, which is a pastry dough that contains butter, water, flour, and eggs. Instead of using a raising agent such as baking powder or baking soda, the high moisture in the dough causes the steam to puff the pastry. This type of dough is used for a wide variety of recipes, such as these Gougères, profiteroles (cream puffs), éclairs, French crullers, and more.

parmesan garlic knots

PREP TIME: 25 minutes

COOK TIME: 17 minutes

YIELD: 12 knots

TOOLS/EQUIPMENT

- Baking sheet
- Parchment paper (optional)
- Plastic wrap
- Small bowl
- Pastry brush

Butter, for greasing the baking
  sheet (optional)

1 prepared Homemade Pizza
  Dough (page 51)

3 to 5 small fresh garlic cloves,
  peeled and minced

4 tablespoons unsalted butter,
  melted

½ teaspoon table salt

½ teaspoon Italian seasoning

¼ cup finely grated Parmesan
  cheese

Preheat the oven to 350°F.

Lightly grease a baking sheet or line with parchment paper.

Form the knots.

Divide the pizza dough into 12 pieces. Roll each piece into a long rope 8 to 12 inches long. Tie each rope into a knot, then tuck the ends underneath the knot. Place the knots on the prepared baking sheet. Lightly cover the knots with plastic wrap and place in a warm, dark, draft-free place for a half hour to an hour, or until risen again.

Bake the knots.

Bake for 13 to 17 minutes, or until very light golden brown.

Make the topping.

Meanwhile, in a small bowl, mix together the garlic, melted butter, salt, and Italian seasoning. Brush over the knots, then sprinkle the cheese on top. Bake an additional 3 to 5 minutes, or until the knots are golden brown.

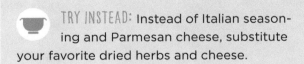

TRY INSTEAD: Instead of Italian seasoning and Parmesan cheese, substitute your favorite dried herbs and cheese.

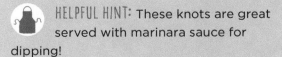

HELPFUL HINT: These knots are great served with marinara sauce for dipping!

raspberry chipotle brie en croûte

PREP TIME: 20 minutes

COOK TIME: 25 minutes

YIELD: serves 8

TOOLS/EQUIPMENT

- Small bowl
- Rolling pin
- Pastry brush
- Baking sheet
- Parchment paper (optional)

½ cup raspberry jam

½ teaspoon ground chipotle chile

Flour, for dusting the work surface

1 frozen puff pastry sheet
(half of a 17-ounce package),
thawed according to package
directions

1 large egg, beaten

1 (8-ounce) wheel Brie cheese

¼ cup sliced almonds

Crackers, for serving

Preheat the oven to 375°F.

Make the raspberry chipotle sauce.
In a small bowl, stir together the raspberry jam and chipotle chile until blended.

Wrap the Brie.
On a lightly floured surface, gently roll out the puff pastry to a 12-inch square. Brush the edges of the pastry with the beaten egg. Place the Brie in the center of the pastry. Top the Brie with the raspberry chipotle sauce, then sprinkle the almonds on top. Wrap the sides of the puff pastry up and over the Brie to fully enclose the cheese. Pinch the seams together to seal. Lightly brush the outside of the pastry with the beaten egg.

Bake the Brie.
Place the enclosed brie on an ungreased baking sheet or a baking sheet lined with parchment paper. Bake for 20 to 25 minutes, or until golden brown.

Cut the Brie.
Cut the pastry so the cheese starts to come out. Serve warm with a variety of crackers.

> TRY INSTEAD: Instead of raspberry jam, you could also try strawberry or cherry. If nut allergies are a concern, omit the almonds.

pesto straws

PREP TIME: 25 minutes (plus 30 minutes chill time)

COOK TIME: 15 minutes

YIELD: 24 straws

TOOLS/EQUIPMENT

- 2 baking sheets
- Parchment paper (optional)
- Rolling pin
- Spatula
- Plastic wrap

Olive oil, for greasing the baking sheets (optional)

Flour, for dusting the work surface

2 frozen puff pastry sheets (17-ounce package), thawed according to package directions

½ cup prepared basil pesto

¼ cup grated Parmesan cheese

DID YOU KNOW? If nut allergies are a concern, you can substitute a store-bought or homemade pesto that does not contain nuts.

Grease the pans.

Lightly grease 2 baking sheets or line with parchment paper.

Roll out the pastry.

On a lightly floured surface, unfold the puff pastry sheets. Roll out each to a 12-inch square. Cut each square in half.

Spread the pesto and cheese.

With a spatula, spread the pesto evenly on two of the pieces of puff pastry, leaving a ¼-inch border. Sprinkle the cheese over the pesto. Top with the remaining two pieces of pastry, pressing lightly around the edges.

Make the straws.

Cut each pastry into 1-inch-wide strips, making 24 straws total. Gently twist each strip, and pinch the ends of each to seal. Place on the prepared baking sheets.

Refrigerate the straws.

Lightly cover the straws with plastic wrap, and refrigerate for at least 30 minutes, or until cold.

Preheat the oven to 400°F.

Bake the straws.

Remove the straws from the refrigerator and remove the plastic wrap. Bake for 10 to 15 minutes or until golden brown. Cool slightly, then serve warm.

pepperoni pinwheels

PREP TIME: 30 minutes

COOK TIME: 20 minutes

YIELD: 24 pinwheels

TOOLS/EQUIPMENT

- 2 baking sheets
- Parchment paper (optional)
- Rolling pin
- Sharp knife

Olive oil, for greasing the baking sheets (optional)

1 prepared Homemade Pizza Dough (page 51)

Flour, for dusting the work surface

⅓ cup tomato sauce

2 cups shredded mozzarella cheese

¼ pound thinly sliced pepperoni

Preheat the oven to 375°F.
Lightly grease 2 baking sheets with olive oil or line with parchment paper.

Roll out the dough.
Divide the dough into 2 even pieces. Roll out each piece of dough on a lightly floured surface to a 10-by-12-inch rectangle.

Make the pinwheels.
Spoon the tomato sauce over each dough rectangle, leaving a ½-inch border. Top the sauce with the cheese, then the pepperoni slices. Starting at the long end, tightly roll up each pizza dough. Pinch along the seam to seal. Using a sharp knife, cut the dough into 1-inch rounds.

Bake the pinwheels.
Place the rounds on baking sheets. Bake for 15 to 20 minutes, or until golden brown.

 HELPFUL HINT: Be sure to roll the dough tightly before slicing.

TROUBLESHOOTING TIP: Deli pepperoni tends to work better than pepperoni that comes in a package because it's larger, making it easier to roll the dough without it falling out.

mini mexican pizzas

PREP TIME: 30 minutes
COOK TIME: 37 minutes
YIELD: 12 pizzas

TOOLS/EQUIPMENT
- 2 baking sheets
- Rolling pin
- Large skillet

Olive oil, for greasing the baking sheets
1 prepared Homemade Pizza Dough (page 51)
Flour, for dusting the work surface
8 ounces ground beef
2 tablespoons taco seasoning
¾ cup plain tomato sauce
2 cups shredded Cheddar cheese
1 cup shredded lettuce
¾ cup finely chopped tomato
¾ cup guacamole
½ cup crushed tortilla chips

Preheat the oven to 375°F.
Lightly grease 2 baking sheets with olive oil.

Shape the dough.
Divide the pizza dough into 12 balls. On a lightly floured surface, roll out each dough ball into thin circles, 4 or 5 inches wide. Place on the baking sheets.

Precook the dough.
Bake for 10 to 15 minutes, or until just light golden brown.

Brown the beef.
Meanwhile, in a large skillet over medium-high heat, heat the ground beef. Cook, stirring occasionally while breaking up the beef, 5 to 7 minutes, or until thoroughly browned. Drain the grease. Add the taco seasoning to the beef, and stir to combine.

Build the pizzas.
Spoon the tomato sauce on top of each pizza crust, leaving about a ½-inch border around the edges. Sprinkle the cheese over the sauce, then spoon the ground beef on top.

Bake the pizzas.
Bake for 10 to 15 minutes, or until the dough is golden brown and cheese is bubbly.

Top the pizzas.
Top each pizza with the lettuce and tomato. Place a dollop of the guacamole on each pizza and sprinkle with the crushed chips.

sausage and ricotta calzones

PREP TIME: 30 minutes

COOK TIME: 25 minutes

YIELD: 6 calzones

TOOLS/EQUIPMENT

- 2 baking sheets
- Parchment paper (optional)
- Rolling pin
- Large skillet
- Large bowl
- Pastry brush

Olive oil, for greasing the baking sheets (optional)

1 prepared Homemade Pizza Dough (page 51)

Flour, for dusting the work surface

8 ounces Italian sausage, casings removed, crumbled

1 (15-ounce) container ricotta cheese

1 large egg

½ teaspoon garlic powder

1 teaspoon dried Italian seasoning

2 cups shredded mozzarella cheese

½ cup grated Parmesan cheese

2 tablespoons olive oil

Tomato sauce, for dipping (optional)

Preheat the oven to 450°F.
Lightly grease 2 baking sheets with olive oil, or line with parchment paper.

Prepare the pizza dough.
Divide the dough into 6 equal pieces. On a lightly floured surface, roll out each piece of dough to circles about 7 or 8 inches wide.

Cook the sausage.
Meanwhile, in a large skillet over medium-high heat, add the sausage. Cook 5 to 7 minutes, or until cooked through, stirring occasionally while breaking up the sausage. Drain the grease. Set sausage aside to cool.

Make the filling.
In a large bowl, stir together the ricotta cheese, egg, garlic powder, and Italian seasoning until well blended. Stir in the mozzarella cheese, Parmesan cheese, and sausage.

Prepare the calzones.
Spoon about ¾ cup of the cheese and sausage mixture on one side of the dough, leaving about a ½-inch border on the filled side edge. Fold the other side of the dough over the filling, pinching to seal. Starting at one end of the border, fold the border dough over, a little at a time, to secure it into place.

Bake the calzones.
Place the calzones on the prepared baking sheets. Lightly brush olive oil over the calzones. Bake for 20 to 25 minutes or until crust is golden brown, rotating the pans halfway through cooking. Serve with tomato sauce for dipping (optional).

mediterranean phyllo triangles

PREP TIME: 45 minutes

COOK TIME: 20 minutes

YIELD: 30 triangles

TOOLS/EQUIPMENT

- 2 baking sheets
- Large bowl
- Plastic wrap
- Pastry brush

Butter, for greasing the baking sheets

1 (10-ounce) package frozen, chopped spinach, thawed and dried

1 cup crumbled feta cheese

¼ cup chopped oil-packed sun-dried tomatoes, drained

2 large eggs, beaten

3 tablespoons onion, minced

3 garlic cloves, minced

1 tablespoon freshly squeezed lemon juice

1 teaspoon dried oregano

¼ teaspoon table salt

⅛ teaspoon freshly ground black pepper

20 sheets frozen phyllo dough, thawed according to package directions

½ cup (1 stick) unsalted butter, melted

Preheat the oven to 375°F.

Generously grease 2 baking sheets with butter.

Make the filling.

In a large bowl, mix together the spinach, feta, tomatoes, eggs, onion, garlic, lemon juice, oregano, salt, and black pepper until well blended.

Prepare the phyllo dough.

Unroll the phyllo dough. Cover well with plastic wrap and keep it covered while working. Place one sheet of the dough on a work surface. Gently brush the sheet of dough with melted butter. Place another sheet of dough on top, and brush it with butter. Cut the dough into 3-inch-wide pieces along the long side to make 3 long strips.

Make the triangles.

Spoon about 2 teaspoons of filling on one side of each strip of dough. Take one corner of the strip and fold over the filling to make a triangle. Gently fold again along the strip of dough, and keep going all the way to the end of the strip to make an enclosed triangle. Repeat with the remaining dough until it's all gone. Place the triangles on the prepared baking sheets, brush with more butter, and cover with plastic wrap until ready to bake. »

Bake the triangles.

Remove the plastic wrap and bake for 15 to 20 minutes, or until golden brown, rotating the pans halfway through baking.

HELPFUL HINT: Squeeze the spinach several times to get out as much liquid as possible. Using paper towels or a salad spinner helps. You could also use fresh spinach, just cook and drain it well first.

TROUBLESHOOTING TIP: Phyllo dough can be very delicate and it dries out fast, so be gentle and keep it covered while working with it. Also, avoid rolling the triangles too tightly so they don't crack when baking.

FOOD FACT: Phyllo dough can be found in the freezer section of your grocery store and is different than puff pastry dough. Phyllo dough is a very thin dough that is generally layered to make flaky pastries.

little chicken and mushroom biscuit pot pies

PREP TIME: 40 minutes
COOK TIME: 20 minutes
YIELD: serves 4

TOOLS/EQUIPMENT

- 4 (8-ounce) ramekins
- Baking sheet
- Large skillet
- Medium bowl
- Pastry cutter (see Cutting in Butter, page 42)

FOR THE FILLING

4 tablespoons unsalted butter
1 cup thinly sliced and coarsely chopped mushrooms
¼ cup finely chopped onion
¼ cup finely chopped celery
¼ cup finely chopped carrot
1 garlic clove, minced
¼ cup all-purpose flour
1¼ cups chicken broth
½ cup heavy whipping cream
⅛ teaspoon table salt
⅛ teaspoon freshly ground black pepper
1 cup shredded precooked chicken

FOR THE BISCUIT TOPPING

1 cup all-purpose flour
1 teaspoon baking powder
¼ teaspoon table salt
4 tablespoons cold unsalted butter, cut into small cubes
⅓ cup cold milk (2 percent or whole)

Preheat the oven to 400°F.
Place 4 (8-ounce) ramekins on a baking sheet.

Cook the vegetables.
In a large skillet over medium heat, melt 4 tablespoons of butter. Add the mushrooms, onion, celery, carrot, and garlic. Cook 4 to 5 minutes, or until soft, stirring occasionally.

Finish the filling.
Stir in ¼ cup of flour to the skillet. Once incorporated, slowly stir in the broth and cream until smooth. Cook and stir until thickened and bubbly, 2 to 3 minutes. Stir in ⅛ teaspoon of salt, the black pepper, and shredded chicken. Spoon the mixture into the ramekins.

Make the topping.
In a medium bowl, mix together 1 cup of flour, baking powder, and ¼ teaspoon of salt until well blended. Cut in 4 tablespoons of cold butter with a pastry cutter or the back of a fork until the mixture is crumbly. Mix in the milk, stirring until the dough is just combined. Spoon the biscuit dough in small pieces over the filling in the ramekins.

Bake the pot pies.
Bake for 15 to 20 minutes, or until the biscuit topping is golden brown. Cool slightly before serving.

> **HELPFUL HINT:** Rotisserie chickens from your local grocery store are handy to use for the precooked chicken in this recipe.

Appendix A
BAKING FOR EVERY OCCASION

Now that you've got a collection of great baking recipes, let's talk about when to make them. Some recipes seem to beg to be made for certain occasions; for example, what sleepover would not be complete without Sticky Monkey Bread Bites? Here are some particularly perfect times to consider using these recipes:

For Bake Sales

- Sprinkle Cake Pops (page 86)
- Snickerdoodle Bites (page 116)
- Thick and Chewy Chocolate Chip Cookies (page 127)
- No Campfire S'mores Bars (page 137)
- Bite-Size Coconut Macaroons (page 121)
- Mini Orange Cookie Tarts (page 179)

For Mother's Day

- Yogurt Banana Bread (page 82)
- Lemon Loaf Cake (page 92)
- Classic Lemon Bars (page 132)
- Chocolate Raspberry Turnovers (page 176)
- Ham and Cheese Quiche (page 182)
- Raspberry Chipotle Brie en Croûte (page 190)

For Father's Day

- Cornbread Muffins with Orange Honey Butter (page 65)
- Rosemary Onion Focaccia (page 76)
- White Chocolate Blondies (page 141)
- Strawberry Cheesecake Bars (page 134)
- Mini Blueberry Peach Crostatas (page 168)
- Banana Cream Pie (page 158)

For Breakfast

- Blueberry Muffin Tops with Cheesecake Drizzle (page 63)
- Cinnamon Nut Coffee Cake (page 95)
- Breakfast Strata (page 184)
- Homemade Mini Cheese Bagels (page 74)

For Sleepovers

- Sticky Monkey Bread Bites (page 66)
- Zebra Marble Cake with Vanilla Frosting (page 99)
- Shortbread Dippin' Sticks (page 118)
- Southern Chocolate Walnut Pie (page 160)
- Mini Mexican Pizzas (page 194)
- Pepperoni Pinwheels (page 193)

For Everyday Snacks

- Soft Pretzel Sticks with Honey Mustard Dip (page 68)
- Very Berry Granola Bars (page 27)
- Honey Roasted Peanut Butter Cookies (page 124)
- Pesto Straws (page 191)
- Rosemary French Cheese Puffs (page 186)
- Cinnamon Sugar Palmiers (page 164)

For Chocolate Lovers

- Mini Triple Chocolate Muffins (page 60)
- Chocolate Chunk Brownies (page 140)
- Chocolate Pecan Pie Squares (page 155)
- Luscious Layered Chocolate Chip Bread Pudding (page 178)
- Dark Chocolate Fudge Lava Cakes (page 106)
- Chocolate Pecan Tassie Cookie Cups (page 129)

Appendix B

CONVERSION CHARTS

Volume Equivalents (Liquid)

US STANDARD	US STANDARD (OUNCES)	METRIC (APPROXIMATE)
2 tablespoons	1 fl. oz.	30 mL
¼ cup	2 fl. oz.	60 mL
½ cup	4 fl. oz.	120 mL
1 cup	8 fl. oz.	240 mL
1½ cups	12 fl. oz.	355 mL
2 cups or 1 pint	16 fl. oz.	475 mL
4 cups or 1 quart	32 fl. oz.	1 L
1 gallon	128 fl. oz.	4 L

Volume Equivalents (Dry)

US STANDARD	METRIC (APPROXIMATE)
⅛ teaspoon	0.5 mL
¼ teaspoon	1 mL
½ teaspoon	2 mL
¾ teaspoon	4 mL
1 teaspoon	5 mL
1 tablespoon	15 mL
¼ cup	59 mL
⅓ cup	79 mL
½ cup	118 mL
⅔ cup	156 mL
¾ cup	177 mL
1 cup	235 mL
2 cups or 1 pint	475 mL
3 cups	700 mL
4 cups or 1 quart	1 L

Oven Temperatures

FAHRENHEIT (F)	CELSIUS (C) (APPROXIMATE)
250°F	120°C
300°F	150°C
325°F	165°C
350°F	180°C
375°F	190°C
400°F	200°C
425°F	220°C
450°F	230°C

Weight Equivalents

US STANDARD	METRIC (APPROXIMATE)
½ ounce	15 g
1 ounce	30 g
2 ounces	60 g
4 ounces	115 g
8 ounces	225 g
12 ounces	340 g
16 ounces or 1 pound	455 g

GLOSSARY

baker's dozen: Thirteen of something. Originated among bakers and tradespeople who gave 13 items for a dozen, to prevent penalties from shorting people.

blind bake: A method to bake a pastry or pie shell by itself before adding a filling.

choux pastry: A pastry dough containing butter, water, flour, and eggs. Instead of a leavening agent (such as baking soda or baking powder), the dough rises because of the steam created from the high moisture content.

clafoutis: Sometimes spelled clafouti, it is a French dessert made with fruit such as cherries, and covered with a thick, flan-like batter.

confectioners' sugar: Finely powdered sugar, usually with cornstarch added. Also called powdered sugar.

crimp: A method of folding, pinching, and/or pleating the edges of a pie crust before baking. Similar to flute.

divided: When the same ingredient is used multiple times in different parts of a recipe.

dollop: A large spoonful of a soft food such as whipped cream.

en croûte: A French term for a food wrapped in some type of pastry dough and baked.

flute: The process of pressing a decorative pattern or design to the edges of a pie crust before baking.

fondant: a thick paste made of sugar, water, food coloring, and often flavoring oils or extracts used for icing and decorating cakes, cupcakes, and candies.

gluten: A mixture of proteins found in wheat and some grains. It makes dough elastic and helps the dough rise, keep its shape, and give a chewy texture to the baked dough.

gougères: A savory French baked good made out of choux pastry and cheese. Sometimes also stuffed with a savory filling.

kneading: Massaging or working the dough by stretching, folding, and pushing the dough to form gluten.

leaven: A substance (such as yeast, baking powder, and baking soda) that lightens dough or batter and causes it to rise.

mise en place: A French term that means "set in place" and is used in cooking to describe getting everything ready, such as ingredients and prep work, before you start cooking.

pâte à choux: See choux pastry.

pith: The white, bitter layer under the skin of some fruit, including citrus.

profiteroles: Small cream puffs that usually have a sweet or savory filling.

score: To cut lines into the surface of foods for a variety of reasons such as to help foods absorb more flavor or cook faster.

serrated: Notched or toothed on the end.

set: To become solid or firm.

tarte Tatin: A French apple tart that is generally baked with pastry on the top then turned over before serving.

tuiles: Thin, crisp French cookies that generally have a curved or rolled shape. They are formed while the cookies are still warm and allowed to cool to set.

zest: the outer colored part of citrus fruit peels. This part of the fruit contains oils that provide concentrated flavor.

RESORCES

....

Listed below are some of my favorite sources for bakeware, serving dishes, specialty ingredients, kitchen gadgets, and more!

- Amazon
  www.amazon.com

- The Baker's Cupboard
  thebakerscupboard.com

- Bed, Bath & Beyond
  www.bedbathandbeyond.com

- Bob's Red Mill:
  www.bobsredmill.com

- Crate and Barrel
  www.crateandbarrel.com

- King Arthur Flour
  www.kingarthurflour.com

- Kitchen Collection
  www.kitchencollection.com

- Michael's
  www.michaels.com

- Penzeys
  www.penzeys.com

- Pampered Chef
  www.pamperedchef.com

- Pottery Barn
  www.potterybarn.com

- The Spice & Tea Exchange
  www.spiceandtea.com

- The Spice House
  www.thespicehouse.com

- Sur La Table
  www.surlatable.com

- West Elm
  www.westelm.com

- Williams-Sonoma
  www.williams-sonoma.com

- Wilton
  www.wilton.com

For more recipes, visit Snappy Gourmet at www.snappygourmet.com.

RECIPE INDEX

....

INDEX

ACKNOWLEDGMENTS

To my daughter, thank you for helping me in the kitchen every day testing recipes, always with a smile on your face. Your enthusiasm kept me going, and I enjoyed every minute baking with you!

To my son, thank you for always being my best taste tester. Your honest opinion and willingness to try anything and everything was extremely helpful.

To my husband, thank you for all your help cleaning up the big messes in the kitchen on a regular basis, even multiple times in one day.

To my mom and dad, thank you for always letting me cook, bake, and experiment in the kitchen when I was a kid.

To all my friends and neighbors, thank you for rushing over numerous times to be my taste testers.

To Meg, Elizabeth, Marthine, and the whole Callisto Media team, thank you for this fabulous opportunity and for all your help! I couldn't have done it without you all!

To Patty, thank you for knowing exactly what I was always trying to say, and thank you and your kids for testing the recipes and all your feedback!

NOTES

NOTES

NOTES

NOTES

NOTES

NOTES

NOTES

NOTES

NOTES

NOTES

NOTES

NOTES

NOTES

kid chef

Nutty Parmesan-Kale Salad (page 121)

kid
chef

The FOODIE KIDS COOKBOOK

HEALTHY RECIPES AND CULINARY SKILLS
FOR THE NEW COOK IN THE KITCHEN

Melina Hammer

Foreword by Bryant Terry

SONOMA
PRESS

For kids everywhere,
May you feel empowered to bop around
the kitchen and create terrific food.

CONTENTS

··

FOREWORD

....

Flipping through *Kid Chef* brings back lots of memories of the time when my wife and I were figuring out how to get our 4-year-old daughter, Mimi, more involved in preparing food with us at home. As I am writing this, Mimi is sitting on her stool tearing rainbow chard leaves from their colorful stems into bite-size pieces. Because we started her off when she was two, this routine is very familiar. Initially, we gave her simple tasks like raking food scraps into the compost pail; washing vegetables; and picking through dried legumes, throwing away any shriveled ones. Maybe you started off doing similar things, helping out in the kitchen too.

It amazes us to see how confident and competent Mimi is becoming. As she gets older, her jobs will become more challenging: pounding spices in a mortar; zesting citrus with a microplane; separating the egg whites from the yolks; using a pan on the stove to sauté veggies. All the things you will learn here, plus so much more.

Preparing and cooking food builds independence when you're completing tasks on your own; it allows you to learn and practice basic math and science; it expands your palate; it gives you ample opportunities to be creative; and most important, cooking is super fun!

I am happy that you will have this book as a personal resource. It is so important to learn about cooking and proper nutrition when you're young so you can establish life-long habits that will decrease your risk of preventable diet-related illnesses. And guess what? With *Kid Chef,* you'll join a larger movement that embraces mindful cooking as a way to address the massive public health crisis facing Americans due to our unhealthy Western diet, filled with too much meat and too many sweets. Before you know it you will be making dishes for family and friends *and* passing on the cooking skills you've learned, inspiring others to join the movement, too.

Bryant Terry
James Beard Foundation Leadership Award-winning chef

INTRODUCTION

Welcome to the world of cooking! You may already have some kitchen know-how—maybe you've helped bake cookies with friends or fixed yourself a homemade snack. Or maybe you've never picked up a pan in your life. That's ok, too, because this book will teach you what you need to know to become a pro in the kitchen.

Cooking is not hard, but we all do start at the beginning. The more you practice, the better you get. Just keep that in mind, and don't get frustrated when a recipe isn't going the way you think it should, because *everyone* makes mistakes. Be patient, and ask for help when you need it.

In this book, you'll learn fundamental skills to secure your success in the kitchen, and tips to develop good cooking habits. Get ready to . . .

- Orient yourself in the kitchen and learn what to stock in your pantry as well as the must-have gadgets and tools you'll need to make great food.
- Participate in several cooking lessons to help you master the essential skills—like prep work, baking, and roasting—that go along with preparing a mouthwatering meal.
- Find a range of recipes to test out on your family and friends, from the impressive Potato-Gruyère Tart (page 93), to the easy—and totally fantastic—Chocolate-Cherry Bark (page 185), to the tasty Hearty Greens Strata (page 142) that works as a breakfast, lunch, or dinner.

As you find your own path to healthy eating, you'll discover that people will have different ideas about what that means. My idea of healthy eating is preparing foods that have little to no processed ingredients, healthy fats (those fats feed our brains!), and plenty of fresh fruits and veggies. Balanced meals like these, with the occasional indulgence of homemade sweets, make for healthy and happy living.

Are you ready to begin your journey into cooking? Put on your apron and let's get started!

PART ONE

culinary school

1

in the kitchen

You may want to jump right in and start cooking, but before you start, it's important to familiarize yourself with your kitchen. Once you know what ingredients you'll need to have on hand and which tool is best for what, the better your results will be. In no time, you'll be using these tools and ingredients with ease to whip up all kinds of delicious food!

BEST PRACTICES

Before you get cooking, there are a few essentials you'll need to check off to achieve good food practices in the kitchen.

1. **Make it official.** One way to make your time in the kitchen official is by putting on an apron. This helps keep your clothes free of stains and gives you an easy place to quickly wipe your hands.

2. **A clean workspace is a safe workspace.** Find a stretch of counter or table space that you can comfortably take over to prepare your recipe and clear out any nonessential items that clutter it. Then, wipe it down with a clean, damp sponge. Dry the area thoroughly before you collect your ingredients and tools.

3. **Always wash your hands.** Before working in the kitchen, always wash your hands in warm, soapy water. A high standard of personal hygiene will keep bacteria away from the food you cook and eat. Be sure to wash your hands after handling raw meat as well, since germs are often concentrated on high-protein foods.

4. **Wash your fruits and veggies.** To remove trace amounts of bacteria (from the soil or from being handled by others before you), give fruits and vegetables a gentle scrub with a soft-bristled brush (for sturdy produce like apples, carrots, and celery) and thorough rinse under cold running water (for more delicate produce like berries, lettuces, and herbs), and pat them dry with a dish towel.

5. **Handle your meat properly.** If you are preparing meat or seafood, pat it dry with paper towels before slicing or cooking. Discard the paper towels, place the meat on a plate or tray, cover, and refrigerate until ready to use.

6. **Cook your eggs safely.** Take these precautions to reduce the risk of salmonella poisoning: Do not allow uncooked eggs to sit at room temperature for more than two hours, and be sure to cook your eggs until the whites are solid.

A CLEANER CLEANER

This homemade nonchemical disinfectant works great sprayed onto counters before wiping down. In a spray bottle, mix:

- a 1:2 ratio of white vinegar to water
- a few drops of orange or lemon essential oil

Citrus fruits are natural disinfectants. Adding these enhance the antibacterial properties and make your cleaner smell nice.

TOOLS OF THE TRADE

It's not necessary to have fancy cooking equipment to get started. A few well-made basics are really all anyone needs to create a terrific dish.

There are a few kitchen tools you'll use on a day-to-day basis, such as:

- A chef's knife and cutting board
- Vegetable peeler
- Colander or strainer
- Mixing bowls
- Measuring cups and spoons
- A skillet, cast-iron preferably
- A medium-size saucepan
- Pot holder
- A heat-tolerant rubber spatula
- Wooden spoon

As you cook more recipes, you may find yourself needing more—and different—tools. Having specialty tools in your kitchen makes it possible to create more advanced dishes. Tools such as tart and springform pans, heavier metal muffin tins, ice pop molds, and appliances such as a stand mixer or immersion blender are not needed every day, but once you use them, you'll understand immediately why they exist.

As you spend time making—and returning to—recipes, you will find your favorite kitchen tools; it's kind of like making good friends over time. In the following pages, I'll cover the tools we'll use in this book.

A WORD ABOUT MICROWAVES

Professional chefs don't cook with a microwave and neither should you. Microwaves destroy the enjoyable textures and nutrients in food. They are simply a well-marketed, "convenient" replacement for other tools that do the same job. You can quickly cook and reheat foods by using a toaster oven or a saucepan, or defrost foods by using a bowl filled with cold water.

COOKWARE

Dutch oven A heavy pot, often enameled, that works on the stove and in the oven. It's good for slow-cooking food, baking bread, and making a large batch of soup.

Grill pan A pan with raised ridges that works like a grill on the stove top. It produces a nice char and grill marks on your food.

Saucepan with lid A deep pan for making soups, stews, and sauces—basically, anything liquid you want to heat. Opt for a medium-size saucepan.

Skillet A shallow pan that's versatile for sautéing, searing, caramelizing, frying, and browning. Cast iron skillets are strongly recommended as they conduct heat really well and can also go into the oven. Avoid Teflon-coated pans as they can chip over time and release chemicals like perfluorooctanoic acid (a known carcinogen), into your food.

Steamer basket A collapsible basket used to hold vegetables and other foods over boiling water for steam cooking. It's also called a steamer insert.

BAKEWARE

Baking dish A shallow glass, metal, or ceramic dish that can go into the oven.

Baking sheet A metal tray, preferably rimmed, for cooking food in the oven. Used for making cookies, as well as to catch spills from overflowing juices while baking pies, lasagna, and other saucy dishes.

Muffin pans A baking pan with built-in cups. They are available in different sizes and materials: silicone works best for easy unmolding and heavier metal tins achieve crispy edges.

Pizza stone A ceramic, stone, or salt cooking surface. Pizza is put on the stone and placed in the oven, though sometimes the stone is heated first. It helps create a crispy crust.

Ramekins Small ceramic dishes used for baking and serving individual portions of food.

Roasting pan Cookware used to cook meats such as whole chicken, leg of lamb, and pork. It can be used with a rack that suspends meat above the pan while catching the drippings (to make gravy or sauce) and helps air to circulate to produce crispy skin.

Springform pan A round cake pan with a removable bottom. It's ideal for baking dishes like cheesecake and quiches, foods with delicate contents that don't allow you to invert them. It cannot be used to bake thin batters, as they will leak out of the pan's seams.

Wire cooling rack A flat wire grid with feet that allows baked goods to rest and cool and prevents them from getting soggy with condensation.

TOOLS AND UTENSILS

Citrus reamer A kitchen tool, often wooden, with a cone-shaped "blade" and deep troughs that extracts juice from citrus fruit.

Colander A bowl with holes throughout used to drain pasta and canned foods and to rinse fruits and vegetables.

Ice pop molds Containers that give shape to liquid ingredients as they freeze. Filling small paper cups or yogurt containers—or even ice cube trays—works in a pinch.

Knives A tool with a blade attached to a handle. For different kinds of knives, see lesson 4: knife skills, page 42.

Ladle A deep-bowled spoon with a long handle. It's ideal for transferring soup, gravy, or stews from a pot to serving bowls.

Measuring cups Kitchen tools made of plastic, metal, or glass used to measure liquid or dry goods like flour or sugar.

Measuring spoons Small kitchen tools, often made of plastic or metal, used to measure small amounts of liquid or dry ingredients, such as spices, salt, and extracts.

 Meat thermometer A device inserted into meat to measure its internal temperature and gauge "doneness," helping you to not overcook. It's useful for cooking steaks and roasts to temperature and for safely cooking poultry and pork.

 Melon baller A utensil that produces sphere shapes from melons and other produce. It's also used to scoop seeds from vegetables, make mini scoops of cookie dough or ice cream, and shape truffles.

 Mortar and pestle A tool consisting of a bowl and a club-shaped implement used to crush seeds, spices, herbs, and vegetables.

 Parchment paper Nonstick baking paper often applied to baking sheets to simplify cleanup.

 Pastry brush A utensil used to spread butter, oil, or glaze. It works well for painting egg wash or cream for a special golden crust and for glazing cakes and cookies.

 Rolling pin A long cylinder with handles used to roll and flatten dough evenly for pies, tarts, and pasta. It's also good for crushing crackers and breadcrumbs for press-in crusts and sprinkled-on toppings.

 Skewers Thin metal or wooden sticks used to hold pieces of food together especially while grilling or roasting meats or vegetables.

 Spatula A tool with a flat, flexible blade—preferably made of heat-resistant rubber, so you can scrape every last bit out of containers.

 Tongs A tool used to grip food. It's great for handling anything you're cooking with precision, whether to turn meat skewers onto the other side while grilling, or rotate carrots in a sauté pan.

Vegetable peeler A tool with a sharp metal blade used to peel the outer layer of sturdy veggies. For more stability, opt for a Y-shaped peeler.

Zester or box grater A device used to grate cheese, zest citrus, grind whole spices like nutmeg and cinnamon, and mince ginger and garlic.

Whisk A handled wire tool used to blend ingredients, smooth and eliminate lumps, and also to emulsify (combine oil and water mixtures together).

APPLIANCES

Blender or immersion blender An electric mixing device used for puréeing soups and making salad dressings, smoothies, whipped cream, and more. An immersion blender is handheld, and the blade *must* be submerged before you turn it on.

Stand mixer or handheld mixer A countertop mixer with different attachments that blends ingredients, beats dough, or whips eggs. A handheld mixer can do many of the things that a stand mixer can, but a stand mixer enables you to work hands free.

Food processor A machine similar to a blender that has a large basin to easily make salsa, pesto, hummus, dips and spreads, dough, bread and cookie crumbs for crusts, and ice cream toppings.

Toaster oven An electrical appliance that serves as a small oven. It's a workhorse for all kinds of heating tasks like toasting, melting, and caramelizing.

9 TIPS THAT WILL MAKE YOU A GOOD COOK

Commit these tips to memory, and then implement them to elevate your cooking game.

1 **Read the recipe. Read it again.** Go through the steps of the recipe mentally before gathering your ingredients and tools to start cooking.

2 **Stay organized.** A well-prepped workspace, free of clutter, is a strong foundation for success in the kitchen.

3 **Prep your ingredients.** Measure and chop your ingredients before you begin cooking, and have them at your workstation, ready to go.

4 **Clean as you cook.** No one likes to deal with a mess after producing a delicious meal. Wiping down counters, clearing your cutting board, and disposing of nonessential items as you go will make a big difference at the end!

5 **Taste, taste, taste.** Taste the food early on as you begin to cook a recipe, and taste throughout as you add ingredients. Don't wait until a dish is almost finished, because flavor is built up in layers. For dishes containing raw or undercooked meats or eggs, wait until they are fully cooked and then taste.

6 **Be patient.** A recipe doesn't always work out perfectly the first time, and that's ok. Making a less-than-perfect dish will

teach you some lessons, and the next time you try it, you can apply what you learned to handle it more skillfully. You'll also get the satisfaction of knowing you stuck with it!

7 **Pay attention.** What does the food you're cooking smell like? What does it look like? How does it sound? Sometimes seconds make the difference in the success or failure of a meal. Focusing will help you save food from burning or becoming too tough or dry, and will help protect you from any cuts or burns.

8 **Use fresh ingredients.** While fresh fruits and vegetables are an important part of a delicious dish, so are fresh herbs and toasted spices: They can transform a so-so meal into one that sings with their bright, aromatic qualities.

9 **Watch others.** The more you study the people you admire and how they cook—as well as *what* they cook—the more you will absorb and the broader your own skill set will become.

STOCKING YOUR PANTRY AND REFRIGERATOR

The magic of making great food starts at the market. Choose the ripest pieces of fruit, the most deeply colored and heaviest vegetables, and the crispest, most "alive-looking" greens—even if that means sorting one piece at a time. Spend extra time choosing the best ingredients, because their flavors help make even the simplest dishes taste truly special. The following ingredients are used repeatedly in countless recipes and helpful to keep stocked in your pantry and refrigerator.

Pasta

Ridged pasta like penne is ideal for creamy, baked, or meaty sauces, while long pasta like fettuccine is great for light olive-oil- or seafood-based sauces. Lasagna noodles, tagliatelle, and other broad or ribbon-like noodles are perfect for richer, meaty sauces. As you experiment, you'll find a pasta for every sauce, and a sauce for every pasta!

- Fettuccine or spaghetti
- Macaroni
- Penne or rigatoni
- Lasagna or tagliatelle

Grains

Try to buy these bulk, because they are a better value. Stored in sealed glass jars, your beautiful array of grains is a window to inspiration and will keep from going stale.

- Barley
- Brown rice
- Quinoa

Legumes

You can buy preservative-free canned beans, but it's best to buy dry beans and soak them when you plan to use them. It's more satisfying knowing you cooked them, and you have more control of what's in your food.

- Black beans
- Cannellini or Great Northern beans
- Chickpeas

Nuts and Seeds

It's helpful to keep a wide variety of these on hand. For snacking, roasted and lightly salted is a good bet. For cooking, buy nuts and seeds shelled and raw and toast them yourself.

- Almonds
- Cashews
- Flaxseed
- Hazelnuts
- Pecans
- Sesame seeds
- Sunflower seeds
- Walnuts

Spices

Whenever possible, use whole spices. They have a longer shelf life, toast more easily—which brings out their flavor—and are more aromatic when grated.

- Bay leaves
- Cayenne
- Chili powder
- Cinnamon
- Coriander
- Cumin
- Mustard seeds
- Nutmeg
- Paprika
- Peppercorns
- Red pepper flakes
- Salt (kosher and sea salt)

Oils

Hands down, you will turn to olive oil again and again as you cook. Select the highest quality that your budget allows. Safflower or peanut oil is good for high-heat cooking such as frying. Raw coconut oil works better for lower-heat cooking and baking.

- Coconut oil, raw
- Olive oil, extra-virgin
- Safflower oil or peanut oil
- Sesame oil, toasted

Flour

You can use all-purpose flour (unbleached is best), but it's a very good idea to incorporate whole-wheat flour for its nutrients and healthful benefits. Whole-wheat flour is heavier and denser and behaves differently from all-purpose flour. In a recipe using all-purpose flour, you may substitute whole-wheat flour for one-third of the called-for amount.

- All-purpose flour
- Whole-wheat flour

Vinegars

If you have to choose between stocking up on vinegars versus oils, I recommend widening your vinegar selection first. They bring so much personality to a wide variety of dishes.

- Apple cider vinegar
- Sherry vinegar
- White vinegar
- White wine vinegar

Sweeteners

Keep honey in your pantry at all times, preferably from a local farmer. Things like confectioners' sugar are really only needed if you plan on baking.

- Brown sugar (light and dark varieties)
- Cane sugar
- Confectioners' sugar
- Honey
- Maple syrup

Dairy

Ideally, use milk, cheese, and butter from grass-fed cows. The label should read "grass fed" or "pasture-raised." The best eggs are from pasture-raised chickens and have bouncy, richly colored yolks.

- Buttermilk
- Cheddar
- Eggs
- Feta
- Gruyère
- Haloumi
- Heavy cream
- Parmesan
- Ricotta
- Whole milk

Fruits and Vegetables

As your budget allows, choose fruits and vegetables that are organic. Not only will you notice a richer flavor, you'll also avoid eating foods with pesticide residue on them.

- Carrots
- Celery
- Kale
- Lemons
- Potatoes
- Sweet potatoes
- Swiss chard

Alliums

Strong-smelling or "aromatic" vegetables such as onions, scallions, garlic, leeks, and chives are a standard in almost every recipe, creating the first layer of flavor in a dish.

- Chives
- Garlic
- Leeks
- Onions
- Scallions

Herbs

Buy fresh herbs whenever available, and comb through the bunches on display for those that have the greenest, most alive-looking shoots. They will taste better and last longer.

- Basil
- Cilantro
- Mint
- Parsley
- Rosemary
- Sage
- Thyme

2

culinary skills

This chapter serves as your cooking class. You will learn proper techniques for reading a recipe, measuring ingredients, using the stove top, cutting with a knife, preparing your ingredients, and baking and roasting in the oven. Do the lessons in order and complete the recipe tutorial with each lesson so you can practice what you've learned. Remember cooking is a skill that gets better with practice!

READING A RECIPE

Recipes are a road map to what you want to cook. But ultimately, you are the chef. Serving suggestions—and even the recipe itself—should be used as a guideline for you to adapt to your own tastes and available ingredients. Using recipes becomes even more fun as you begin to feel more confident in your personal cooking style. Then you know you can modify elements and turn out something wonderful—maybe even better than the original recipe!

Always read the entire recipe and the instructions a couple times fully to be sure you know how to perform each task and that you have all the tools and ingredients you need. I've created the **Glossary** (page 189) to provide definitions for any recipe terms that you might not understand.

Here are the parts that make up a recipe:

A **Title** This is what you are going to make. Sometimes the title also tells you about how you'll prepare the food, such as "Roasted Chicken."

B **Time required** Prep—short for preparation—includes time spent chopping, measuring, or stirring. Cook time indicates the actual time in the oven or on the stove. Freeze time is listed as well for certain recipes that need it. This helps you plan your time accordingly.

C **Servings** This is important to note, as it tells you if the recipe makes enough to feed your guests. If not, it's usually easy to double a recipe.

D **Ingredients** A list of foods you need to make the recipe, organized in the order in which they are used.

■ Some lists indicate how to prep the food before you get to the instructions (i.e., "2 tablespoons finely chopped fresh parsley").

■ Salt and pepper may not include an exact measurement. This means you will add these to your taste.

E **Tools / Equipment** These are the devices you'll need to make the recipe. However, basic equipment such as spoons, pot holders, and measuring cups will not be included in this list. Also, since you'll probably use the chef's knife most of the time, knives will only appear in the list if a different kind is required, such as a bread knife or paring knife. Sometimes you can substitute a different tool for one you don't have, for example, a thick wooden dowel instead of a rolling pin.

PREP TIME
5 minutes

COOK TIME
8 minutes

SERVES
4

**TOOLS /
EQUIPMENT**

Fine grater

Small bowl

Bread knife

Aluminum foil

Baking sheet

1 stick butter, at room temperature

2 garlic cloves, finely grated

2 tablespoons finely chopped fresh parsley

Freshly ground black pepper

1 baguette or ciabatta loaf

Flake salt, such as Maldon

Preheat the oven to 375°F.

Mix ingredients.
In a small bowl, mix together the butter, garlic, and parsley, and season with pepper.

Slice the baguette, and spread the butter mix.
Using a bread knife, cut the baguette on the diagonal into 2-inch segments without slicing all the way through. Use a butter knife to spread all slices, both sides, with the butter mixture, and sprinkle with salt. Cut the baguette in half, and wrap each half in aluminum foil.

Bake the garlic bread.
Lay the foil parcels on a baking sheet. Using a tea towel, remove one parcel after 5 minutes and give it a gentle squeeze. If it is warm to the touch and feels firm from developing a crust, then it is ready. If the bread is still soft and has more give, put the parcel back in the oven for 2 to 3 more minutes.

Serve.
Open the foil parcels and allow to cool for a few minutes. Serve warm alongside a hearty dish of pasta, like Pasta with Homemade Tomato Sauce (page 134).

TRY INSTEAD For extra-crispy garlic bread, after 5 minutes of baking, open the foil to expose the bread and turn the oven to broil. Broil for 1 to 2 minutes, until the garlic bread becomes deeply golden brown.

YOUR GROCERY BAG

When it comes to shopping, the best approach is to make a weekly plan of what you're going to cook, consult your recipes, and create a detailed shopping list.

■ **Make a list.** Jot down all the ingredients you don't already have in your refrigerator or pantry. Make your shopping trip more efficient by organizing your list by aisle or section: produce, meat and seafood, freezer, dairy, and specialty.

■ **Get inspired.** If you come across a new or unusual food (for example, maitake mushrooms or celeriac) that draws your attention, give yourself permission to add it to your basket. Make a point of learning about it, and create a dish to highlight its delicious qualities.

■ **Swap as needed.** This is a pro move: Swap an ingredient for another like it that looks fresher at the market. Your recipe will turn out all the more flavorful for it.

■ **Avoid overly processed foods.** As much as possible, choose whole foods that are products of nature, not food products that have been processed in a number of ways, often loaded with preservatives, artificial colors and flavors, and added sugar. Read product labels carefully and investigate unfamiliar ingredients.

■ **Choose fresher, better ingredients.** Whenever possible, choose organic, fresh ingredients. Organic foods have no harmful chemicals applied to them while they grow, making them a healthier option.

■ **Know your meat and fish.** Get familiar with pasture-raised meats (which means the animals lived in their natural environment and ate their natural diet, instead of being confined to a cage and fed industrialized feed). These animals have been treated more humanely than their counterparts and will be healthier. For fish, opt for wild instead of "farm-raised."

■ **Find a farmers' market.** Farmers' market foods are local and fresher by nature, and shopping there supports your local community. Farmers' markets can also be a lot of fun! Farmers display their stands in unique ways, showing off the literal fruits of their labor. Feel free to ask questions, especially if they aren't busy.

■ **Minimize spoilage.** Make the most of the food you bring home by using it in the order it was purchased. This is known as "first in, first out." Check expiration dates on packages, and use foods expiring soonest.

MEASURING SKILLS

While liquid and dry measuring cups hold the same volume, dry measuring cups are meant to be filled to the brim and then the excess leveled off for precision (often with the edge of a knife). Liquid measurements end below the lip of the cup or are ideally measured using a transparent glass or plastic spouted cup.

Dry Measuring

Flour should be kept in a wide-mouth jar or bag for ease. Choose a measuring cup that fits the amount you need. With a scoop or spoon, fill the cup until it overflows. Do not pack the flour down or use the measuring cup to scoop the flour, as it will cause compression. Using the straight edge of a butter knife, level the flour even with the rim of the measuring cup.

Sugar is more dense. To measure it, scoop directly using the measuring cup and shake it a couple times to settle the amount level to the cup rim. For brown sugar, scoop into the measuring cup, then pack it in with the flat of your palm until it is level with the rim. Next, tap it out into a bowl. If you packed it well, it should keep its shape.

When you fill and then level the ingredients flush with the rim, you know your measurement is correct. The same goes for measuring spoons: Scoop and sweep the excess away with a straight edge, measuring to the rim of the spoon.

Liquid Measuring

Measure liquids in a spouted, transparent measuring cup set on an even surface. Pour liquid so that it reaches the measurement line. Be sure your eyes are even with the level of the measurement. If need be, bend down to read the measurement at eye level.

PREP TIME
10 minutes

COOK TIME
50 minutes

MAKES
5–6
CUPS

**TOOLS/
EQUIPMENT**

Whisk

Large bowl

Small bowl

Rubber spatula

Rimmed
baking sheet

Parchment paper

Wire cooling rack

3 cups rolled oats

¾ cup raw almonds, coarsely chopped

½ cup raw hulled pumpkin, sesame,
or sunflower seeds, or a mix

¼ cup flaxseed

¼ cup quinoa or millet

¼ cup wheat bran

⅓ cup olive oil

½ cup pure maple syrup or honey

¼ cup packed light brown sugar

1 teaspoon ground cinnamon

¾ teaspoon freshly grated nutmeg

1 teaspoon flake salt, such as Maldon

1 egg white, beaten until foamy

½ cup dried cranberries, blueberries,
figs, cherries, or other dried fruit

¼ cup unsweetened coconut flakes

Preheat the oven to 300°F.

Mix the dry ingredients.
In a large bowl, mix the oats, almonds, pumpkin seeds, flaxseed, quinoa, and bran. Set aside.

Combine with the spices and wet ingredients.
In a small bowl, use a rubber spatula to stir together the oil, maple syrup, brown sugar, cinnamon, nutmeg, salt, and egg white. Pour the liquid over the oat mixture, and fold until well combined.

Bake the granola.
On a rimmed baking sheet lined with parchment paper, spread the granola evenly. Bake for 30 to 40 minutes, stirring every 10 minutes for even browning.

Add the fruit.
Add the dried fruit and the coconut flakes, stir to combine, and bake until the granola is fragrant and a beautiful, toasty brown, about 10 minutes more.

Store and serve.
Set the sheet on a cooling rack to cool completely. Transfer the granola to jars or airtight containers, and store at room temperature. Enjoy as a snack, as a topping for yogurt or ice cream, or as cereal with milk.

DID YOU KNOW? You can also make a savory granola. Instead of maple syrup, swap in a little cayenne or soy sauce, and add chopped rosemary and more nuts, like cashews, pecans, and walnuts.

USING THE STOVE

When using the stove it's important to practice safe cooking habits. Even when being careful, a kitchen fire is a real possibility. For the most part, fires are avoidable if you follow these important safety tips:

- Never leave cooking food unattended.
- Keep the stove top clean of any food, oil, or grease, which can ignite while cooking.
- Always tie back long hair (standard restaurant procedure)
- Roll up long sleeves, and remove any hanging jewelry that can get caught on burners or pan handles.

Turning on the Stove

Gas stoves have a continuously burning tiny flame called a pilot light under the cooktop. This flame lights the burners when you turn them on. To ignite the burner, turn the knob all the way, often to a spot marked "Lite," until you hear a clicking sound. Once the burner has ignited, adjust the flame to the temperature called for in the recipe.

Burners on electric stoves consist of coiled heating elements that normally range in temperature from Low (1) to High (10). The temperature is controlled by the knob. Flat, glass-ceramic cooktops are also electric, but they conduct heat in a different manner. This type of cooktop heats more quickly and also cools more quickly. Only the burner area heats up, while the adjacent cooktop remains cool. Depending on the stove, you may control the heat via a knob, or you may control the temperature digitally through a panel on the stove.

Making Sure the Pan Is Hot

The first step in stove-top cooking is heating your pan. Heat it while dry, over medium-high heat. To test the pan for readiness, sprinkle a drop of water: If the drop sizzles and jumps around, it's ready.

Adjust the flame to the specific recipe's requirements, and add your cooking oil or butter. You need only a little, as the heat will disperse it across the pan's surface area as it melts down. This will make your food less likely to stick. Heat the butter and allow it to foam—then add your food. If you are using oil, heat it until it pulls to the edge of pan, also known as when oil "smiles," and then add the food. Do not heat oil so much that it smokes; that means it has burned.

Resisting the Temptation to Fuss

Resist the urge to fuss with the food as it cooks; instead, be patient. You must give the pan—and the food—enough time to work its magic. Use the timing in the recipe as a guide for how frequently to stir or for when to turn food to the other side.

As you wait for the next step in a recipe, pay attention to how your food looks, smells, and sounds: These are cues that will make you an expert cook. Sliced onions sautéing in the pan turn from opaque to transparent. Nuts are aromatic just when they become ready during toasting. A sauce will bubble quietly once it has come to a simmer. Each detail is important, and when observed, it will give you the information you need to become a confident chef.

BURNER DOS AND DON'TS

DON'T leave a burner on that does not have a filled pot or pan on it.

DON'T leave an empty pan on a hot burner.

DON'T put a glass or ceramic pan or lid on a hot burner.

DO use appropriately sized burners for the size pot or pan you are using.

DO turn any pot or pan handle away from the edge of the stove, as it could get knocked over if turned out.

DO keep oven mitts as well as other cloth and paper goods away from stove burners.

DO assume pots and pans are hot, and handle them with dry pot holders.

DON'T hover over the pan while cooking, since food often splatters.

DO turn food away from you rather than toward you when turning food over, so any hot liquid or grease is directed away from your skin.

Stove-Top Techniques

Here are the main stove-top cooking techniques you'll use over and over again:

Simmer Liquids over high heat boil rapidly, while liquids over a lower heat simmer. Simmering is a way of gently cooking ingredients until they are tender.

After bringing your ingredients to a boil over high heat, turn the heat to low or medium-low for gentle bubbling in the pot: You should see the liquid shimmer and a bubble or two form every few seconds.

Boil Boiling means high heat and continuous bubbles popping out of vigorously moving liquid in the pot. Boiling helps keep food in motion, prevents sticking, and cooks food quickly. This process is most often used for cooking pasta and some grains, boiling eggs, and blanching vegetables.

Fry Frying is cooking food in oil over moderate to high heat. There are two basic types of frying: shallow frying and deep-frying. Shallow frying is cooking food in oil that comes up to partially cover the food. Deep-frying is cooking food by submerging it in hot oil.

Some oils are meant for cooking, others for flavor. Cooking oils have a mild flavor and scent and a high "smoke point"—the temperature at which oil starts to smoke and burn—making them ideal for frying. If the frying oil isn't hot enough, food will become soggy. If it's too hot, food will burn before fully cooking.

Butter has a low smoking point, making it a poor choice for frying. Good frying oils include canola, grapeseed, peanut, safflower, and sunflower oils.

Grill Grilling is great for many reasons: It is a fast way of cooking; few seasonings aside from olive oil, salt, and pepper are needed; and the textures of charred, juicy foods are delicious. For the purposes of this book, you'll focus on stove-top grilling using your grill pan.

HOW TO HANDLE A FIRE

In the unlikely event of a fire, turn off the burners or the oven. If the fire is small and contained in the pan, smother it with baking soda or cover it with a metal lid to extinguish it. Study the instructions on how to use an ABC or UL-rated dry chemical fire extinguisher, and keep it, baking soda, and metal lids nearby to put out fires quickly. Never use flour or fan the flames, and never use water to put out a grease fire.

Place a fire extinguisher close to an exit so you can back out of the kitchen or leave your home if the fire becomes uncontrollable. Keep a stocked first aid kit near the fire extinguisher. If you have been burned, apply ice and then aloe vera to the affected area.

If the fire cannot be extinguished, exit your home and call 911 for emergency help.

Melt Melting is the process of turning a solid into a liquid using low heat. You can melt butter or cheese in a sauce pan, but for chocolate or custards, the best method is to use a double boiler on your stove top. You can buy a double boiler, but it's easy to fashion your own. Use a tempered glass or metal mixing bowl, or small saucepan, and a larger saucepan. The bowl or small saucepan should fit into the large saucepan for best heat distribution, with only a small gap between them. To use the double boiler, add 1 to 2 inches of water to the larger pan, and place the bowl or small saucepan into it, filled with whatever you intend to melt, and bring the water to a simmer.

Sauté In sautéing, you'll move the pan or stir occasionally to keep food from sticking and to cook each piece at the same rate. Use a large, wide pan to sauté so that you don't crowd the food. This helps air circulate around each piece, allowing the heat of the pan to cook some of the natural moisture out of the food, intensifying flavors.

When you add food to the hot pan to sauté, you should hear a sizzle immediately upon contact. Oil, butter, and grease can splatter while cooking, so take extra care and lay food down gently into the pan. Cook over medium-high heat according to the recipe (until softened; until browned), and stir the food occasionally, every 30 seconds or so.

PREP TIME
1 minute

COOK TIME
2–4 minutes

SERVES

1

**TOOLS/
EQUIPMENT**

Small bowl

Small cast-iron or
enameled skillet

Spatula

1 large egg

1 teaspoon olive oil or butter

Pinch sea salt (optional)

Freshly ground black pepper (optional)

HELPFUL HINT

How long you cook the egg is a
matter of personal preference.
Sunny-side up (runny yolk): no
more than 3 minutes. Over easy
(semi-solid yolk): no more than
4 minutes. Over hard (solid yolk):
5 minutes or so. To gauge "doneness," gently shake the pan to see
if the yolk jiggles.

Crack the egg.
Tap the egg firmly on the rim of a bowl to crack
it, then empty it into a small bowl. This low-stress
method helps prevent broken yolks.

Heat the skillet.
Heat a small skillet to medium temperature.

Coat the skillet.
Drizzle the olive oil (or place the butter) into the
skillet. When the oil becomes shimmery and pulls
to the edges of the skillet (or the butter sizzles),
it is ready.

Cook the egg.
Pour the egg gently into the skillet, holding the bowl
just above it for an easy transfer. You should see
the egg bubble and sizzle. If it doesn't, your pan
was not hot enough. Gently tilt the skillet to one
side and then the other, spreading the white in an
even layer to help it cook fully. Cook to your ideal
"doneness" (see Helpful Hint).

Serve.
When your fried egg is ready, turn off the burner, hold
the skillet handle with a pot holder, and with your
other hand, slide a spatula under the egg to transfer it
to a plate. Season with salt and pepper (if using), and
eat immediately. This easy, delicious, nourishing dish
works for breakfast or dinner and pairs nicely with
toast, a salad, or even pasta and veggies.

KNIFE SKILLS

The knife is probably the most commonly used tool in the kitchen and also the most important to learn how to use properly so that you avoid hurting yourself. You will develop these skills over time, but technique and the right knife for the job are key. As you practice these skills and become familiar with knives, using this essential kitchen tool will begin to feel like second nature. Cutting food doesn't just make it easier to eat, it also allows foods of different sizes to cook at the same rate and helps you create more delicious-looking dishes!

What Knife Is Best?

A knife may feel large or awkward at first—so you can ask for the help of an adult or use a mini chopper until you gain more practice. While some knives are better for certain cutting tasks than others, at this stage, I recommend choosing a knife that feels comfortable and natural in your hands.

KNIFE SAFETY RULES

1. Above all else: Always pay attention to what you are doing!

2. Always cut on a cutting board made of a material other than glass, marble, or metal to avoid slipping. Wood and plastic are good choices. Place a dampened tea towel under the cutting board to keep it in place as you cut.

3. Keep your knives sharp. If you use dull knives, you'll end up pushing harder, which may lead to an accident.

4. If you have to carry a knife from one area of the kitchen to another, always carry it point down, parallel to your side, as you walk.

5. This is not the circus. Never attempt to catch a falling knife—step back and allow it to fall. You should also wear closed-toe shoes as a precaution.

6. Never leave a knife in the sink. Anyone who reaches into the sink may not know it is there and could be injured.

Bread knife This serrated-blade knife is great for sawing through the crusty exterior of bread but is also useful for cutting tomatoes or pineapple, shaving chocolate, and more.

Chef's knife This is one of the larger of the knives you'll use in the kitchen. It works in a rocking motion and should feel comfortable in your hand. Go to a store with a wide selection, and try out different brands. Find one that feels neither too heavy nor too light and that is not too long or too short. It will become your trusted friend.

Paring knife A small paring knife is a good beginner knife, especially if you don't feel adept at holding a larger knife like a chef's knife yet. It's also great for younger kids with smaller hands. This knife is good for small chopping tasks, like trimming ends off of green beans, shaving the pith from lemon peel, skinning a tomato, or hulling strawberries.

Sharpening Knives

There is no substitute for using sharpening stones for your knives, but it's a skill that needs to be developed, even for adults. You may consider using knife-sharpening kits while you get your cutting and cooking skills up and running.

Learning to Cut

Learning to safely and efficiently make even cuts is essential to becoming a good cook. The proper way to hold a larger knife, like a chef's knife, is to grab it as if you were shaking hands: wrap your middle finger, ring finger, and pinkie finger around the handle to hold it, but then rest your index finger on one side of the blade, curling it up a little so you do not cut yourself. Rest your thumb on the opposite side, and pinch the blade between your thumb and index finger to guide it, with the other fingers holding the handle firmly. This will give you leverage and control over the knife and keep you from cutting yourself. Practice this grip to strike the right balance without holding the knife too tightly so you don't tire out your hand.

For smaller knives, like a paring knife, you use the same gripping technique. You may extend your index finger along the top of the knife for greater control.

Always use two hands when cutting. Your less dominant hand will hold the food. Make a claw shape with your fingers, curling the fingertips back (including your thumb) and sticking the knuckles out, then rest your fingertips on the food you plan to cut. As you slice, rest your knuckles against the side of the knife to steer it, make slices of equal size, and keep your fingers stable as you move up the food, keeping them out of the way of the sharp blade. Move in smooth, even strokes, using the blade's sharp edge to do the cutting rather than forcing the blade through the food.

PRACTICE ROUND: CUTTING CELERY

1. Place the curved side of a celery stalk up and the flat edges down to stabilize the food on the cutting board.

2. Get your holding hand "claw" in place, and with the chef's knife in your other hand, place the tip of your knife on the cutting board.

3. As you cut, the tip of your knife should not leave the cutting board but should stay anchored there, pivoting as you smoothly work with the knife.

4. Move ¼ inch onto the celery, and with a sliding motion, make a cut.

5. You did it!

Use the same practice to continue cutting the whole stalk. As you cut, the chopped pieces may cling to the knife. It is helpful to pause after a few slices to brush them off and reposition your holding hand, moving farther up the food as you continue to make slices.

Cutting Styles

With any of these methods, first trim veggies and fruit of any unwanted things like stems, cores, and roots. You may also need to cut a sliver off any round or wobbly vegetable or halve it to stabilize it on the cutting board as you slice or chop.

A **Chop** To cut items into small pieces uniformly. It doesn't mean to hack the food up but to create an emphasis on same-size pieces.

B **Dice** To cut items into small cubes. You first cut the food into long, equal-size, matchstick-shaped pieces (see Julienne), then chop those into whatever size dice is called for in the recipe.

C **Julienne** To cut foods into long, thin strips, like matchsticks.

D **Mince** To cut into very small pieces. Mincing requires the use of your holding hand to keep the tip of the knife in place as you rock the blade back and forth across the food.

E **Slice** To cut broad, thin pieces and can be the finished cut or the first step in creating other cuts.

salsa fresca

PREP TIME
15 minutes

COOK TIME
none

SERVES
4

**TOOLS /
EQUIPMENT**

Large bowl

Rubber gloves
or plastic bag

Citrus reamer

2 large tomatoes

1 small white or red onion

1 jalapeño pepper

½ cup fresh cilantro

1 lime

¼ teaspoon cumin

Flake salt, such as Maldon

Freshly ground black pepper

delicious additions

*Diced fresh mango, pineapple,
or jicama*

Chopped tomatillos or cucumbers

Minced chipotle or poblano pepper

Prepare the tomatoes.
Dice the tomatoes and transfer them, along with
any juices, from the cutting board into a large bowl.

Prepare the onion.
Peel and trim the onion and mince it, rocking the
knife back and forth, until it is almost the size of
confetti. Use the side of the knife to scrape the
onion into the bowl with the tomatoes.

Clean your tools.
Rinse the knife and board under cold water, and
wipe dry if the sharp onion juices have made you
tear up.

Prepare the pepper.
Wearing a rubber glove or a plastic bag secured
with a rubber band around your wrist, slice the
jalapeño in half lengthwise. Remove the core and
seeds, and discard. Mince the jalapeño, and add
it to the bowl. Remove the glove or plastic bag
and discard.

Prepare the cilantro.
Chop the cilantro, and add it to the mixture.

Prepare the lime.
Slice a lime in half widthwise, and squeeze its juice
over the mixture in the bowl.

Combine the ingredients.
Stir, adding cumin, and salt and pepper to taste.
Taste and add more salt or lime juice if needed.
Refrigerate for 15 minutes, up to 1 hour, to let the
flavors meld.

PREP WORK

As the headline implies, you must do work in preparation to cook a recipe so that you'll be ready to execute each step as needed. The difference between harmony and a disaster often lies in how well you have prepared. If you measure, slice and dice, and get all the ingredients ready in advance, then lay them out in order of use *before* getting into the cooking, you will guarantee a less stressful experience.

Beating

To beat an egg, crack it into a bowl. Use a whisk to stir vigorously in a circular motion to break the yolk and combine it with the whites. Beating also brings air into a mixture, creating volume. Beat lightly or well to incorporate the mixture, depending on what the specific recipe calls for. This common technique is used when making scrambled eggs, omelets, cakes, mayonnaise, and meringue.

Mixing

To mix, use a rubber spatula or wooden spoon to stir ingredients together. It may be dry or wet ingredients you are asked to mix, and depending on their respective thicknesses, mixing may either take a moment or require a few minutes to incorporate.

Separating Eggs

Cold eggs are easier to separate. Crack an egg on the lip of a bowl or on a flat surface. Open the egg over the bowl, and allow the yolk to settle in its shell. Carefully transfer the yolk back and forth from one shell half to the other. The slippery white will drip into the bowl. Transfer the yolk into another bowl. If separating more than one egg, use a third bowl to pour successfully separated whites into so that if any yolk drips into your egg-separating bowl as you go, you can discard without contaminating all the egg whites.

After cracking an egg, you can also cup your hand over a small bowl and pour the yolk into it. Allow the thick white to seep between your fingers and drop into the bowl as you separate them slightly, leaving the yolk in your palm. Slip the egg yolk into a bowl designated for yolks, transfer the white into a larger bowl reserved for whites, and repeat until you have enough for the recipe. This method lets you really "get into" your food! If you choose this version, wash your hands thoroughly before and after handling the eggs.

Separated eggs are incorporated into recipes from meringues (whites) to aioli (yolks).

Peeling

Allow the small end of the vegetable to rest on the cutting board, holding it at a slight angle at the other end or from underneath. With the other hand, use fluid movements to glide the peeler along the vegetable away from you, in a top-down motion, rotating the vegetable as you go, until you return to where you started. Flip the vegetable so that the bottom is now the top, and repeat on any missed areas until the vegetable is fully peeled.

If no harmful chemicals were used to grow your vegetables and the skins aren't very tough, you don't have to peel them. Plus, that is where much of the nutrition lives. Pesticide-free veggies just need to be scrubbed free of dirt under cold running water.

Juicing

Use a citrus reamer to juice whole lemons, limes, oranges, and other citrus fruits. First, roll the fruit back and forth along the surface of the counter with your palm while gently pressing down. This breaks down some of the fibers, making the juice easier to extract.

Lay the fruit on its side, tip-end and stem-end parallel to each other. Hold one end, and slice it in half down the middle. Position the cut side over a bowl to catch the juice. Hold the fruit cupped in one hand, and press the pointed mound of the reamer into the fruit with the other, twisting the reamer back and forth to get all the juice out.

Another way to juice is by using a citrus reamer mounted in a bowl. Here, the reamer remains stationary. Twist the fruit back and forth on its ridges, pressing gently down as you do so to extract the juice. Some versions of this type of reamer include a sieve-catch in the bowl with an additional compartment beneath it to easily separate the seeds and pulp from the juice.

If you don't have a citrus reamer, you can use a fork and achieve the same results. Use the tines of a fork as you would a handheld reamer, but alternate twisting the fork, then the fruit, to extract the most juice.

If you only need a small amount of citrus juice, cut a wedge from the fruit, saving the rest (up to three days) in a sealed container in the refrigerator. To squeeze a little lemon juice to season a dish, cut a wedge from the lemon, then, holding one hand underneath it to catch any seeds, squeeze the wedge over your food.

Citrus juice is a universally used flavor; use it for salads and soups, in drinks, on cooked meat, fish, and grains—anytime you want a little extra zing.

Mincing or Pressing Garlic

You can choose to mince garlic with a knife or use a garlic press if you have one on hand. For speedy results, grate garlic on a zester to get a fine texture that will cook evenly.

Grating and Zesting

Box graters have four sides, each with different-size blades: zesting (the finest), shredding, grating, and slicing. To grate cheese or vegetables on a box grater, position the grater over a dish or bowl to collect the shredded results. Hold the grater handle, and press down to stabilize it. Hold the vegetable at one end and run it top-down along the grater, so that the blades catch the edge of the veggie to grate it.

The blades of box graters are very sharp and can cut you; as you grate food, be careful to reposition your hand further up the food, keeping a safe distance between your knuckles and the sharp edges. It is nearly impossible to grate the last end of the food without cutting yourself, so save the last bit to use for stock or discard it.

Many recipes often call for citrus zest, or the skin of a citrus fruit minced finely. If possible, find unwaxed, organic citrus, and wash and pat them dry beforehand. Use a zester, like a Microplane. Hold the handle, and position its end down against the cutting board surface to stabilize it. You can also rest the zester teeth-up over a bowl and press the top and handle ends onto the opposite sides of the bowl, zesting directly into your recipe rather than transferring the zest from the cutting board.

Hold the citrus fruit with your other hand and, pressing moderately, move in short strokes in the opposite direction of the teeth, grating the topmost colored skin only. The white part underneath the skin, called the "pith," is bitter and unpleasant. Check after a few strokes to see if you have exposed the pith, then rotate the fruit, moving it to zest the skin in a new spot. Repeat until you have fully zested the fruit, or until you have enough for the specific recipe.

CLEANLINESS AND SAFETY

Be serious about cleanliness. Wash your hands thoroughly when handling food. Never prepare food directly on the countertop. Use cutting boards or plastic cutting mats, incorporating different ones for preparing different types of foods—one for raw fruits and veggies and a different one for raw meats. Wash cutting boards in hot, soapy water and then pat or air dry, and wipe down counters with hot water.

Keep hot foods hot and cold foods cold. Check the temperature of your refrigerator. It should be set to 40°F (5°C). Your freezer should be set to 0°F (−18°C) or lower. These chilly temperatures will keep your food from spoiling.

Refrigerate leftover cooked food as soon as possible to prevent the spread of bacteria. Eat leftovers within 3 to 4 days. Food left at temperatures between 40 and 140°F will spoil quickly and can carry bacteria that transmit food-borne illnesses.

bacon-herb frittata sandwich

PREP TIME
10 minutes

COOK TIME
25 minutes

SERVES
4

**TOOLS/
EQUIPMENT**
Box grater
Medium bowl
Whisk
Large skillet
Tongs
Rubber spatula
Small bowl

5 eggs

2 scallions, finely chopped

⅓ cup buttermilk

2 tablespoons crème fraîche

¼ teaspoon freshly grated nutmeg

⅛ teaspoon cayenne pepper

1 cup grated sharp Cheddar or
Swiss cheese , divided

Kosher salt

Freshly ground black pepper

3 slices bacon, cut into half-inch strips

3 whole-grain tortillas

3 tablespoons chopped fresh parsley,
to top, plus a handful of chopped salad
greens such as arugula or mesclun mix

Preheat the oven to 425°F.

Mix the eggs, spices, liquids, and cheese.
In a medium bowl, whisk together the eggs, scallions,
buttermilk, crème fraîche, nutmeg, cayenne, and half
the cheese. Season with salt and pepper.

Cook the bacon.
In a skillet large enough to fit the tortillas, cook the
bacon until crisp over medium heat, stirring occasionally, about 6 minutes. Using tongs, transfer the
bacon to the egg-scallion mixture. Pour all but a
spoonful of the rendered fat into a small bowl.

Cook the tortillas.
Add 1 tortilla to the fat in the skillet and toast over
medium heat, about 5 minutes. Flip halfway through
to toast both sides. Transfer to a plate. Repeat with
the reserved fat and remaining tortillas. Leave the
last toasted tortilla in the skillet.

Cook the frittata.
Pour half of the egg mixture over the tortilla, and
on medium heat, gently stir the mixture with a
rubber spatula for about 30 seconds as the eggs
begin to set. Add a second tortilla, followed by the
rest of the egg mixture, and stir gently again for
another 10 seconds or so. Top with the final tortilla
and sprinkle remaining cheese on top. Transfer the
skillet to the oven to bake for 8 to 10 minutes, until
the frittata is puffed and golden.

Finish and serve.
Remove from the oven, top with the parsley and
greens, cut into wedges, and serve warm.

BAKING SKILLS

Baked goods can be quite straightforward to make, but to bake, you must be more precise than when you cook. Baking measurements are precise for a reason: The proportions of ingredients perform a special chemistry in the finished baked goods, such as the proper rise in a crusty loaf of bread, a flaky crumb in the perfect pie, or the silky creaminess in a frosting. Pay close attention as you bake, and you will learn to make treats everyone drools over.

Oven Safety

Before preheating, check the oven for anything inside and position the racks as you need them. You should avoid storing things in the oven to reduce the risk of fire.

When opening the oven, move back from the initial blast of heat before reaching in to handle a pan so the hot air doesn't hit you in the face. Use pot holders to remove your food and close the oven door immediately afterward. Place the hot pan on a wire cooling rack, a pot holder, or a trivet.

If you discover a fire in the oven, keep the door closed and turn the oven off. Do not open the oven door until the pot or pan has completely cooled.

Creaming Butter and Sugar

Creaming butter and sugar is one of the first steps to making delicious baked goods. Use room-temperature butter (which is still solid, but if you pressed your thumb into it, it would leave a dent). Allow 30 to 60 minutes for it to soften on the countertop. With a handheld or stand mixer on low speed, beat the butter smooth for 10 to 20 seconds. Gradually pour in the sugar, and continue to beat at moderate speed, scraping the sides of the bowl periodically with a rubber spatula.

It should take 2 to 5 minutes to properly cream them together (depending on which mixer you use), resulting in a fluffy, smooth, pale yellow mixture. The mixer beats air in, and that air suspended in the mixture helps create a light texture in cakes and muffins and makes cookies light and crisp instead of hard and dense.

Cutting in Butter

"Cutting in" means incorporating butter into flour in such a way that little lumps of the butter remain whole in the mixture. When the dough is baked, these small lumps create separation in the structure of the crust, creating a flaky texture. Use unsalted butter; this will allow you to control the amount of salt in the overall recipe. When you cut butter into flour, start with the required amount cut into smaller cubes, and keep it very cold.

There are a couple of ways to incorporate butter and flour together. Before specialty tools existed, using two knives to literally cut butter into the flour was standard. You can still do it that way, though it takes patience, as the process is slow going.

A more common and faster method is to use a food processor. Pulse the processor in brief spurts to incorporate the very cold cubed butter into the measured flour. The risk in using this machine is that you could overwork the flour, stiffening the gluten in it and making it tough, not tender. There is also less control in creating those ideal pea-size bits of butter. Be conservative and pulse in fewer, short bursts. You can pulse more if needed, but you cannot go back once you have overworked it. Just like everything else with cooking and baking, if you choose this method and do it regularly, it will become more natural.

Using a Rolling Pin

Once you make pastry, do not attempt to use it immediately. The pastry is stickier and therefore harder to roll at this point. It benefits from mellowing in the refrigerator for at least 20 minutes. When the dough is ready, use a rolling pin to flatten the dough on an even surface.

Here are some tips for successfully rolling out dough:

- Sprinkle only a small amount of flour onto your work surface; too much flour will cause the dough to become dry and tough.
- Place even pressure on the rolling pin as you work; roll from the center of the pastry toward you to the edge, stopping just before rolling over the edge.

- Give a one-eighth turn to the pastry with each pass of the rolling pin so that you aren't overextending your reach.
- Roll, turn, and repeat until your dough is the required thickness.
- Patch any cracks in the dough rather than rerolling the crust; over-handling will make the dough tough.
- Work gently but quickly. If the dough becomes too warm (denting or smearing rather than spreading), refrigerate it before rolling it again. To plan for this, roll pastry out on lightly floured parchment paper, using that as your "work surface." This makes it easy to transfer pastry to chill.

Keeping Pastry Cold

Before mixing, butter needs to remain as cold as possible so that once in the hot oven, its water content can release steam, which is what creates air pockets and a flaky crust. The same is true for pastry, as it has the butter suspended throughout it. Uncooked pastry becomes flabby and stretchy when it is not cold enough, making it difficult to work with.

There's no such thing as pastry that's too cold before being baked. You can even place a fully formed, ready-to-go pie or tart into the freezer for a while to make sure it'll hold its shape once met with the blazing-hot oven. The old adage is true: "Cold with the making, hot with the baking."

Even Baking

Position cake pans or muffin tins as close to the center of the oven as possible. They should not touch each other or the oven walls. If your oven isn't wide enough to put pans side by side, place them on different racks and stagger them to allow air to circulate.

Every oven is hotter in a certain area; for example, maybe the back is hotter than the front. If you don't correct for that, you may end up with unevenly cooked pastries. To account for this, rotate your pans halfway through the process. If you are using more than one rack, also switch pan position when you rotate. However, do not open the oven constantly to check on progress. This will lower the temperature and alter the baking time.

Bake pies on the lowest oven rack, on a preheated baking sheet to prevent soggy bottom crusts. For double-crust fruit and meat pies, cut slits in the top crust or use decorative cutters to allow steam to escape. This ensures an evenly baked final creation. If crust edges brown too quickly during the long bake time, loosely fold 2-inch-wide strips of foil and press them around the edges of the crust until it's time to remove the pie from the oven.

Checking for Doneness

To test a baked good like a cake or muffin for doneness, insert a toothpick or wooden skewer into the center—it should come out clean. Cake should spring back when lightly touched and should be just pulling away from the sides of the pan.

For fruit pies to thicken properly, they need to be hot enough for the filling to boil. If your pie isn't bubbling, it isn't ready yet.

Cookies will continue to set from the heat of the pan after being removed from the oven. Remove the cookie tray, close the oven, and place the tray on your stove top. Slide the edge of a spatula under the edge of one cookie and lift gently. If the cookie stays flat across the bottom without bending or breaking in the middle, it's ready to come out.

If you prefer soft cookies, slightly underbake them or substitute brown sugar for some or all of the granulated sugar in the recipe. In many instances, this will produce softer cookies because brown sugar contains more moisture.

rosemary shortbread cookies

PREP TIME
20 minutes,
plus 40 minutes
to chill

COOK TIME
15 minutes

MAKES

2

**DOZEN
COOKIES**

**TOOLS /
EQUIPMENT**

Medium sieve
for sifting

2 large bowls

Electric mixer

Rubber spatula

Baking sheets

Wire cooling rack

Parchment paper

1 ¾ cups all-purpose flour

¼ cup flax meal

1 tablespoon finely chopped fresh rosemary

¾ teaspoon sea salt

2 sticks unsalted butter, at room temperature

½ cup confectioners' sugar, sifted

Mix the dry ingredients.
In a large bowl, mix the flour, flax meal, rosemary, and salt until well combined. Set aside.

Cream the butter.
In another large bowl, use an electric mixer to cream the butter, about 4 minutes. Add the sugar and blend until fluffy, scraping down the sides with a spatula.

Form the dough.
Add the flour mixture to the butter mixture, and blend on low, just until a dough forms. Test by squeezing the dough between your fingers—if it holds together, it's ready. Working quickly, roughly squeeze dough into a cylindrical shape. Wrap the parchment over it and roll dough back and forth into an even, solid roll, about 12 inches long. The ends should be the same thickness as the center.

Chill the dough.
Refrigerate the dough log for 20 minutes.

Preheat the oven to 350°F.

Cut the cookies and bake them.
Remove the dough from the refrigerator, and unwrap the parchment paper. Use a sharp knife to cut the dough into ¼-inch-thick disks. Arrange them on baking sheets and refrigerate until firm, about 20 minutes. Bake for 15 minutes, or until the edges and bottoms are golden.

Serve.
Transfer the cookies onto a wire cooling rack to cool fully. Cookies will keep for 4 days between layers of parchment, sealed, at room temperature.

ROASTING SKILLS

Roasting is a wonderful way to prepare food and is one of the oldest cooking methods in history! Besides the convenience of putting food in the oven and walking away rather than standing at attention cooking at the stove, the flavors and texture produced by roasting transform ingredients in a most delicious way. Roasted squash makes you think it's candy; roasted potatoes become crisp *and* fluffy; roasted fish is made buttery and flaky. As long as you pay attention toward the end of the cooking cycle—neither burning nor drying out the dish—roasting foods is an easy path to yummy eating.

Opt for Pasture-Raised Meat

Pasture-raised—and some organic—meats come from animals that are treated humanely. These chickens, pigs, and cows live outside rather than in confining cages, and they eat what would be natural for them. This diet honors the animal and makes their cuts more flavorful.

When animals are fed organic feed, that also means they ate no genetically modified ingredients (GMOs) such as corn and soy, which have chemicals inserted into their seeds or genes to tolerate heavy doses of pesticides as they grow. Pasture-raised or grass-fed meats are widely available at farmers' markets, as well as at green grocers. These meats cost more, but when you buy them, you support humane animal farming.

Handling Meat

When you bring your raw meat home to cook, here's how to safely handle it:

- Never prepare raw meat, poultry, or fish where it can come into contact with cooked foods or raw vegetables—this is known as "cross-contamination prevention."
- Wash your hands if they come into contact with raw meat, poultry, or fish.
- Designate one cutting board for raw meat, poultry, and fish.
- Never put cooked food on an unwashed dish that held raw meat, poultry, or fish.

- Plan ahead: Thaw meat, poultry, and fish in the refrigerator.
- Pat dry raw meat, poultry, and fish with paper towels before cooking. Immediately dispose of the used towels.
- Cook poultry until the juices run clear.
- Use a meat thermometer to tell whether meats are cooked properly.

Food Storage

In the refrigerator, store raw meats in a pan or bag so meat juices don't drip onto other foods. Smell the meat before you begin to work with it: If it has a strong, unpleasant, or "off" odor, do not use it. Freeze or cook raw ground meat, fish, and poultry within three days. Freeze or cook steaks, roasts, and chops within five days.

USING A MEAT THERMOMETER

Insert the stem end of the meat thermometer in the thickest portion of the meat, away from any bones. Cooking times may vary from oven to oven and based on meat thickness, so use a meat thermometer to make sure food has reached a safe minimum internal temperature. Wash the stem between uses.

Always allow meat to rest before cutting into it. You will retain internal juices better by resting meat fresh out of the pan, grill, or oven for at least 10 minutes (up to 20 minutes for larger cuts) under a piece of aluminum foil bent into a tent-like shape. This keeps your meat warm while retaining that glorious crust the cooking produced. The juicy steak or roast this technique produces is a definite sign of a skilled chef!

MEAT	INTERNAL TEMPERATURE	INTERNALLY, MEAT LOOKS LIKE
Beef, whole cuts (steaks, roasts, and chops), medium rare	120°F to 130°F	Deep pink, juicy
Beef, whole cuts (steaks, roasts, and chops), medium	140°F	Pink
Ground beef, pork, and lamb	160°F	Light pink
Lamb, whole cuts (steaks, roasts, and chops), medium rare	120°F to 130°F	Deep pink, juicy
Lamb, whole cuts (steaks, roasts, and chops), medium	140°F	Pink
Pork, whole cuts (roasts and chops), medium	145°F	Light pink
Poultry, whole, pieces	165°F	White, no red meat

PREP TIME
10 minutes

COOK TIME
35 minutes

SERVES
4

**TOOLS/
EQUIPMENT**

Large cast-
iron skillet

Wooden spoon

Tongs

4 sweet Italian or bratwurst sausage
links, uncooked

4 small Granny Smith or Braeburn
apples, cored and cut into wedges

5 shallots, peeled and sliced
into wedges

1 handful fresh sage leaves, torn

2 tablespoons olive oil

Kosher salt

Freshly ground black pepper

½ cup apple cider vinegar

Dijon or grain mustard, for serving

Salad greens (optional), for serving

Crusty bread (optional), for serving

Preheat the oven to 425°F.

Pat the sausages dry with a paper towel.

Roast the apple mixture.
In a large cast-iron skillet, toss the apples, shallots, and sage in the olive oil, and season with salt and pepper. Transfer to the oven, and roast for 15 minutes.

Add the sausage, and continue cooking.
Using pot holders, remove the skillet from the oven, and use tongs to turn the roasted apple mixture. Nestle the sausages in between. Roast until the sausage is browned and cooked through and the apple mixture is tender and caramelized, 15 to 20 minutes more.

Serve.
Add the apple cider vinegar to the pan, and use a wooden spoon to scrape up any browned bits, letting it bubble. Bring the skillet tableside, and set it on a trivet. Serve at once alongside your favorite mustard, a pile of greens, and crusty bread (if using) to mop up the juices.

YOU MADE IT!

Congratulations! You learned how to read a recipe, measure ingredients, use the stove, cut and prep ingredients, and bake and roast—and along the way, you built your confidence in the kitchen!

Maybe you had some hiccups and didn't master a lesson as well as you hoped to. Try the recipe tutorials again and study as you go. When you understand what went wrong the first time and persist—taking the time to do it right—the better your skills will be when you encounter new recipes that use the same techniques.

The following chapters are some of the most exciting: you get to pick recipes to cook! If you want to ease in, start with simpler recipes and work your way up. Here are some recipe suggestions:

IT'S A CINCH

SHOW YOUR SAVVY

FEELING BOLD

PART TWO
recipes

Dutch Baby (page 76)

3

breakfast

simple scrambled eggs

PREP TIME
5 minutes

COOK TIME
5–10 minutes

SERVES
4

**TOOLS /
EQUIPMENT**

Small bowl

Whisk

Medium sauté pan

Heat-tolerant
rubber spatula

6 to 8 eggs

Kosher salt

Freshly ground black pepper

4 tablespoons butter

Flake salt, such as Maldon, for finishing

delicious additions

Sautéed broccoli or mushrooms

*Shredded cheese, folded in or
finely shredded to top*

Minced scallions or chives

Diced tomatoes

Bacon or ham

Beat the eggs.
Crack the eggs into a small bowl, and whisk until
frothy. Season with salt and pepper.

Add the eggs to the pan.
Melt the butter in a medium sauté pan over
medium heat, and then turn the heat to low as the
butter foams. Pour the eggs in and let sit for a few
seconds.

Cook the eggs.
Use a spatula to nudge and stir the eggs, scraping
the bottom continuously as you move them around
the pan to help prevent sticking. Use the spatula to
push the eggs from center-out, and then scrape the
pan edge, swirling the outermost eggs into the center. Keep doing this until the eggs begin to look like
pudding and then form into dense, rich egg curds,
about 4 minutes.

Serve.
Remove the pan from the heat while the eggs are
still a little loose; they will continue to cook on the
way from the pan to your plate. Sprinkle with a little
flake salt and pepper, and eat at once.

HELPFUL HINT You want the eggs to cook
slowly, so if they start sticking, turn your
heat even lower and keep stirring; not fast, but
continuously.

cheesy egg sandwich

PREP TIME
5 minutes

COOK TIME
10 minutes

SERVES
4

**TOOLS /
EQUIPMENT**

Bread knife

Box grater

Toaster oven

Small cast-
iron skillet

Metal spatula

Olive oil, for drizzling and frying

1 baguette or other crusty bread,
sliced into 5-inch sections and halved
horizontally

⅔ cup grated sharp Cheddar
cheese, divided

4 eggs

1 handful greens (arugula or spinach)
per person, rinsed and patted dry

Sea salt

Freshly ground black pepper

Toast the bread.
Drizzle a little olive oil onto the cut sides of the
bread, and lay the slices on a toaster tray. Toast until
golden and crispy, about 3 minutes. Turn the slices
cut-side up, transfer to plates, and sprinkle the
cheese evenly on the toast.

Melt the cheese.
Return the bread to the toaster oven and broil until
the cheese bubbles, about 5 minutes. Carefully
transfer the toast to the plates.

Fry the eggs.
In a small cast-iron skillet over medium-high heat,
fry the eggs in enough olive oil to coat the pan once
it is hot. Turn the heat to medium after 1 minute,
allowing the whites to cook fully while keeping the
yolks soft. Season with salt and pepper.

Serve.
Pile the greens onto the toast sandwich bottoms,
followed by the fried egg; then top with broiled
cheesy toast. Eat at once, with a plate underneath
to catch any drips of liquidy golden yolk.

TRY INSTEAD This recipe has many
options! Swap sautéed spinach for
the fresh greens, or pepper Jack cheese
for the Cheddar. Add mustard, mayonnaise
or avocado. Add a sausage patty or ham.

breakfast burrito bar

PREP TIME
10 minutes

COOK TIME
12 minutes

SERVES
4

**TOOLS/
EQUIPMENT**

Different-size
festive bowls

Dish towel

Box grater

Colander

Sauté pan

Aluminum foil

4 to 8 whole-grain (8- or 10-inch)
tortillas

6 to 8 eggs, scrambled

2 cups canned black beans, drained
and rinsed

3 strips cooked bacon, crumbled

1 cup Greek yogurt or sour cream

1 cup bite-size cilantro sprigs

1 ½ cups Salsa Fresca (page 46)

½ cup orange, red, or green bell
peppers, diced

1 ½ cups shredded sharp Cheddar
or Monterey Jack cheese

1 ½ cups diced avocado or
No-Nonsense Guacamole (page 101)

Sriracha or Cholula hot sauce,
for garnish

Preheat the oven to 375°F.

Warm the tortillas.
Wrap a stack of 4 tortillas in aluminum foil and warm
for 5 to 10 minutes. If you are preparing 8 tortillas,
make 2 wrapped bundles. Wrap the warmed foil
bundles in a dish towel to keep them toasty.

Serve.
Serve the fillings and toppings in festive, colorful
bowls. Arrange them together on the table or counter, along with the towel-wrapped tortillas, and allow
your guests to assemble their own burrito creations.

DID YOU KNOW? Many burrito bar items
can be made ahead and refrigerated,
such as the salsa, No-Nonsense Guacamole,
and diced pepper mix.

shakshuka (tomato-egg bake)

PREP TIME
10 minutes

COOK TIME
20 minutes

SERVES
4

**TOOLS/
EQUIPMENT**

Toaster oven

Mortar and pestle

Large
enameled skillet

Wooden spoon

1 onion, chopped

2 tablespoons olive oil

2 garlic cloves, chopped

1 (28-ounce) can tomatoes, or
Homemade Tomato Sauce (page 134)

1 tablespoon za'atar

2 teaspoons cumin seeds, toasted
and ground in a mortar and pestle
(see No-Nonsense Guacamole recipe,
page 101)

Kosher salt

Freshly ground black pepper

4 eggs

¼ cup fresh cilantro leaves, for garnish

⅔ cup Greek yogurt or sour cream

Crusty bread, torn, for serving

delicious additions

Chickpeas
Artichoke hearts
Feta

Preheat the oven to 375°F.

Cook the onion and garlic.
In a large enameled skillet over medium heat, sauté the onion in olive oil for 3 to 5 minutes. Add the chopped garlic, and cook for another minute.

Add the tomatoes and aromatics.
Add the tomatoes, and bring to a simmer. Add the za'atar and cumin, season with salt and pepper, and simmer uncovered for a few minutes, until the sauce thickens. Break the tomatoes into chunks using the edge of a wooden spoon. Taste and adjust seasoning as needed.

Add the eggs.
Use the wooden spoon to make four nests in the sauce and crack an egg into each. Season the eggs with salt and pepper, and transfer the skillet to the oven, cooking for 7 to 10 minutes, or until the eggs are just set.

Serve.
Serve from the skillet on a trivet at the table. Season with salt and pepper to taste, and garnish with fresh cilantro and a few dollops of yogurt. Serve with the bread to mop up the sauce and yolks.

DID YOU KNOW? This one-skillet dish originated in North Africa; *shakshuka* means "a mixture."

savory sausage hash

PREP TIME
15 minutes

COOK TIME
15 minutes

SERVES
4

**TOOLS /
EQUIPMENT**

Large enameled or
cast-iron skillet

Fine grater

Wooden spoon

2 tablespoons olive oil, divided

1 onion, finely chopped

3 Yukon gold potatoes, scrubbed and
diced into ½-inch cubes

1 pound hot or Italian pork sausage,
casings removed

2 garlic cloves, finely grated

1 small jalapeño, cored and seeded,
finely chopped

2 tablespoons minced fresh rosemary

1 teaspoon dried smoked paprika

Sea salt

Freshly ground black pepper

Cook the onion and potatoes.
Place a large skillet over medium heat, and add
1 tablespoon of olive oil when the pan is hot. Add
the onion and sauté for 5 minutes, or until they
become translucent, stirring occasionally. Add the
potatoes and the remaining 1 tablespoon of olive
oil, and stir to incorporate. Sauté the mixture for
another 5 minutes, stirring only a few times during
this step so the potatoes can form a nice crust.

Cook the sausage.
Add the sausage, garlic, and jalapeño, and brown
the meat, crumbling it into smaller pieces with the
edge of a wooden spoon. Add the rosemary and
paprika, and season with salt and pepper. Stirring
occasionally, lower the heat if needed as you cook
the mixture, until the potatoes become crispy and
fork tender and the meat is browned all over.

Serve.
Serve from the skillet on a trivet at the table.

spiced-orange french toast

PREP TIME
10 minutes

COOK TIME
20 minutes

SERVES
4

**TOOLS/
EQUIPMENT**

Citrus reamer

Zester

Shallow
baking dish

Large cast-
iron skillet

Metal spatula

5 eggs

1⅓ cup whole milk

2 tablespoons fresh-squeezed
orange juice

Zest of 1 orange

1 teaspoon ground cinnamon

Sea salt

1 tablespoon butter, plus more as
needed for the pan and for serving

1 tablespoon grapeseed oil, plus
more as needed

8 (½-inch-thick) slices brioche
or challah bread

Maple syrup, for serving

Whisk the ingredients.
In a shallow baking dish, use a fork to beat together
the eggs, milk, juice, zest, cinnamon, and a large
pinch of salt.

Prepare to cook the French toast.
In a large cast-iron skillet over medium heat, heat
the butter and grapeseed oil. Dip the brioche one
slice at a time into the egg mixture to coat, punc-
turing it a couple of times with a fork. Don't let
the bread sit in the custard for very long, as it will
become soggy.

Pan fry in batches.
When the butter foams, carefully place the bread
into the skillet, two slices at a time. Pan fry the bread
in batches until golden brown on both sides, flipping
when one side is done, about 5 minutes per batch.
Repeat with the remaining slices, adding more butter
and oil to the pan as needed.

Serve.
Serve the French toast warm with butter and
maple syrup.

HELPFUL HINT Always zest citrus before
you juice it. It's much easier to hold onto
the fruit before its juice has been squeezed.

PRO TIP Keep cooked French toast
warm on a baking sheet in a 300°F
oven as you cook the rest.

dutch baby

PREP TIME
5 minutes

COOK TIME
15 minutes

SERVES
4

TOOLS/ EQUIPMENT

Small, shallow ramekins

Baking sheet

Blender

¾ cup all-purpose flour

¾ cup whole milk

4 eggs, lightly beaten

2 tablespoons cane sugar

Pinch freshly grated nutmeg

¼ teaspoon sea salt

4 tablespoons butter, divided into 4 pats

Confectioners' sugar, for dusting

Lemon wedges, for serving

delicious additions

Jam

Cinnamon sugar

Fresh berries

Stewed apples

Whipped cream or crème fraîche

Preheat the oven to 425°F.

Prep the ramekins.
Arrange the ramekins on a rimmed baking sheet, and place in the oven to heat.

Blend the ingredients.
In a blender, mix the flour, milk, eggs, sugar, nutmeg, and salt until frothy.

Butter the ramekins.
When the ramekins are hot, add a pat of butter to each and, using pot holders for protection, swirl to coat. Butter should foam. Replace in oven until fully melted.

Bake the Dutch Babies.
Remove baking sheet from the oven. Divide the batter evenly among the ramekins, and bake until the Dutch Babies are puffed and golden brown, 10 to 15 minutes.

Serve.
Working quickly while the pancakes are still puffy, transfer the ramekins to larger plates. At the table, sprinkle a little confectioners' sugar on top, followed by a squeeze of lemon. Eat immediately.

DID YOU KNOW? This custardy pancake puffs up in a delightful way as it cooks. It also deflates quickly once out of the oven, perfect for absorbing a final pat of butter and some freshly squeezed citrus. For the tastiest results, eat it right away!

banana-maple breakfast quinoa

PREP TIME	TOOLS / EQUIPMENT
10 minutes	Medium glass bowl with lid
COOK TIME	Fine grater
5 minutes	Medium saucepan
SERVES	Heat-tolerant rubber spatula
4	

1 cup red or golden quinoa

2 cups almond or cashew milk, plus more for drizzling

½ teaspoon ground cinnamon

¼ teaspoon freshly grated nutmeg

¾ cup fresh or frozen blueberries

Pinch kosher salt

2 bananas

Maple syrup, for serving

Soak the quinoa overnight.
Transfer the quinoa to a glass bowl or container with a lid. Add the nut milk, cinnamon, and nutmeg. Soak on the counter overnight, lid slightly askew.

The next morning, heat the quinoa.
In a medium saucepan over medium-low heat, add the frozen berries and a pinch of salt to the quinoa mixture and warm, about 5 minutes. Have a few tablespoons of water or more nut milk nearby to drizzle in case the quinoa sticks as you stir. If using fresh berries, add them when the porridge is almost warm enough to eat.

Serve.
Spoon the quinoa into bowls, and slice bananas on top. If you like, add more freshly grated nutmeg and a dash of cinnamon. At the table, drizzle maple syrup over the top and eat at once.

TRY INSTEAD Fresh-grated ginger added to the overnight soak makes this dish peppery and bright. You can also try other fruit. Swap diced apples or pears or a handful of grapes cut in half in for the berries.

open sesame nut bars

PREP TIME
10 minutes

COOK TIME
25 minutes

TOTAL TIME
1 hour 5 minutes

MAKES
16
BARS

**TOOLS/
EQUIPMENT**

8-inch-square
glass baking dish

Parchment paper

Large bowl

Small bowl

Rubber spatula

Wire cooling rack

Butter, for greasing

1 ¼ cups white and/or black sesame seeds

¾ cup unsweetened shredded coconut

½ cup dried apricots, chopped

¼ teaspoon sea salt

¼ cup honey

⅓ cup crunchy peanut butter

¼ teaspoon pure vanilla extract

DID YOU KNOW? These tasty, energy-boosting bars can be made three days ahead.

Preheat the oven to 350°F.

Prep the baking dish.
Butter an 8-inch-square glass baking dish, and line it with parchment paper long enough so that it extends beyond the dish by at least 2 inches on all sides. Cut slits at the corners so the parchment lays flat.

Mix the ingredients.
In a large bowl, mix together the sesame seeds, coconut, apricots, and salt. In a small bowl, stir the honey, peanut butter, and vanilla extract. Add the honey mixture to the seed-and-fruit mixture, and stir well to combine.

Transfer the ingredients and bake.
Use a rubber spatula to scrape the mixture into the prepared baking dish, using the broad side of the spatula to press everything into an even layer. Bake until golden around the edges, 20 to 25 minutes. Transfer the baking dish to a wire cooling rack and let cool until firm, about 30 minutes.

Serve.
Use the parchment tabs to lift the seeded block out of the baking dish—if it starts to crumble, let it cool longer. Using a sharp knife, cut 16 bars. Eat the fruit-seed-nut bars at room temperature. Store any leftovers in a sealed container at room temperature for up to 5 days.

creamy blueberry bliss

**TOOLS/
EQUIPMENT**

Blender
Rubber spatula

1 ½ cups nonfat Greek yogurt

2 cups frozen blueberries

1 banana, cut into chunks,
or 2 tablespoons honey

3 tablespoons flax meal

¼ cup almond milk or whole milk

Ice, as desired

Purée the ingredients:
Spoon the yogurt into the blender, followed by the berries, banana, and flax meal. Purée until smooth, adding milk to thin the consistency slightly and ice as desired to keep it slushy. Stop the blender to scrape the sides down as needed.

Serve.
Pour into glasses and drink chilled.

> TRY INSTEAD Consider adding a tablespoon of peanut butter for a PB&J theme. Swap blueberries for frozen strawberries and mango for a tropical vibe, or add raspberries and blackberries to the mix to make it extra berry.

fruity-nutty breakfast bowl

PREP TIME
10 minutes

COOK TIME
none

SERVES
4

**TOOLS/
EQUIPMENT**

Toaster oven

2 cups Greek yogurt

4 tablespoons flax meal

2 tablespoons chia seeds

4 tablespoons peanut butter

3 cups fresh fruit, such as pomegranate seeds, blueberries, raspberries, or chopped apples, persimmon, or pears

½ cup unsweetened coconut flakes, toasted

2 tablespoons nuts, toasted and coarsely chopped, such as almonds or pistachios (see Colorful Crunch Salad recipe, page 122)

Assemble the breakfast bowls and serve.
Stir the yogurt until creamy. Divide the yogurt evenly into bowls. Sprinkle the flax meal and chia seeds evenly into each. Spoon the peanut butter on top, then the fruit. Scatter the toasted coconut and chopped nuts to finish each bowl, and eat immediately.

HELPFUL HINT For easy toasted coconut, arrange the flakes in a single layer on a small piece of parchment on the toaster oven tray. Once coconut is golden, carefully lift parchment from the tray and sprinkle directly onto the bowls. No fussing or cleanup required!

ginger-lemon green juice

PREP TIME
10 minutes

COOK TIME
none

SERVES
4

TOOLS / EQUIPMENT
Vegetable peeler
Blender

1 (2-inch) piece fresh ginger, peeled and cut into chunks

4 green apples, peeled and cored

2 lemons, peeled, seeds removed

1 orange, peeled, seeds removed

2 stalks lacinato kale, stems removed and coarsely chopped

2 sprigs fresh parsley, leaves only

1 ½ cups ice water

Purée the ingredients:
In a blender, purée the ginger and apples with the lemons and the orange, followed by the kale and parsley. Stop the blender to scrape the sides down as needed. If you prefer a thinner consistency, drizzle ice water through the feeder cap as the motor runs, stopping every few seconds to check the consistency.

Serve.
Pour into glasses and drink at once.

PRO TIP It's best to drink these juices right away. The purées themselves will keep for a day in the refrigerator without losing their vitamin potency, but they will oxidize, losing their bright color.

Perfect Hummus (page 98)

4

snacks & small bites

mini quiches

PREP TIME
10 minutes

COOK TIME
15 minutes

TOTAL TIME
30 minutes

MAKES

24

QUICHES

**TOOLS/
EQUIPMENT**

Mini muffin tin

Medium bowl

Whisk

Baking sheet

Measuring cup

Butter, for greasing

4 whole eggs

1 egg yolk

⅓ cup heavy cream

¼ teaspoon freshly grated nutmeg

Pinch ground cayenne pepper

½ teaspoon kosher salt (if you choose bacon, ham, or smoked fish as your "delicious addition," reduce to a pinch of salt instead)

½ teaspoon freshly ground black pepper

¾ cup shredded Gruyère cheese, divided

Preheat the oven to 375°F.

Grease a 24-cup mini muffin tin.

Mix the ingredients.
In a medium bowl, whisk together the eggs, yolk, cream, nutmeg, cayenne, salt, and pepper until frothy. Stir in ½ cup of shredded cheese.

Add the quiche mixture to the pan.
Place the prepared muffin pan on a baking sheet to catch any drips. If you chose any delicious additions, add a teaspoonful to each cup. Transfer the egg mixture by ladling it into a measuring cup, and from there, pour the egg mixture into each cup, filling to just below the rim. The measuring cup's pour spout makes this a no-mess operation! Top the egg mixture with the remaining ¼ cup of shredded cheese, adding a small pinch to each quiche.

delicious additions

Steamed broccoli florets or chopped asparagus

Diced red bell pepper or chopped tomatoes

Sautéed sliced mushrooms

Sautéed spinach

Sautéed onions or shallots

Finely chopped chives or scallions

Bacon, cooked and crumbled, or ham

Smoked whitefish or salmon

Cook the quiches.

Bake until the tops are puffed and golden, 10 to 15 minutes. Let them cool for about 5 minutes.

Serve.

Invert the tin over the baking sheet to pop out the quiches. Arrange them on a platter or individual plates, and serve.

TRY INSTEAD Feel free to use a different cheese: grated Comté, Swiss, or sharp Cheddar.

DID YOU KNOW? You can freeze extras after they have cooled completely on a small plate or tray. Once they are frozen (about 30 to 45 minutes), seal them in a freezer-safe container or bag. From there, they're good for up to two months! To reheat them, warm them in a 375°F oven for 8 to 10 minutes.

mighty meatballs

**TOOLS/
EQUIPMENT**

Box grater

Fine grater

Small bowl

Medium bowl

Aluminum foil

Baking sheet

2 tablespoons buttermilk

¼ cup fresh bread crumbs

12 ounces ground beef

½ cup grated Parmesan cheese

2 pieces bacon, finely chopped

Pinch freshly grated nutmeg

1 egg

⅓ cup chopped fresh parsley

2 garlic cloves, grated

2 tablespoons olive oil

¼ teaspoon Kosher salt

¼ teaspoon freshly ground
black pepper

Mix the ingredients.

In a small bowl, add the buttermilk to the bread crumbs, and allow the crumbs to absorb the milk, 5 to 7 minutes. Meanwhile, put the ground beef in a medium bowl. Add the cheese, bacon, nutmeg, milk-soaked bread crumbs, egg, parsley, garlic, and olive oil to the meat, and sprinkle with salt and pepper. Overworking the mixture will produce tough, chewy meatballs, so mix everything just until combined.

Form the meat into balls.

Use 2 teaspoons to form the meat mixture into bite-size balls. Use the spoons to place them onto an aluminum-foil-lined baking sheet so that the heat of your hands doesn't warm them prior to cooking. Pre-heat the broiler with a rack in the topmost position.

Cook the meatballs.

Broil the meatballs until browned on top, checking them at about 5 minutes. Lower the heat to 350°F, and bake until tender and fully cooked, about 10 minutes.

Serve.

Serve warm on a serving platter or plates.

ricotta-jam toast

PREP TIME
5 minutes
plus 30 minutes
to warm

COOK TIME
5 minutes

SERVES
4

**TOOLS /
EQUIPMENT**

Zester
Toaster oven

2 to 4 tablespoons preserves of
your choice—raspberry, blueberry,
blackberry, or red currant

4 slices whole-grain, sourdough, or
seeded bread

1 cup whole-milk ricotta cheese,
well-stirred

Zest of 1 lemon

Prepare the preserves.
Let the preserves come to room temperature
if you brought a jar from the refrigerator, about
30 minutes.

Assemble the toasts.
Toast the bread until golden and crispy at the
edges, about 5 minutes. Spread the ricotta onto
the toasts. Add a spoonful—or more, to your
taste—of the preserves, and garnish with the
lemon zest.

Serve.
These toasts are tasty served warm or at room
temperature.

TRY INSTEAD Replace the lemon zest
with freshly ground black pepper along
with marmalade, applesauce, or persimmon
preserves. Crumble a pinch of pink peppercorns over strawberry, fig, or apricot preserves.

from-scratch pizza

PREP TIME
20 minutes
plus 3–24 hours
to rest and rise

COOK TIME
10 minutes

SERVES
4

**TOOLS/
EQUIPMENT**

Fine grater

Large bowl

Small bowl

Pizza stone

Baking sheet

Tea towel

Parchment paper

Metal spatulas

1 cup plus 2 tablespoons all-purpose flour, plus extra for dusting

1 teaspoon kosher salt

1 cup water, mildly warm

¾ teaspoon active dry yeast

1 teaspoon olive oil

1 cup fresh mozzarella, torn

6 slices prosciutto, torn (optional)

½ cup Parmigiano-Reggiano, finely shredded

Flake salt, such as Maldon

Olive oil

2 to 3 cups fresh arugula, rinsed and patted dry

1 lemon, halved

Combine the dry ingredients.
In a large bowl, use a fork to stir the flour and salt together well.

Mix the yeast and knead the dough.
In a small bowl, stir the water and yeast together, add the olive oil, and stir again. Add this mixture to the flour mixture, and knead with your hands until well combined, about 3 minutes. Let the dough rest for 15 minutes.

Knead it again.
Knead the rested dough for 3 more minutes. Bring it out onto a heavily floured work surface, cut it in half, and use the outer edge of your palms to shape each into a ball. Cover the dough with a damp tea towel. Let rest and rise for 3 to 4 hours at room temperature, or 8 to 24 hours in the refrigerator.

Heat the pizza stone.
Place the pizza stone on the middle rack in your oven and preheat it to its highest setting for at least 1 hour.

Stretch the dough.
Place a dough ball on a well-floured surface, and use your fingertips, all together, to indent half an inch from the edge to make a border all the way around. Lift the dough and stretch it across your knuckles, pulling the thick areas thinner. Then lay it down and gently pull with your fingers to shape and stretch it farther as needed, until it is 12 inches wide. »

TROUBLESHOOTING To make this pizza, stretch your dough until it's pretty thin for a crispier pizza crust. There's a fine line between stretching and poking a hole, so pay attention to the thinning parts, and lay the dough down at any point if it becomes too fragile. Be patient; even if you "mess it up," the results will still taste delicious.

HELPFUL HINT Dough can be made three days in advance and should be made one day before making this recipe. If you refrigerated the dough, remove it 30 to 45 minutes before you shape it for the pizza.

Add the toppings.
Lay the stretched dough on a sheet of parchment paper laid on a well-floured overturned baking sheet and top the dough inside the border with the torn mozzarella and prosciutto, the shredded Parm, a pinch of salt, and a drizzle of olive oil.

Bake the pizza.
Use a quick, firm sliding motion to transfer the parchment and pizza to the pizza stone in the hot oven. Bake until the crust is golden and the cheese bubbles, about 10 minutes.

Dress the greens.
While the pizza cooks, transfer the arugula to a large bowl. Squeeze the lemon halves over the greens, cupping a hand underneath to catch any seeds, and toss to combine.

Serve.
Remove the pizza by lifting it from the parchment edges, then transfer the pizza with two spatulas to a cutting surface or platter. Top with the lemon-dressed greens, add another scatter of salt, cut into wedges, and eat at once. Repeat stretching and topping the second pizza, and cook it while you munch on the first.

potato-gruyère tart

PREP TIME
15 minutes
plus 10 minutes
to chill

COOK TIME
30 minutes

SERVES
4–6

**TOOLS /
EQUIPMENT**

Vegetable peeler

Box grater

Rolling pin

Baking sheet

Parchment paper

Paring knife

Large bowl

All-purpose flour, for dusting

1 package puff pastry, such as Dufour brand, thawed in the refrigerator

4 waxy potatoes, such as Yukon gold, peeled and sliced into ¼-inch-thick rounds

1 small onion, halved and sliced thin

1 to 2 tablespoons olive oil

3 to 5 fresh thyme sprigs, leaves only

Sea salt

Freshly ground black pepper

¾ cup Gruyère cheese, grated

Handful of fresh chives, minced, or arugula (optional)

Preheat the oven to 400°F.

Prepare the dough.
On a lightly floured work surface, unfold the dough and roll it out into a large rectangle about ⅛ inch thick. Arrange on a baking sheet lined with parchment paper, and prick the dough all over with a fork—this will ensure the dough doesn't swell up as it bakes. With a paring knife, make a border by gently scoring the dough along all four sides ¼ inch from the edge.

Chill the dough.
Refrigerate the dough for 10 minutes.

Prepare the toppings.
In a large bowl, toss the potatoes and onion in olive oil with the thyme leaves, and season with salt and pepper.

Assemble the tart.
Remove the baking sheet with dough from the refrigerator. Inside its border, sprinkle the grated cheese, then arrange the potato mixture on top. Season with salt and pepper.

Bake the tart.
Bake for 20 to 30 minutes, or until the potatoes are golden brown and cooked through.

Serve.
Cut into slices and enjoy! For added color and flavor, try garnishing the cooked tart with freshly snipped chives or fresh arugula.

moroccan pickled carrots

PREP TIME
10 minutes

COOK TIME
5 minutes

MAKES

1

PINT

TOOLS/
EQUIPMENT

Vegetable peeler

Mason jar with lid

Small saucepan

Whisk

Peel of 1 organic lemon, pith shaved off

2 dried chile peppers

2 garlic cloves

1 bay leaf

1 pound carrots, peeled and cut into
3- to 4-inch spears

½ teaspoon whole cumin seeds

1 teaspoon mustard seeds

Pinch black peppercorns

½ cup white or apple cider vinegar

⅓ cup filtered water

1 teaspoon honey

½ teaspoon kosher salt

Fill the jar.
Put the lemon peel, chiles, garlic, and bay leaf in the jar. Gently place it on its side, and pack the carrots in as tightly as they'll fit, tucking in the spices as you go.

Make the pickling liquid.
Turn the jar upright, and top with the cumin, mustard seeds, and peppercorns. In a small saucepan, heat the vinegar, water, honey, and salt until they dissolve, about 5 minutes, whisking the ingredients together to help speed the process.

Pickle the carrots.
Carefully pour the hot liquid into the jar over the carrot spears. The carrots should be completely covered by the liquid. Allow the liquid to cool to room temperature before sealing. Refrigerate for at least 1 week to allow the seasonings to take effect. Pickled carrots keep refrigerated for up to 1 month.

easy tzatziki

PREP TIME
15 minutes
plus 20 minutes
to drain

COOK TIME
none

MAKES
2 1/2
CUPS

**TOOLS /
EQUIPMENT**
Fine grater
Colander
Large bowl

5 Persian cucumbers (or half an English cucumber), scrubbed and diced

1 teaspoon kosher salt

2 cups Greek yogurt

2 garlic cloves, finely grated

3 tablespoons fresh dill, chopped

1 tablespoon red wine vinegar

1 tablespoon olive oil

Freshly ground black pepper

Prep the cucumbers.
In a colander in the sink, sprinkle salt over the cucumbers, toss to combine, and let them sit for 20 minutes or so to drain their juices.

Release excess liquid.
Press the cucumbers to release any excess liquid, and transfer them to a large bowl.

Make the tzatziki.
Add the yogurt, garlic, dill, vinegar, and olive oil to the cucumbers, season with pepper, stir well to incorporate, and taste. Adjust to your liking, transfer to a sealed container, and refrigerate until ready to use. The dip keeps for 2 weeks.

DID YOU KNOW? Tzatziki can be made three days in advance and goes great with smoked fish, on toast, on grilled meats, swapped for salad dressing, and so much more.

FOOD FACT If your cucumbers are not organic, peel them first, as much of the pesticide residue is concentrated in the skin.

crispy fish sticks

PREP TIME
10 minutes

COOK TIME
15 minutes

SERVES
4

**TOOLS/
EQUIPMENT**

Zester

Citrus reamer

Baking sheet

2 shallow dishes

Whisk

Metal spatula

Olive oil, for greasing

1 pound flounder or cod fillets,
cut into 1-inch strips

Flake salt, such as Maldon

Freshly ground black pepper

1 egg, beaten

Zest and juice of half a lemon

1 cup panko bread crumbs

1 tablespoon Old Bay or
Italian seasoning

Tartar sauce, for serving

Lemon wedges, for serving

Preheat the oven to 425°F.

Prep the fish.
Lightly grease a baking sheet with olive oil. Pat the fish strips dry with paper towels and discard. Season the fish with salt and pepper, and set aside.

Prepare the egg mixture and breading.
In a shallow dish, whisk together the egg, lemon zest, and juice. In another shallow dish, stir the bread crumbs, Old Bay seasoning, and black pepper with a fork to combine.

Bread the fillets.
Dip the fish first in the egg mixture, letting any excess drip off, then press into the bread crumb mixture to adhere. Arrange the fish sticks in a single layer on the baking sheet, more toward the edges of the pan for better browning.

Bake the fish sticks.
Bake in the oven for 10 to 15 minutes, or until golden and the fish flakes easily with a fork, turning the pan halfway through for even baking.

Serve.
Use a spatula to transfer the fish sticks to a serving dish, and serve alongside tartar sauce and lemon wedges.

perfect hummus

PREP TIME
20 minutes
plus 8 hours to
soak and
10 minutes to sit

COOK TIME
1 hour

MAKES
4
CUPS

**TOOLS/
EQUIPMENT**
Citrus reamer
Mortar and pestle
Medium bowl
Colander
Large saucepan
Food processor
Rubber spatula

1 cup dried chickpeas

2 teaspoons baking soda, divided

4 garlic cloves

½ cup freshly squeezed lemon juice

1 teaspoon kosher salt, plus more
to season

¾ cup tahini

3 teaspoons cumin, toasted and ground

¼ cup ice water

Extra-virgin olive oil, for drizzling

Soak the chickpeas overnight.
In a medium bowl, cover the chickpeas and
1 teaspoon of baking soda with cold water by
2 inches. Cover with a pan lid, and let sit 8 hours
to overnight at room temperature, allowing
chickpeas to rehydrate. Drain and rinse.

Cook the chickpeas.
In a large saucepan over high heat, cover the
soaked chickpeas and remaining teaspoon of
baking soda with water by at least 2 inches. Bring to
a boil, skimming foam from the surface as needed.
Reduce the heat to medium-low, place pan lid to
mostly cover, and simmer until the chickpeas are
tender and falling apart, about 45 minutes to an
hour. Drain and set aside.

Process the mixture.
In a food processor, pulse the garlic, lemon juice,
and salt until the mixture becomes a coarse paste.

Add the tahini and water.
Add the tahini to the garlic mixture, and pulse to
combine. With the motor running, add the ice water
1 tablespoon at a time and pulse until the mixture is
smooth, pale, and thick. The initial shock of the cold
water may make the mixture seize up at first.

delicious additions

Smoked paprika

Chopped fresh parsley

Ground sumac

Roasted red peppers

Aleppo pepper

Lemon zest

Add the chickpeas and spices.

Add the chickpeas and cumin to the mixture, and pulse until the hummus is very smooth, about 3 minutes, stopping as needed to scrape down the sides. Add more ice water if you want a thinner consistency. Taste and season with more salt, cumin, and/or lemon juice if needed. Let the hummus sit for 20 minutes to allow flavors to meld, up to overnight.

Serve.

Transfer the hummus to a shallow dish and swirl to make a well in the center of it. Drizzle with olive oil, and serve with veggie spears, pita bread, chips, grilled meats, on toast—really, just about anything.

HELPFUL HINT In warmer weather, soak chickpeas overnight in the fridge to reduce the risk of bacteria. Give them a quick rinse, cook as instructed, and you're good to go!

pita veggie pockets

PREP TIME
10 minutes

COOK TIME
3 minutes

SERVES
4

**TOOLS /
EQUIPMENT**

Toaster oven

2 whole grain pita pockets, sliced in half

CREAMY—CHOOSE 1

1 cup Perfect Hummus (page 98), black bean dip, avocado, scrambled eggs, Labneh, or Greek yogurt

CRUNCHY—CHOOSE 3

2 carrots, cut into disks or matchsticks

2 Persian cucumbers, chopped

2 radishes, sliced thin

1 colorful bell pepper, diced

Handful arugula, baby spinach, or lettuce

⅓ cup almonds, toasted and slivered

BRIGHT AND ZINGY—CHOOSE 2 TO 3

Handful fresh parsley, dill, or mint

Handful olives

1 tablespoon pickled onions

⅓ cup crumbled feta cheese or shaved Parmesan

Toast the pockets.
Toast the pita pockets in the toaster oven—it may take two rounds of toasting depending on the size of your toaster oven.

Assemble the pockets.
Spread or spoon your creamy element onto the insides of each pita pocket. Divide the crunchy ingredients evenly among the pockets, pressing in the ends to open the pocket up like a purse and layering the fillings in. Sprinkle the bright and zingy elements to top or tuck them in between the crunchy and creamy layers.

Serve.
Eat immediately or within 24 hours for best result. Refrigerate the sandwiches in a sealable bag or container if you make them more than 4 hours in advance of when you plan to eat them.

DID YOU KNOW? Labneh is a custard-like cheese most similar to Greek yogurt. It is prized for its rich texture and bright tanginess. You can find it at Middle Eastern grocers, specialty shops, and online.

no-nonsense guacamole

PREP TIME
10 minutes

COOK TIME
3 minutes

SERVES
4

**TOOLS /
EQUIPMENT**

Fine grater

Citrus reamer

Small skillet

Mortar and pestle

Medium bowl

Wooden spoon

2 teaspoons cumin seeds

4 avocados, halved and pitted

1 garlic clove, finely grated

½ teaspoon chili powder

Juice of 3 limes

⅓ cup chopped fresh cilantro

Flake salt, such as Maldon

Tortilla chips, for serving

Toast the spice.
In a small dry skillet over medium heat, toast the cumin until fragrant, about 3 minutes. Transfer to a mortar and pestle, and grind into a powder.

Combine the ingredients.
Scoop the avocado flesh into a medium bowl, and coarsely mash with a fork. Add the garlic, chili powder, lime juice, and cilantro, season with salt, and stir to combine. Taste and adjust seasoning as needed.

Serve.
Serve the guacamole with tortilla chips, on tacos, or with eggs, grilled meats and seafood, and more. To store any leftovers, squeeze a little lime or lemon juice onto the guacamole, stir to combine, and immediately seal in an airtight container so it does not oxidize. Keeps for up to 2 days in the refrigerator.

anything quesadillas

PREP TIME
5 minutes

COOK TIME
10 minutes

SERVES
4

**TOOLS/
EQUIPMENT**

Box grater

Large skillet

Metal spatula

6 (10-inch) flour tortillas

Olive oil, for pan frying

Kosher salt

Freshly ground black pepper

**AS A GENERAL RULE, USE THIS
RATIO, PER QUESADILLA:**

3 to 4 tablespoons condiments
(such as herbs, mustard, or onions)

⅓ cup main ingredient (such as sliced
meat, mashed squash, roasted veggies)

⅔ cup grated cheese of your choice

Prep the tortilla.

Generously spread one tortilla with any sauce-like, condiment. It may be cream cheese to go with the smoked salmon, mustard to go with the corned beef, etc. Set it aside; this will be the tortilla to sandwich the layers once they are in the pan.

Layer the elements.

Set a large skillet over medium heat. When the pan is hot, drizzle with oil and swirl to coat. Place a tortilla into the skillet, and spoon your main ingredient item onto it, spreading it all the way to the edge.

Sandwich the quesadilla, and cook.

Sprinkle the cheese over, all the way to the edge. If you have any herbs, add them to top the cheese. Lay the prepped tortilla facedown onto the rest, pressing down on it evenly with a metal spatula to compress the layers. Cover the pan with a lid, and if needed, lower the heat slightly so that you do not burn the bottom tortilla.

Cook and flip the quesadilla.

Cook covered for 2 to 3 minutes, or long enough for the cheese to begin melting. This is the "glue" to hold the fillings together when you flip the tortilla. In one swift move, use the spatula to flip the quesadilla over. You may use another spatula or serving spoon to steady the top side as you prepare to flip. This requires some coordination but helps guarantee that the fillings stay put.

delicious combinations

Any of these flavor combos are great, listed here in the order of main ingredient, condiment, cheese:

BLT with sharp Cheddar or blue cheese

Tuna melt with pepper Jack

Corned beef, sauerkraut, and mustard with Swiss

Ham, honey mustard, and Swiss cheese

Sage-roasted and mashed sweet potato or butternut squash with Parmesan or blue cheese

Sliced tomatoes, chives, and mayo with dill Havarti

Turkey, roasted peppers, and mashed avocado with Gouda

Smoked salmon, dill, cucumbers, and cream cheese

Cooked steak, peppers, and onions with Muenster

Roasted zucchini or mushrooms, parsley, olives, and mozzarella

Refried beans, lime, cilantro, and queso fresco

Continue cooking.

Once the quesadilla is flipped, add a drizzle of olive oil to the pan as needed. Swirl to coat and cook for another 2 minutes, using the spatula to compress the layers together, until the cheese is well-melted and the quesadilla is brown and crispy.

Serve.

Transfer the quesadilla to a cutting board, and slice into wedges. Allow to cool for at least 2 minutes so the hot cheese does not burn you. Serve with fresh herbs, if desired.

GET CREATIVE

As you explore the world of food, you'll discover all kinds of flavor combos. Get creative and adapt your favorites here, with the added yum of melty, gooey cheese, just like the name "queso" in quesadillas says.

gazpacho gulps

PREP TIME
10 minutes plus
3 hours to chill

COOK TIME
none

SERVES
4

**TOOLS/
EQUIPMENT**
Blender
Rubber spatula

2 pounds tomatoes, cored and cut
into chunks

1 cubanelle pepper, cored, seeded, and
cut into chunks

1 cucumber, peeled and cut into chunks

1 small white or red onion, cut
into chunks

1 or 2 garlic cloves, halved

1 teaspoon kosher salt

1 teaspoon freshly ground
black pepper

2 teaspoons sherry vinegar, plus more
to taste

½ cup olive oil, plus more for drizzling

Purée the vegetables.
In a blender, blend the tomatoes, pepper, cucumber, onion, and garlic at high speed until very smooth, about 2 minutes, stopping periodically to scrape down the sides with a rubber spatula. Season with salt and pepper.

Add the remaining ingredients.
With the motor running, add the vinegar and slowly drizzle in the olive oil through the feeder cap. The mixture will turn bright orange or pinkish. Blending as you add the oil will emulsify the mixture, making it creamy.

Serve.
Transfer the gazpacho to a glass pitcher and refrigerate for 3 hours, or until well chilled. Before serving, season with additional salt and vinegar to taste. Serve in small glasses with a drizzle of olive oil—preferably sipped in the sun.

HELPFUL HINT Leftover gazpacho will last up to five days, kept refrigerated and covered. Give leftovers a good stir just before serving.

crispy sesame seaweed

PREP TIME
5 minutes
plus 15 minutes
to marinate

COOK TIME
5 minutes

MAKES
16
SHEETS

**TOOLS/
EQUIPMENT**

Small bowl

Parchment paper

Pastry brush

Rubber band

Large cast-
iron skillet

Tongs

Metal spatula

2 tablespoons safflower or
grapeseed oil

2 tablespoons sesame oil

Kosher salt

16 sheets nori seaweed

Prepare the marinade.
In a small bowl, stir the safflower and sesame oils
to combine.

Dress the seaweed.
Set a sheet of nori, shiny-side up, on a piece of
parchment large enough to extend a couple inches
beyond the nori in all directions. Brush a light layer
of oil onto it, and lightly sprinkle with salt. Repeat
with the remaining seaweed sheets as you stack
them, shiny-side up, on top of each other on the
parchment.

Marinate the seaweed.
Roll the nori stack in the parchment, and fasten it
with a rubber band, helping to keep the parchment
rolled around the seaweed as it marinates. Let the
rolled bundle sit for at least 15 minutes before
toasting.

Crisp the seaweed.
Place a large cast-iron skillet over medium heat.
Once hot, place one nori sheet from the bundle in
the pan shiny-side up, and pressing on it with the
back of a spatula, toast for 15 seconds, or until it
begins to get crispy and turn a brighter green. Add
another piece of seaweed on top of the first, rough
side facing up. Use tongs to flip the stack over, and
add another nori sheet rough-side up. Toast for
about 15 seconds again. Repeat this process until
all 16 sheets have been added, flipping and toasting
until they become crispy and green.

Serve.

When all the sheets have been crisped, you can use kitchen shears to cut the nori into smaller rectangles or other shapes, as you like. Keep leftovers in a resealable bag or an airtight container, at room temperature, and use within 10 days.

> **HELPFUL HINT** The oil mixture and salt will distribute evenly on both sides of the seaweed sheets, since they were rolled in a stack together. For best results, the key in this preparation is to keep the rough side facing out as you toast.

Delicious Delicata Rings (page 131)

5

salads & veggies

savory cabbage slaw

PREP TIME
15 minutes
plus 20 minutes
to sit

COOK TIME
none

SERVES
4

**TOOLS/
EQUIPMENT**
Citrus reamer
Small bowl
Whisk
Large bowl

4 tablespoons olive oil

3 tablespoons fish sauce

1 tablespoon sherry vinegar

Juice of 1 lime

1 teaspoon brown sugar

Flake salt, such as Maldon

½ head red cabbage

½ head green cabbage

Freshly ground black pepper

Make the dressing.

In a small bowl, combine the olive oil, fish sauce, vinegar, lime juice, sugar, and a small pinch of salt, whisking vigorously to dissolve the sugar. Taste, adjust seasoning as needed, and set aside.

Make the slaw.

With the flat side of the cabbage flush against your cutting board, use a very sharp knife to slice the cabbage very thinly and transfer to a large bowl. Use two forks to toss half the dressing in with the cabbage mix. Add the remainder, and toss again to coat. Season with pepper.

Serve.

The slaw is best once the acids in the dressing soften the crunchy cabbage slightly, at least 20 minutes. Before serving, toss the slaw to reincorporate the dressing accumulated at the bottom of the bowl, then pile the slaw onto sandwiches or serve as a super-flavorful, crunchy side. Keeps in the refrigerator, covered, for 1 week.

TRY INSTEAD The addition of a couple julienned carrots and a thinly sliced, seeded jalapeño make this zippy slaw even more festive.

asian cucumber salad

PREP TIME
10 minutes
plus 10 minutes
to sit

COOK TIME
3
minutes

SERVES

4

**TOOLS /
EQUIPMENT**

Medium bowl

Whisk

Small skillet

3 tablespoons rice wine vinegar

1 tablespoon toasted sesame oil

1 tablespoon soy sauce

½ teaspoon sugar

4 cups Persian, hothouse, or other
thin-skinned cucumbers, scrubbed
and chopped

2 scallions, ends trimmed and sliced
thin on a diagonal

⅓ cup chopped fresh cilantro

Pinch flake salt, such as Maldon

1 tablespoon sesame seeds

delicious additions

Minced pickled or fresh ginger

Minced garlic

Red pepper flakes

Bonito flakes

Make the dressing.
In a medium bowl, whisk to combine the rice wine
vinegar, sesame oil, soy sauce, and sugar, dissolving
the sugar.

Compose the salad.
Add the cucumbers, scallions, cilantro, and salt, and
toss to coat well. Taste and adjust seasoning as necessary. Allow the salad to sit for at least 10 minutes
for the flavors to meld.

Toast the seeds.
In a small dry skillet over medium heat, toast the
sesame seeds until golden, about 3 minutes.

Serve.
Serve chilled with the toasted sesame seeds sprinkled on top. Pairs well with grilled meats, seared fish
or shrimp, brown rice, or broiled, marinated tofu.

PRO TIP Think about how you'll use the
cucumber salad before you chop. For
a stand-alone salad, thin circle slices have a
delicate presentation. Paired with grilled meat
or fish, diced cucumber offers a crunchy
contrast to the juicy main attraction.

summery corn and watermelon salad

PREP TIME
15 minutes

COOK TIME
none

SERVES
4

**TOOLS/
EQUIPMENT**

Zester

5 fresh basil leaves

½ small watermelon, seeded, rind removed, cut into 1-inch cubes

2 ears fresh sweet corn, cooked and cut off cob

1 teaspoon ground sumac

¼ teaspoon ground cayenne

Zest of ½ lemon

Flake salt, such as Maldon

Assemble the salad.

Transfer the cubed watermelon and any accumulated juices to a serving platter. Add the corn cut off the cobs (it is okay if there are rows of corn left intact; that is part of the fun). Sprinkle the sumac and cayenne over the mixture, followed by the lemon zest.

Cut the basil into a chiffonade.

Do this immediately prior to serving the salad, as the edges of the basil will darken from being cut (known as oxidation). Stack the basil leaves on top of each other, and roll into a tight bundle. Slice your knife across the roll, creating very thin strips (called chiffonade). Fluff the chiffonade to separate the strips, and scatter onto the salad.

Serve.

Season with salt, and serve immediately.

FOOD FACT The fresher corn is, the juicier, more tender, and sweeter its kernels. To tell when a watermelon is its ripest, look for a light spot on one side of the skin: This means it was allowed to ripen on the vine rather than being harvested prematurely.

panzanella salad

**TOOLS/
EQUIPMENT**

Bread knife

Baking sheet

Small bowl

Whisk

1 loaf crusty bread, torn into bite-size chunks and left to dry out on a baking sheet for 1 to 2 days

2 tablespoons olive oil, plus extra for soaking, drizzling, and frying

Flake salt, such as Maldon

Freshly ground black pepper

5 large heirloom tomatoes, cut into wedges

1 ½ cups Sun Gold tomatoes, halved

2 cups fresh basil leaves, rinsed and patted dry

4 chives, finely chopped

2 teaspoons red wine vinegar

TRY INSTEAD Substitute shallots cut into wedges and slowly sautéed until soft and translucent, or thinly sliced raw or pickled red onion for the chives.

Preheat the oven to 425°F.

Toast the bread.
Arrange the bread on a baking sheet, and drizzle with olive oil, and season with salt and pepper. Toast the bread in the oven until golden and crisp on the edges, turning once halfway through as needed, about 8 minutes total.

Assemble the salad.
Arrange the tomatoes on a serving platter, alternating shapes and colors. Add the basil, and nestle the crispy bread into the mixture, then scatter the chives all around.

Make the dressing.
In a small bowl, whisk the olive oil and red wine vinegar to combine.

Serve.
Drizzle the dressing over the salad, saving some for at the table, season with salt and pepper, and dig in. You just made an edible work of art!

DID YOU KNOW? This salad is best made when tomatoes are in season during summertime. Look for heirlooms that are heavy, as they'll be bursting with juice and flavor. Different heirloom tomatoes, such as Green Zebras, Cherokee Purples, Yellow Pineapples, or Brandywines add a rainbow of color to the panzanella, as well as subtly different flavors.

minty avocado-melon mix

PREP TIME
15 minutes

COOK TIME
10 minutes

SERVES
4

**TOOLS/
EQUIPMENT**

Citrus reamer

Small bowl

Small cast-
iron skillet

Metal spatula

Melon baller

⅓ cup plus 1 tablespoon
olive oil, divided

2 limes, one juiced and one cut into
wedges for serving

¼ cup chopped fresh mint

Sea salt

Freshly ground black pepper

1 (8-ounce) block Haloumi cheese,
sliced into ¼-inch slices

1 cantaloupe, halved and seeded

2 avocados, halved and pitted

HELPFUL HINT Set aside
any cantaloupe pieces
that are too small for use later,
served over yogurt or with
granola or for making into ice
pops. You can save any
leftover avocado for making
No-Nonsense Guacamole
(page 101).

Make the dressing.
In a small bowl, stir together ⅓ cup of olive oil with
the juice of 1 lime, mint, and salt and pepper to
taste. Set aside.

Fry the cheese.
In a small cast-iron skillet over medium-high heat,
heat the remaining 1 tablespoon of olive oil. Add
the cheese slices, and lower the heat to medium.
Moisture from the cheese can cause the oil to spat-
ter, so be careful as you lay them in. Sear the cheese
for a few minutes—you should hear them sizzle.
Flip to the second side when the first is caramelized
and browned. The second side takes only a couple
minutes. Transfer to a serving platter.

Prepare the melon.
Use a melon baller to make spheres from the cantaloupe's flesh, and then arrange them on the platter
beside the Haloumi.

Prepare the avocado.
Repeat the process with the avocados. Do this just
before serving time so that the avocado doesn't
oxidize, and squeeze a wedge or two of fresh lime
juice over the avocado spheres, tossing to coat.

Serve.
Layer the mixture of avocado and melon balls next
to the Haloumi, and spoon the chopped mint dressing over all. Serve with the remaining lime wedges,
and eat immediately.

salade niçoise

PREP TIME
10 minutes

COOK TIME
7 minutes

SERVES
4

**TOOLS/
EQUIPMENT**

Paring knife

Vegetable peeler

Small bowl

Whisk

Large saucepan

Large
slotted spoon

Large bowl

Colander

FOR THE DRESSING

½ cup olive oil

2 tablespoons white wine vinegar

1 teaspoon Dijon mustard

1 small shallot, minced

3 tablespoons finely chopped
fresh parsley

Kosher salt

Freshly ground black pepper

[INGREDIENT LIST CONTINUES ON NEXT PAGE]

To make the dressing.
In a small bowl, whisk to combine the olive oil, vinegar, mustard, shallot, and parsley. Season with salt and pepper, and set aside.

Boil the eggs.
In a saucepan large enough to fit the eggs in a single layer, add enough water to cover them by 1 inch, and bring the water to a boil. Use a large spoon to carefully lower refrigerator-cold eggs into the water, one at a time, and return to a simmer, adjusting heat as necessary. Simmer for 6 minutes for a liquid-gold yolk, 7 to 9 minutes for a custardy yolk. After your preferred cook time, use a slotted spoon to transfer the eggs to a large bowl filled with ice water.

Peel the eggs.
Once the eggs are cool enough to handle, tap them on the counter to crack the shells all over, and carefully peel them. Rinse each briefly under cold water to remove any stray shell bits, then quarter them.

Cut the potatoes.
Once they are cool enough to handle, slice potatoes into bite-sized wedges and set aside.

Cut the haricots verts.
Stack the haricots verts and slice them into bite-size pieces on a sharp diagonal.

FOR THE SALAD

4 eggs, cold

Ice water

5 potatoes, peeled and boiled until fork tender

2 handfuls very fresh haricots verts, scrubbed, stem ends trimmed

1 head romaine, Bibb lettuce, or arugula, leaves rinsed and patted dry

5 radishes, sliced into thin wedges

½ cup pitted Niçoise (or other oil-cured) olives

1 lemon, sliced into rounds

2 cans oil-packed tuna, drained

2 tablespoons finely chopped chives or thinly sliced red onion

1 tablespoon capers, rinsed

6 anchovies (optional)

delicious additions

Cooked artichoke hearts

Steamed asparagus

Cherry tomatoes or tomato wedges

Marinated beets

Assemble the salad and serve.

On a serving platter, arrange salad leaves to cover. Stack the quartered eggs, haricots verts, sliced radishes, olives, lemon wheels, and boiled potatoes into piles or rows, alongside the chunks of tuna. Scatter the chives and capers over everything, add the anchovies (if using) piled either in the center or laid out over the other elements, and spoon the dressing over all. Serve immediately.

HELPFUL HINT The vinaigrette, potatoes, and eggs can be prepared two days in advance. When thin green beans such as haricots verts are very fresh, they do not need to be cooked. Leaving them raw adds more crunchy nuance to the salad and saves on prep time.

DID YOU KNOW? Niçoise salad is a famous French composed salad that traditionally has tuna and anchovies on top of piles of colorful ingredients.

not-your-average caesar

PREP TIME
10 minutes
plus 30 minutes
to chill

COOK TIME
10 minutes

SERVES
4

TOOLS/
EQUIPMENT
Citrus reamer
Box grater
Blender
Rubber spatula
Mason jar with lid
Baking sheet
Large bowl

5 anchovies, plus extra for garnish

2 garlic cloves

2 tablespoons Dijon mustard

1 tablespoon freshly squeezed lemon juice

1 tablespoon white wine vinegar or champagne vinegar

1 large egg

¾ cup olive oil, plus additional oil for drizzling

¼ cup Parmigiano-Reggiano cheese, finely grated, plus more for serving

½ loaf crusty bread, 1 to 3 days old, diced or torn into bite-size pieces

2 heads romaine lettuce, root ends trimmed, quartered, and coarsely chopped

Pinch freshly ground black pepper

Preheat the oven to 400°F.

Make the dressing.

In a blender, blend the anchovies and garlic until they become a rough paste. Add the mustard, lemon juice, and vinegar, crack in the egg, and blend until the mixture is smooth and creamy. With the blender on, remove the feeder cap and gradually drizzle in the olive oil in a steady stream. Turn the blender off. Add the cheese, and blend again until all ingredients are well combined. Scrape the dressing into a mason jar with a rubber spatula, seal it, and refrigerate for 15 to 30 minutes, or until it thickens.

Make the croutons.

Meanwhile, on a baking sheet, spread the bread pieces in a single layer and drizzle with olive oil. Bake for 12 minutes, or until golden and crisp at the edges.

Assemble the salad.

In a large bowl, pour half the dressing over the chopped lettuce, and toss with a large fork and spoon. Add some of your croutons and toss a little more, so that some are coated in the dressing.

Serve.

Pile the salad into bowls, adding a few more croutons to each serving as you like and one or two anchovies to garnish. Drizzle on additional dressing to taste, grate more cheese on top, and finish with the pepper. The dressing will keep for up to 3 days, sealed in the refrigerator.

emerald salad with buttermilk dressing

PREP TIME
10 minutes

COOK TIME
none

SERVES
4

TOOLS/
EQUIPMENT
Fine grater
Mason jar with lid

½ cup buttermilk

2 to 3 tablespoons sour cream

1 teaspoon Dijon mustard

1 tablespoon apple cider vinegar

2 tablespoons chopped fresh chives, tarragon, dill, or parsley, or a combination

1 garlic clove, finely grated

Few dashes hot sauce

¼ teaspoon freshly ground black pepper

Pinch flake salt, such as Maldon

3 heads lettuce (such as gem, Bibb, or butter), root ends trimmed and quartered lengthwise

Make the dressing.

In a mason jar with a lid, combine the buttermilk, sour cream, mustard, vinegar, chives, garlic, hot sauce, pepper, and salt. Close it tightly, then shake it like crazy. After 30 seconds to a minute of vigorous shaking, open the jar and taste, adjust the seasonings as needed, seal, and shake again.

Serve.

Divide the lettuce wedges and herbs evenly onto plates. Spoon the dressing directly from the mason jar onto the greens. Sprinkle salt and pepper to taste. Any remaining dressing will keep sealed, in the refrigerator, for up to 5 days. You'll want to use it on everything: roasted potatoes, carrot spears, roast chicken, and more!

FOOD FACT All that shaking emulsifies— or blends—the ingredients, suspending the water molecules inside the fat molecules. What results is a creamy, dreamy dressing.

grainy mustard-potato salad

PREP TIME
10 minutes

COOK TIME
10 minutes

SERVES
4

TOOLS / EQUIPMENT

Large saucepan
Colander
Large bowl

6 medium Yukon gold potatoes, scrubbed and cut into chunky wedges

3 medium Red Bliss potatoes, scrubbed and cut into chunky wedges

4 to 5 tablespoons olive oil

2 tablespoons whole-grain mustard

1 tablespoon capers, well-rinsed and chopped

1 shallot, sliced thin

3 tablespoons dill, torn into small sprigs

Sea salt

Freshly ground black pepper

Boil the potatoes.
In a large saucepan, cover the potatoes with water and gently boil them for 8 to 10 minutes, until fork-tender. Drain the potatoes in a colander, and transfer to a large bowl.

Dress the potatoes.
In a large bowl, toss the olive oil, mustard, capers, and shallot to combine with the potatoes.

Serve.
Once the potato mixture has cooled to room temperature, add the dill sprigs, and toss again. Season to taste with salt and pepper. Enjoy warm, at room temperature, or chilled.

nutty parmesan-kale salad

PREP TIME
15 minutes

COOK TIME
10 minutes

SERVES
4

**TOOLS/
EQUIPMENT**

Citrus reamer

Zester

Vegetable peeler

Large bowl

Baking sheet

Toaster oven

Small serving bowl

1 bunch lacinato kale, also known as Tuscan or dinosaur kale, rinsed, ends trimmed

Zest and juice of 1 lemon

2 tablespoons olive oil

Flake salt, such as Maldon

Freshly ground black pepper

1 cup hazelnuts

½ cup shaved Parmigiano-Reggiano

Chop the kale.

Gather the kale into a tight bunch or stack the leaves on top of each other, and slice into very thin strips, about ⅛ inch wide. Transfer to a large bowl.

Dress the salad.

Add the lemon zest and juice and the olive oil to the bowl, season with salt and pepper, and toss to combine. Taste and adjust seasoning, and set aside.

Prepare the nuts.

Toast the hazelnuts for 5 minutes or until fragrant. When cool enough to handle, gently rub off their skins. Arrange the nuts on a cutting board. Coarsely crush them by leaning your weight onto the side of a chef's knife placed on them. Transfer nuts to the toaster oven tray and toast again until golden, about 3 minutes more. Empty the nuts into a small serving bowl.

Serve.

At the table, scatter the hazelnuts and shaved Parm over the salad, and serve immediately.

> **HELPFUL HINT** Chopping and dressing the kale can be done a day in advance, giving time for the citrus to break down the leaves' sturdiness. If you do make it ahead, toss again before adding final toppings to redistribute the dressing.

colorful crunch salad

PREP TIME
15 minutes

COOK TIME
5 minutes

SERVES
4

TOOLS/
EQUIPMENT
Toaster oven

4 red, orange, and yellow bell peppers, cored and sliced into thin, bite-size strips

2 celery stalks, diced

1 handful green beans, ends trimmed, sliced into thin coins

¼ cup chopped fresh parsley

2 tablespoons capers, rinsed and chopped

2 tablespoons olive oil

2 teaspoons sherry or champagne vinegar

Freshly ground black pepper

⅓ cup slivered almonds

Toast the nuts.
Arrange almonds in a single layer on a toaster oven tray. Toast for 4 minutes, or until they become fragrant and their edges turn golden. You may agitate pan halfway through, circulating the almonds for even toasting. Transfer them to a small dish.

Assemble the salad.
Layer the peppers, celery, green beans, parsley, and capers onto a serving platter. Toss slightly to incorporate.

Serve.
Drizzle the salad with the olive oil and vinegar, season with pepper, and scatter the toasted almonds on top. Serve immediately.

egg salad and toast points

PREP TIME
10 minutes

COOK TIME
15 minutes

SERVES
4

**TOOLS/
EQUIPMENT**
Citrus reamer
Large saucepan
Large bowl
Large
slotted spoon
Toaster oven
Medium bowl

8 eggs

Ice water

4 slices crusty bread, such as
sourdough or seeded wheat, crusts
removed, and cut diagonally in half,
into triangles

2 tablespoons mayonnaise

2 teaspoons Dijon mustard

1 teaspoon freshly squeezed
lemon juice

1 celery stalk, finely chopped

1 tablespoon finely chopped
cornichons

1 tablespoon finely chopped parsley

Sea salt

Freshly ground black pepper

Cook the eggs.
In a saucepan large enough for the eggs to sit in
a single layer, bring to a boil enough water to submerge the eggs by at least 1 inch. Carefully lower
the eggs into the water, return to a boil, and simmer
for 10 minutes. Have a large bowl filled with ice
water nearby.

Transfer and peel the eggs.
Use a slotted spoon to transfer the eggs to the
water to chill them for peeling. Let the eggs sit in
the ice bath until cool to the touch. Tap the eggshell
on your work surface, turning it and cracking it
throughout. Peel the shells and discard.

Toast the bread.
Toast the bread pieces in the toaster oven until
golden and crisp. Transfer to individual plates or
a serving dish.

Assemble the salad.
In a medium bowl, use a fork or potato masher to
mash the hard-cooked eggs, combining them with
the mayonnaise, mustard, and lemon juice. You
may opt to keep the consistency chunky, or for a
creamier consistency, mash until well combined.

DID YOU KNOW? If the eggs are very fresh, adding ¼ teaspoon kosher salt to the cooking water will make them easier to peel. Eggshells and other vegetable clippings make great nutrients for compost. Save them in a plastic bag in the refrigerator, and when it becomes full, empty it in a designated spot in your backyard to break down into the soil. There is a wealth of information in your local library or online about how to make proper compost, which is the best food for plants, flowers, and trees.

Finish assembling.
Add the celery, cornichons, and parsley, and season with salt and pepper. Stir gently to combine.

Serve.
Serve with the toast points chilled or at room temperature. Any leftovers will keep, sealed in the refrigerator, for up to 4 days.

roasted cauliflower with dipping sauce

PREP TIME
10 minutes

COOK TIME
55 minutes

SERVES
4

**TOOLS/
EQUIPMENT**

Citrus reamer

Box grater

Dutch oven

Rubber spatula

Small bowl

Roasting pan

FOR THE CAULIFLOWER

1½ cups dry white wine or white wine vinegar

6 cups water

⅓ cup olive oil, plus more for serving

3 tablespoons kosher salt

3 tablespoons freshly squeezed lemon juice

2 tablespoons orange juice

2 tablespoons butter

1 tablespoon crushed red pepper flakes

Pinch black peppercorns

1 bay leaf

1 head cauliflower, stem trimmed

Flake salt, such as Maldon, for serving

[INGREDIENT LIST CONTINUES ON NEXT PAGE]

Poach the cauliflower.

In a Dutch oven or other heavy-bottomed pot over high heat, bring the wine, water, olive oil, kosher salt, lemon juice, orange juice, butter, red pepper flakes, peppercorns, and bay leaf to a boil. Add the cauliflower, then reduce the heat to simmer. Turn occasionally, using a pair of serving spoons to submerge each side in the poaching liquid, until a knife easily inserts into center, 15 to 20 minutes.

Preheat the oven to 475°F.

Make the dipping sauce.

In a small bowl, mix together the crème fraîche, Greek yogurt, cheese, and capers, and season with pepper. Set aside.

Roast the cauliflower.

Using tongs or the serving spoons, transfer cauliflower to a roasting pan. Roast, rotating the sheet if browning unevenly, until deep golden and crispy in parts, about 35 minutes.

FOR THE SAUCE

½ cup crème fraîche

3 tablespoons nonfat Greek yogurt

¼ cup finely shredded Parmigiano-Reggiano

3 teaspoons capers, rinsed and chopped

Freshly ground black pepper

Serve.

Bring the roasted cauliflower to the table, set on a trivet, and serve directly from the roasting pan with the dipping sauce—and a spoon to dispense it—alongside.

FOOD FACT Capers are the pickled flower buds of a shrub that grows in dry climates in the Mediterranean, and to harvest them, people pick them off the plant one by one. If you can find salt-packed rather than brined capers, they will keep in your pantry indefinitely and are more robust in flavor. Find them in specialty shops or online.

PRO TIP After cooking the cauliflower, the poaching liquid can be reserved and used again: to cook rice or quinoa, or as stock for soup.

honey-roasted carrots with rosemary

PREP TIME
10 minutes

COOK TIME
35 minutes

SERVES
4

TOOLS/ EQUIPMENT

Small saucepan

Whisk

Baking sheet

Rubber spatula

2 tablespoons butter

2 tablespoons honey

Flake salt, such as Maldon

2 to 3 bunches small carrots, scrubbed and greens trimmed, halved lengthwise if thick

2 fresh rosemary sprigs, quills stripped from stems and coarsely chopped

Freshly ground black pepper

Preheat the oven to 425°F.

Prepare the glaze.
In a small saucepan over medium heat, melt the butter. Add the honey, and whisk to dissolve. Season with a pinch of salt, and set aside.

Toss the ingredients together.
On a baking sheet, drizzle the honey mixture over the carrots, toss to coat, and scatter the chopped rosemary on top. Season with salt and pepper.

Roast the carrots.
Bake for 30 to 35 minutes, or until the carrots are tender and caramelized in spots, rearranging them for even browning halfway through.

Serve.
Transfer to a serving platter or plates and eat warm.

PRO TIP While there's no need to peel the carrots in this recipe, you can save the peels and cut the ends from carrots, along with the ends, skins, and stems of onions, parsley, and celery, in a resealable bag kept in the freezer for making homemade stock. When the bag is full, you know it's time to make stock.

roasted brussels sprouts and shallots

PREP TIME
10 minutes

COOK TIME
30 minutes

SERVES
4

TOOLS / EQUIPMENT

2 baking sheets

Tongs

1 ½ pounds Brussels sprouts, trimmed and halved

6 shallots, quartered

3 tablespoons olive oil

Sea salt

Freshly ground black pepper

1 lemon, cut into wedges, for serving

Arrange oven racks and preheat oven.
Place one oven rack in the top third of the oven and another in the bottom third, then preheat oven to 450°F.

Prep the veggie mixture.
On two baking sheets, toss the Brussels sprouts and shallots with the olive oil, placing most of the Brussels halves cut-side down. Season with salt and pepper.

Roast the vegetables.
Swap the pans halfway through, and use tongs to turn the veggies over for even roasting. Cook until caramelized and tender, 25 to 30 minutes.

Serve.
Transfer the Brussels sprouts and shallots to a serving dish, with lemon wedges to squeeze at the table.

delicious delicata rings

PREP TIME
15 minutes

COOK TIME
30 minutes

SERVES
4

**TOOLS/
EQUIPMENT**

Pointy teaspoon
2 baking sheets
Metal spatula

3 delicata squash, halved widthwise

Olive oil, for drizzling

Flake salt, such as Maldon

Freshly ground black pepper

HELPFUL HINT When choosing delicata squash, look for ones that are firm and heavy for their size.

DID YOU KNOW? Delicata squash have a skin so thin you can eat it, and once roasted, the flesh is so sweet you'd think it was candy. You can store this squash in a cool, dry place away from direct sunlight for up to three months.

Arrange oven racks and preheat oven.
Place one oven rack in the top third of the oven and another in the bottom third, then preheat oven to 425°F.

Prepare the squash.
Use a pointy teaspoon to scrape the seeds and any stringy bits from each squash half and discard (or save for compost). Slice the squash into ½-inch rings, discarding the stem ends.

Prep the squash for roasting.
Drizzle 1 to 2 tablespoons of olive oil onto each baking sheet, and spread it around with your fingers to coat the pans. Lay the delicata rings flat in a single layer on each sheet, and lightly drizzle with olive oil. Season with salt and pepper.

Roast the squash.
Cook for 10 to 15 minutes, until the rings begin to brown on the bottom, then the flip rings to the other side, season again, and swap the pans, returning them to roast for another 10 to 15 minutes, until the squash is tender and deeply golden in spots. Test by seeing if you can pierce them with a fork— if you can, they are ready.

Serve.
Serve warm for a delicious snack or side dish.

Mini Pot Pies (page 161)

6

main dishes

pasta with homemade tomato sauce

PREP TIME
10 minutes

COOK TIME
15 minutes

SERVES
4

TOOLS/ EQUIPMENT

Medium saucepan
Paring knife
Slotted spoon
Large bowl
Wooden spoon
Tongs
Large pot
Colander
Fine grater

8 tomatoes—heirloom varieties are ideal, with a few Roma tomatoes in the mix

Ice water

2 tablespoons butter

Olive oil, for drizzling

2 anchovies

2 garlic cloves, sliced thin

Kosher salt

1 pound rigatoni or other ridged pasta

Parmigiano-Reggiano, for serving

Freshly ground black pepper

Blanch tomatoes and peel the skins.
Set a medium saucepan filled with water to boil. Using a paring knife, cut an "X" shape into the bottom of each tomato. Carefully lower 1 or 2 tomatoes into the water at a time and blanch for 1 minute. Use a slotted spoon to transfer the blanched tomatoes to a bowl filled with ice water. When cool enough to handle, peel the skins and discard, then cut larger tomatoes into chunks and smaller ones in half over a bowl to collect their juices. Repeat with the remaining tomatoes, and set aside.

Make the sauce.
In the same saucepan over medium heat, melt the butter and a drizzle of olive oil together. When the butter foams, add the anchovies, letting them sizzle and melt into the buttery mix. Use tongs to break them apart as they dissolve. After a minute or two, add the garlic slices and stir to combine. When the garlic becomes fragrant, add the tomatoes.

Stir the mixture together, and bring to a boil.
Once bubbling, lower the heat to a simmer so the mixture still bubbles, but less vigorously. Stir occasionally, simmering for 7 to 10 minutes, while you cook the pasta.

Cook the pasta.

In a large pot, boil enough water to cook 1 pound of pasta, 2 to 3 quarts. Add 1 tablespoon kosher salt to the water once it reaches a rolling boil, just before adding the pasta. Cook the pasta according to package instructions, stirring immediately after adding it to the water so that the noodles don't stick together. Once the water returns to a boil, stir occasionally until al dente. Drain the pasta in a colander, reserving 1 cupful of the cooking liquid.

Serve.

Add a spoonful or two of the cooking liquid to the sauce and stir to incorporate. Transfer the pasta into shallow bowls, and top with the chunky tomato sauce. Use a fine grater to shower the pasta with a little fresh Parm, followed by salt and pepper to taste. Leftover sauce can be refrigerated for up to 5 days or frozen up to 2 months.

herby pesto pasta

PREP TIME
15 minutes

COOK TIME

10 minutes

SERVES
4

**TOOLS /
EQUIPMENT**

Box grater

Citrus reamer

Food processor

Large pot

Colander

Large bowl

Rubber spatula

Toaster oven

⅓ cup nuts, such as pine nuts, walnuts, almonds, or pistachios

1 garlic clove

½ cup Parmigiano-Reggiano cheese, freshly shredded, plus extra for serving

Olive oil, as needed

2 cups loosely packed fresh basil leaves

½ cup fresh parsley leaves

1 tablespoon kosher salt

1 teaspoon freshly squeezed lemon juice, to prevent oxidizing

1 pound fettuccine

Flake sea salt, such as Maldon

Freshly ground black pepper

Toast the nuts.

Arrange nuts in a single layer on a toaster oven tray. Toast for 4 minutes, or until they become fragrant and their edges turn golden. You may agitate pan halfway through, circulating the them for even toasting. Transfer nuts to a small dish to cool.

Make the pesto.

Using a food processor, pulse the nuts, garlic, cheese, and enough olive oil to make a rough paste. Stop as needed to scrape down the sides of the bowl. Add the basil and parsley, a pinch of salt, and more olive oil, and pulse to combine. The mixture should resemble a bright green sauce. Drizzle the fresh lemon juice over the mixture once you are happy with the consistency.

Boil the pasta.

In a large pot, boil enough water to cook 1 pound of fettuccine, about three quarts (12 cups). Add 1 tablespoon kosher salt to the water once it is at a rolling boil just before adding the pasta. Cook the pasta according to package instructions, stirring immediately after adding the pasta so that it doesn't stick together. Once the water returns to a boil, stir occasionally until al dente. Drain the pasta in a colander, and transfer to a large bowl, reserving 1 cupful of the cooking water for later.

HELPFUL HINT The proportions here work for any amount of basil. You really just need to think about what quantity of herbs is available to you and how much pesto you're prepared to make.

PRO TIP The fresher your herbs, the better the pesto will taste. Only include the smallest of stems, picking the rest out for compost, or discard. Always rinse all herbs and pat them dry before using.

Empty the pesto into the bowl of pasta.
Use a rubber spatula to thoroughly scrape the bowl and underneath the blade, getting all the good bits out. Add a few spoons of the pasta water as you toss the noodles and pesto together. Use a large spoon in one hand and the rubber spatula in the other to combine them well, coating the noodles in the sauce.

Serve.
Twirl tangles of pasta into shallow bowls, spooning additional pesto on top as you like. Shower the pasta with a little more freshly grated cheese, season with salt and pepper, and enjoy at once. Leftover pasta will last up to 3 days, kept sealed in the refrigerator. If you saved any pesto separate from the pasta, transfer it to a jar and cover its surface directly with plastic wrap to slow oxidation, seal it, and keep refrigerated for up to 1 week.

butternut mac 'n' cheese

PREP TIME
20 minutes

COOK TIME
50 minutes

SERVES
4

**TOOLS/
EQUIPMENT**

Box grater

4 ramekins

Toaster oven

Small saucepan

Large pot

Colander

Steamer basket

Tongs

Whisk

Baking sheet

Ladle

Wire cooling rack

4 tablespoons butter, divided, plus more for greasing ramekins

2 thick slices rustic bread, crusts removed and torn into bite-size pieces

½ teaspoon kosher salt, plus a hefty pinch

12 ounces macaroni

½ butternut squash, peeled, seeded, and sliced into inch-long bite-size pieces

2 cups milk

3 tablespoons all-purpose flour

¼ teaspoon freshly grated nutmeg

¼ teaspoon freshly ground black pepper

¼ teaspoon cayenne pepper

1½ cups grated sharp white Cheddar cheese, divided

1 cup grated Gruyère cheese, divided

Prepare the ramekins.

Butter 4 ramekins, and set aside on a baking sheet.

Toast the bread.

Place the bread onto a toaster oven tray. In a small saucepan over medium heat, melt 1 tablespoon of butter, and drizzle the butter over the bread, stirring the pieces around the tray to coat. Toast the croutons until lightly crispy, about 5 minutes, and set aside.

Cook the pasta.

Set a large pot filled with water over high heat, and bring to a rolling boil. Add 1 tablespoon salt, add the pasta, and stir well. Cook 3 minutes less than the package instructions say, so that the pasta exterior is cooked and the inside is underdone. Transfer the pasta to a colander, and shake it a few times to drain well. Rinse the pasta briefly to stop it from cooking further and set aside.

Steam the squash.

Fit a steamer basket inside a saucepan and add 1 inch of water. Cover and steam the squash pieces until slightly softened, 3 to 5 minutes. Use tongs to remove the squash from the basket, rinse under cold water, and set aside.

Preheat the oven to 375°F. »

TROUBLESHOOTING
Not keeping your workspace organized when creating a recipe with many steps can backfire on you. This recipe has a number of components to attend to. Pay close attention and they should be a cinch, especially if you keep your workspace uncluttered. Plus, the finished dish is outrageously delicious and well worth the effort!

Make the béchamel.
In a small saucepan over medium-low heat, warm the milk. In the same pot you used for cooking the pasta, over medium heat, melt the remaining 3 tablespoons of butter. When the butter foams, add the flour. Whisk the flour into the butter, stirring to fully combine.

Continue whisking.
Gradually pour in the hot milk. After pouring half in, whisk until the mixture has no lumps, then slowly add the remainder. Whisk constantly, until the mixture bubbles and becomes thick, 8 to 10 minutes.

Combine the ingredients for baking.
Remove the pan from the heat, and stir in the salt, nutmeg, black pepper, cayenne pepper, 1 cup of Cheddar cheese, and ½ cup of Gruyère.

Add pasta and squash.
Stir the cooked pasta and steamed squash into the cheesy béchamel sauce. Ladle the mixture into the ramekins. Sprinkle the remaining ½ cup of Cheddar cheese and ½ cup of Gruyère over the tops, then arrange the toasted croutons on top. Bake until the surfaces are golden, about 25 minutes.

Serve.
Transfer the casseroles to a wire cooling rack, and allow to cool for 5 minutes. Serve the little mac-and-cheese ramekins warm on large plates.

pan-roasted fish

PREP TIME
5 minutes

COOK TIME
10 minutes

SERVES
4

**TOOLS /
EQUIPMENT**

Large cast-
iron skillet

Metal spatula

4 (5-ounce) skin-on fish fillets (such as red snapper, flounder, haddock, or salmon), ½ to 1 inch thick

Kosher salt

Freshly ground black pepper

4 tablespoons olive oil

3 tablespoons butter

3 fresh thyme sprigs, leaves stripped from stems, coarsely chopped

Chopped fresh parsley and lemon wedges (optional), for garnish

Prep and season the fillets.

Pat the fish dry with paper towels and season on both sides with salt and pepper.

Sauté the fish.

Place a large cast-iron skillet over high heat. When the skillet is hot, add the oil. Place the fillets skin-side down away from you into the pan, so if any splattering happens, you'll have less risk of being burned. Press down gently with a metal spatula for about 20 seconds around the edges so that the fillets don't curl up.

Lower the heat and continue to cook.

Lower the heat to medium and let sizzle until the fish is caramelized and becoming opaque around the edges, 2 to 3 minutes. Carefully flip the fillets to the second side, and add the butter and thyme to the pan.

Baste the fish.

Tilt the pan slightly to pool the melted butter on one side. Use a spoon to baste the fish with the melted butter. Baste the fillets repeatedly, until they are golden all over and cooked through, 1 minute or so, depending on the thickness of your fish.

Serve.

Serve immediately, with chopped parsley and lemon wedges, if desired.

hearty greens strata

PREP TIME
15 minutes plus
2 hours to soak
and 30 minutes
to sit

COOK TIME
30 minutes

SERVES
4–6

**TOOLS/
EQUIPMENT**

Box grater

Large cast-
iron skillet

Medium bowl

Whisk

Medium glass
or ceramic
baking dish

Baking sheet

Olive oil, for sautéing

1 medium onion, chopped

1 bunch Swiss chard or kale, stems
removed and finely chopped, leaves
coarsely chopped

¼ teaspoon freshly grated nutmeg

Freshly ground black pepper

Kosher salt

5 eggs

1 cup buttermilk

½ cup whole milk

1 tablespoon Dijon mustard

1 ½ cups grated Gruyère cheese

1 cup finely shredded Parmesan cheese

Butter, for greasing

5 slices day-old bread,
cut into large cubes

1 teaspoon red pepper flakes

Sauté vegetables and aromatics.
Into a large cast-iron skillet over medium heat, drizzle enough olive oil to coat the hot pan. Add the onion, and sauté until tender, 5 to 7 minutes. Add the chard stems and nutmeg, and season with black pepper and salt. Stir to incorporate, cooking for another 2 to 3 minutes.

Add the greens and continue cooking.
Add the chard leaves, mix with the other ingredients, and sauté until the leaves have wilted, about 2 minutes. Transfer the mixture to a plate.

Whisk the egg mixture.
In a medium bowl, whisk together the eggs, buttermilk, milk, and mustard.

Combine the cheeses.
In a shallow dish, toss the two cheeses together. Set aside a third of the cheese for final sprinkling before the strata goes into the oven.

Layer the strata.
Butter a medium baking dish well. Arrange a layer of cubed bread. Don't be fussy, a little textural inconsistency will make for pleasing, savory custard layers once the strata is cooked. Add a layer of the onion-greens mixture. Sprinkle a layer of cheese over the surface. Repeat again with each, finishing the top layer with the remaining cubed bread and a sprinkle of red pepper flakes.

delicious additions

Sautéed and added to the mix:

Broccoli

Leeks

Mushrooms

Tomatoes

Zucchini

Saturate the strata.

Carefully pour the egg mixture evenly over the whole surface to saturate the bread layers. Allow the bread to absorb the mixture for at least 2 hours, preferably overnight. If it stands overnight, cover in plastic wrap and refrigerate.

Prepare to bake.

Allow the strata to sit at room temperature for 30 minutes before baking.

Preheat the oven to 350°F.

Bake the strata.

Scatter the reserved cheese on top. Place the strata on a baking sheet and bake uncovered for 30 minutes, or until golden and set in the center.

Serve.

Cool for 10 minutes and serve while still warm. Leftover strata can be kept, refrigerated, for up to 5 days and can be reheated in the toaster oven.

tomato soup with broiled cheesy toasts

PREP TIME
10 minutes

COOK TIME
35 minutes

TOTAL TIME
1 hour

SERVES

4

**TOOLS/
EQUIPMENT**

Box grater

Paring knife

Medium saucepan

Slotted spoon

Large bowl

Dutch oven

Immersion blender

Wooden spoon

Toaster oven

Ladle

4 cups tomatoes (6 to 8 medium tomatoes), skins peeled, chopped

1 tablespoon olive oil, plus more for drizzling

2 tablespoons butter

1 medium onion, chopped

½ teaspoon freshly grated nutmeg

½ teaspoon smoked paprika

Sea salt

Freshly ground black pepper

2 cups chicken stock

FOR THE TOASTS

4 slices country loaf

½ cup grated Gruyère cheese

Blanch the tomatoes and peel the skins.
Set a medium saucepan filled with water to boil. With your knife, cut an "X" into the bottoms of the tomatoes. Carefully lower 2 tomatoes into the water at a time and blanch for 1 minute. Use a slotted spoon to transfer the blanched tomatoes to a large bowl filled with ice water. When cool enough to handle, peel the skins and discard, then slice the tomatoes into large chunks over a bowl to collect their juices. Repeat with the remaining tomatoes, and add them to the bowl.

Make the soup.
In a Dutch oven or other heavy-bottomed pot over medium heat, heat the oil and butter, and swirl the pan to coat. Sauté the onion until translucent, 5 to 7 minutes. Add the tomatoes and their juice, and bring to a boil. Lower the heat, and simmer, stirring occasionally, for about 5 minutes.

Incorporate the spices and stock, and continue cooking.
Add the nutmeg and paprika, season with salt and pepper, and add the stock. Stir to incorporate, return the heat to medium, and bring to bubbling again. Lower the heat and simmer with the lid on for 20 to 25 minutes. ≫

TRY INSTEAD For a creamier soup, add ⅔ cup heavy cream and then purée it. Or, swap a dollop of crème fraîche for the toast.

FOOD FACT This soup stores well and tastes even better the second day. You can keep it in the refrigerator for up to five days, as long as you bring it to a boil every two days. You can freeze it as well, and there it keeps for up to three months.

Purée the soup.
Remove the pot from heat, take the lid off, and let cool for at least 15 minutes. Pulse an immersion blender to purée the soup. Always keep the blender fully submerged in the liquid while puréeing to avoid an enormous mess, and most important, to avoid being burned. Blend thoroughly for a creamy consistency, less if you prefer it chunky.

Make the broiled toasts.
Toast the bread in a toaster oven until crisp, about 5 minutes. Divide the grated cheese evenly between the slices, turn the toaster oven to broil, return the toasts, and broil until the cheese is melted and bubbling, about 3 minutes more.

Serve.
Ladle the soup into bowls, and top with the cheesy toasts. Drizzle with olive oil, add pepper, and eat at once.

chicken skewer sandwiches

PREP TIME
20 minutes, plus
overnight to
marinate

COOK TIME
20 minutes

SERVES
4

**TOOLS /
EQUIPMENT**

Citrus reamer

Zester

Bread knife

Large bowl

Metal skewers

Tongs

Grill pan

⅔ cup olive oil, plus extra for drizzling

⅓ cup red wine vinegar

2 lemons, juiced, and one zested

4 garlic cloves, chopped

1 tablespoon fresh thyme leaves

1 tablespoon fresh oregano leaves

1 tablespoon fresh basil leaves, rolled
and chiffonaded (see Summery Corn
and Watermelon Salad, page 112)

1 teaspoon red pepper flakes, or
to taste

1 bay leaf

1 teaspoon cane sugar

1 teaspoon kosher salt

1 teaspoon freshly ground
black pepper

1 pound boneless chicken thighs,
cut into 1½-inch cubes

1 baguette, cut into 4 sections, each
split open lengthwise

1 tablespoon coarsely chopped fresh
mint or parsley, or a mix, for garnish

Make the marinade.
In a large bowl, stir together the olive oil, vinegar, lemon juice and zest, garlic, thyme, oregano, basil, red pepper flakes, bay leaf, sugar, salt, and pepper. Add the cubed chicken and refrigerate, covered tightly or in a large, resealable bag, overnight to marinate.

Grill the skewers.
Thread the chicken onto skewers, folding the meat on itself to skewer if it is uneven. Heat a grill pan over high heat until hot. Grill the chicken for 3 to 5 minutes per side, until cooked through and charred in spots.

Grill the bread.
Transfer the grilled skewers to a large plate while you grill the bread. Drizzle olive oil onto the bread and grill for 3 to 5 minutes apiece, rotating as needed, until blackened in spots.

Serve.
These skewers are delicious laid on top of the grilled bread with a scatter of chopped fresh herbs—like parsley or mint—to garnish.

HELPFUL HINT Plan ahead: This recipe requires marinating overnight. This marinade also is great with pork, beef, and lamb as well as chicken.

winter white bean stew

PREP TIME
20 minutes
plus 6 hours
to soak

COOK TIME
1 hour

SERVES
4–6

**TOOLS/
EQUIPMENT**

Large bowl

Dutch oven

Aluminum foil

Small baking dish

Food processor

Wooden spoon

Ladle

Rubber spatula

3 cups dry white beans, such as cannellini, flageolet, or northern beans, or a mix

2 bay leaves

2 Parmigiano-Reggiano rinds or 2 small Parmesan wedges

1 head garlic

2 tablespoons olive oil, plus more for drizzling

1 jalapeño

Kosher salt

Freshly ground black pepper

2 small onions, chopped

5 to 7 small carrots, chopped

3 celery stalks, chopped

1 tablespoon finely chopped fresh rosemary quills

1 teaspoon red pepper flakes

1 cup chicken stock or water

Crusty bread, for serving

Prepare the beans.
In a large enough bowl for them to double in volume (more than one, if using different beans), soak the dry beans in enough cold water to cover by at least 2 inches. After soaking for 6 hours or overnight, drain and rinse, then transfer to a Dutch oven or other large, heavy-bottomed stewpot. Rinse the bowl, and set it aside.

Preheat the oven to 375°F.

Cook the beans.
Place the stewpot over high heat and add enough water to cover the beans by at least 2 inches. Add the bay leaves and cheese rinds, and bring the water to a boil. Once the water is bubbling, lower the heat, and cook the beans on a low simmer for 45 minutes to an hour, until the beans are tender.

Roast the garlic and jalapeño.
While the beans cook, cut the top third off the head of garlic. Nestle it in a sheet of aluminum foil, and drizzle olive oil over it. Fold the foil to seal the garlic, and place in a small baking dish. Do the same with the jalapeño in a small baking dish. Roast the two in the oven for as long as you cook the beans, then remove and set aside to cool.

Transfer the beans and sauté the veggies.
When the beans are finished cooking, they will still look a little soupy. Pull out the cheese rinds and discard, and carefully transfer the beans back into the soaking bowl. Season with salt and pepper, and set aside.

Cook the aromatics.

Return the pot to the burner on medium heat. Add the olive oil and onions, and sauté, stirring occasionally. As they start to become translucent, add the carrots and celery, as well as the rosemary and red pepper flakes. Sauté, stirring occasionally, for 7 minutes. Season with salt and pepper.

Purée the beans with the stock and the aromatics.

In a food processor, pulse together 2 cups of the cooked bean mixture, the roasted jalapeño minus its stem, the chicken stock, and the cloves squeezed out of half the head of roasted garlic until creamy. (You will have a half-head of roasted garlic leftover, which can be used in other soups or whipped into yogurt or cream cheese and spread on toast.) This mixture will add body to the finished stew.

Stir to combine.

Empty the purée into the veggie pot, along with the bowl of cooked beans and their liquid, and give it all a good stir.

Serve.

If the stew needs to be rewarmed, do so over medium-low heat, then ladle the stew into wide bowls and enjoy with crusty bread. Any leftovers can be refrigerated for up to 1 week, or frozen for up to 2 months.

fresh fish tacos

PREP TIME
15 minutes
plus 50 minutes
to marinate

COOK TIME
15 minutes

SERVES
4

**TOOLS/
EQUIPMENT**

Small sauté pan

Small mason jar
with lid

Mortar and pestle

Small bowl

Baking sheet

Aluminum foil

Tea towel

FOR QUICK-PICKLED ONIONS

½ red onion, sliced thin

Pinch black peppercorns

1 bay leaf

¾ cup white vinegar

[INGREDIENT LIST CONTINUES ON NEXT PAGE]

Marinate the onion.

In a small mason jar with a lid, arrange the onion slices, adding a pinch of peppercorns and a bay leaf, and pour in enough white vinegar to cover. Set aside to marinate for at least 30 minutes.

Marinate the fish.

Grind the toasted cumin into a coarse powder with a mortar and pestle. In a small bowl, mix the olive oil, chili powder, cumin, chopped cilantro, and jalapeño, and season with salt. Place the fillets on a baking sheet and pour the marinade over, making sure to coat the fillets well on both sides. Marinate for 20 minutes at room temperature.

Cook the fish.

Heat the broiler with the oven rack in the highest position. Season the fish with salt and pepper. Broil until the fillets are browned on top and the flesh is opaque throughout, about 5 minutes. Remove the pan from the oven and flake the fish with a fork. Taste and adjust seasoning as needed, then set aside.

Heat the tortillas.

Lower the oven temperature to 400°F. Place the tortillas in two stacks of 4, and wrap the bundles in aluminum foil. Heat in the oven for 7 to 10 minutes, until the tortillas are warmed through. Place the tortillas, still wrapped in foil, in a tea towel to keep warm. ≫

FOR THE TACOS

1 teaspoon cumin seeds, toasted (see the No-Nonsense Guacamole, page 101)

⅓ cup olive oil

1½ teaspoons chili powder

¼ cup chopped fresh cilantro leaves, plus more for garnish

½ to 1 jalapeño pepper, seeded and minced

Kosher salt

1 pound flaky white fish (such as flounder, red snapper, or cod), cut into 4 pieces

Freshly ground black pepper

8 fresh corn or flour tortillas

1 recipe of Salsa Fresca (page 46) and/or Savory Cabbage Slaw (page 110), for serving

Sour cream, for serving

2 limes, quartered

Assemble and serve:

To assemble the tacos, place a heaping spoonful of Savory Cabbage Slaw on the center of a tortilla. Add the flaked fish and Salsa Fresca, and top with the marinated onions. Serve accompanied by cilantro sprigs, sour cream, and lime wedges.

PRO TIP You will most likely have leftover pickled onions. Keep them submerged in the vinegar in a refrigerated airtight container. You can then use the vinegar for other cooking, such as in salad dressings, and the pickled onions on anything from scrambled eggs to grilled chicken. Both will keep for several weeks.

miso-grilled shrimp skewers

PREP TIME
20 minutes plus
20 minutes to
marinate

COOK TIME
5–7 minutes

SERVES
4

**TOOLS /
EQUIPMENT**

Citrus reamer

Fine grater

Large bowl

Whisk

Grill pan

Metal skewers

2 tablespoons freshly squeezed lime juice, with extra wedges for garnish

2 tablespoons mirin

2 tablespoons yellow miso

1 tablespoon sesame oil

1 tablespoon fresh ginger, peeled and finely grated

1 large garlic clove, finely grated

1 pound large shrimp, shelled and deveined

**OPTIONAL EXTRAS,
FOR SERVING**

Chopped scallions

Sunflower sprouts

Green beans, steamed and crunchy

Sliced English or Persian cucumbers

Salad greens

Fresh cilantro leaves

Cooked rice or steamed buns

Make the glaze.

In a large bowl, whisk together the lime juice, mirin, miso, sesame oil, ginger, and garlic. Add the shrimp, and toss to coat. Let marinate for 20 minutes.

Grill the shrimp.

Preheat a grill pan over medium-high heat. Thread the shrimp onto metal skewers, piercing the shrimp at the tail end and at the thickest part of the body to secure. Grill the shrimp over medium-high heat until lightly charred and opaque, turning once, about 5 minutes.

Serve.

These glazed and grilled shrimp are great served in steamed buns with chopped fresh scallions and cilantro, over rice, or alongside crunchy green beans, greens, or Asian Cucumber Salad (page 111).

DID YOU KNOW? Miso and mirin are staples in Japanese cuisine. Miso paste is made from fermented soybeans, sometimes with the addition of rice, barley, or wheat, and is rich in vitamin B and protein. Mirin is a sweet, golden Japanese wine made from rice. Both are available at Asian markets or the Asian food section at specialty grocers as well as online.

spring rolls and dipping sauces

PREP TIME
35 minutes

COOK TIME
5 minutes

SERVES
4

**TOOLS/
EQUIPMENT**

Citrus reamer

Box grater

2 small bowls

Small saucepan

Whisk

Medium saucepan

Colander

Large bowl

Dish towel

FOR THE DIPPING SAUCES

4 teaspoons fish sauce

¼ cup water

2 tablespoons freshly squeezed lime juice

1 small garlic clove, grated

1 teaspoon cane sugar

½ teaspoon chili sauce (such as sambal oelek); less if you prefer less spice

2 tablespoons crunchy peanut butter

4 tablespoons hoisin sauce

[INGREDIENT LIST CONTINUES ON NEXT PAGE]

Make the two sauces.

In a small bowl, stir together the ingredients for the first sauce: fish sauce, water, lime juice, garlic, sugar, and chili sauce. Set aside. In a small saucepan over medium heat, mix together ingredients for the second sauce: peanut butter and hoisin sauce. Add a few spoonfuls of water to thin the sauce slightly, and whisk until incorporated. Transfer to another small bowl, and set aside.

Prep the vermicelli.

In a medium saucepan, soak the rice noodles in hot water until they turn opaque and soften. You may turn on the heat to expedite this, but do not boil them, as they may become soggy. Transfer the noodles to a colander and rinse under cold water. Drain and set aside.

Prep the wrappers.

Have enough "bathwater-warm" water in a bowl large enough so that when you dip the wrappers, the water comes up halfway. Dunk and lift, rotate a quarter-turn, and repeat until you have gone all the way around with the wrapper. The time spent dunking takes maybe 2 seconds total, as you are only trying to soften it. With this method, the wrapper becomes pliable but isn't as likely to tear.

FOR THE ROLLS

1 ounce rice vermicelli

Hot water, for soaking

8 rice wrappers (8½-inch diameter)

12 large shrimp, peeled, cooked, and halved lengthwise

2 tablespoons fresh Thai basil leaves

3 tablespoons fresh mint leaves

3 tablespoons fresh cilantro leaves

2 lettuce leaves (such as butter or romaine), halved

½ cup mung bean sprouts

1 carrot, julienned

FOOD FACT Vermicelli often comes in 2-ounce bundles, but using it all makes for a noodle-heavy spring roll. Cook the bundle, and save the remainder for another use.

TRY INSTEAD Swap the shrimp for sautéed chicken breast, thinly sliced into 8 pieces. Swap the mung beans for half a hothouse cucumber, cut into thin strips. Swap the Thai basil for regular basil. And add more crunch with julienned celery, radishes, cabbage, or jicama.

Assemble the rolls.

Place the wet wrapper on a damp dish towel laid flat on your work surface. Arrange 3 shrimp halves pink-side down followed by a pinch of the Thai basil, mint, and cilantro leaves, then a cluster of the crunchy elements: lettuce, bean sprouts, and carrots, then a small handful of vermicelli, folding the length of noodles back and forth until you have a neat pile. Leave a 2-inch border on either side as you layer the ingredients.

Bundle the ingredients, and roll.

Your aim is to make a tight bundle when rolling. Gently pull the edge of the wrapper up over the fillings. Simultaneously use your fingers to press the fillings into a small bundle under the wrapper. Compressing them into a little bundle will keep all the ingredients together and help the roll remain firm and even.

Create a firm seal.

Roll away from you, and tuck the fillings toward you. After a full rotation, fold the sides of the wrapper in. Continue rolling to the edge, gathering fillings in until the roll is sealed.

Serve.

Spring rolls can be served whole with dipping sauces on the side or cut on the diagonal to display their colorful fillings. Refrigerate the finished rolls for up to 2 hours before serving, each wrapped individually in plastic wrap. The rice wrappers will toughen if stored longer than a few hours, increasing their likelihood of cracking.

sopa de lima (chicken lime soup)

PREP TIME
20 minutes

COOK TIME
30 minutes

SERVES
4–6

TOOLS / EQUIPMENT

Fine grater

Citrus reamer

Large cast-iron skillet

Wooden spoon

Tongs

Slotted spoon

Wire cooling rack

Large bowl

Ladle

Safflower oil, for frying

3 corn tortillas, cut into ¼-inch strips

Flake salt, such as Maldon

1 white onion, chopped

4 bone-in, skinless chicken thighs

3 Roma tomatoes, cored

1 serrano or jalapeño chili, cored, seeded, and chopped

½ teaspoon dried thyme

2 garlic cloves, finely grated

3 cups chicken stock

Juice of 3 limes, plus 2 cut into wedges for serving

1½ cups frozen peas, blanched

2 avocados, sliced or cubed, for garnish

Fresh cilantro leaves, for garnish

Freshly ground black pepper

Fry the tortilla strips.
Into a large cast-iron skillet, pour enough oil so that it comes up a quarter inch. Heat the oil, and when very hot, fry the tortilla strips in small batches until golden and crisp, 30 seconds to 1 minute per batch. Tortilla strips should sizzle immediately upon contact with the oil, but not burn. If the oil is smoking, lower the heat.

Transfer the tortilla strips.
Use a slotted spoon or tongs to transfer the fried tortillas to a paper towel-lined wire cooling rack to soak up excess oil. Sprinkle with a pinch of salt. Repeat until all the tortilla strips have been fried. Set the tortilla strips aside and reserve the oil.

Sauté the onion and the chicken.
In a large saucepan over medium heat, use 1 tablespoon of the frying oil to sauté the onion until translucent, about 5 minutes. Add another tablespoon of the oil, and brown the chicken thighs, turning to brown all sides.

Simmer the soup.
Add the tomatoes, jalapeño, thyme, garlic, and stock, and bring the mixture to a boil. Reduce the heat to simmer and cook for 20 minutes, or until the chicken is cooked through, breaking up the tomatoes with the edge of a wooden spoon halfway through simmering.

Shred the meat.

Remove the saucepan from the heat. Use tongs to transfer the chicken from the soup into a large bowl. When cool enough to handle, discard the bones and shred the meat, either with your fingers or using two forks. Return the shredded chicken to the soup, and add the lime juice and peas. Stir thoroughly to combine, taste, and adjust the seasoning as needed.

Serve.

Ladle the soup into bowls, and top with the avocado, cilantro leaves, and fried tortillas. Squeeze the lime wedges over the soup and eat immediately. Allow any leftover soup to come to room temperature, and store refrigerated in sealed containers for up to 3 days. Fried tortilla strips will keep at room temperature, stored between layers of parchment and sealed, for 2 days. Reheat tortillas in the toaster oven or a sauté pan.

roasted chicken with onions and lemons

PREP TIME
10 minutes

COOK TIME
55 minutes

TOTAL TIME
1 hour,
20 minutes

SERVES
4

**TOOLS/
EQUIPMENT**
Large cast-
iron skillet
Tongs
Slotted spoon
Large plate

1 (3- to 4-pound) whole chicken

Sea salt

Freshly ground black pepper

1 tablespoon olive oil, plus more
for drizzling

4 onions, cut into wedges

5 lemons, halved

1 head garlic, top third cut off

5 fresh thyme sprigs

Preheat the oven to 425°F.

Season the chicken.
Season the entire chicken well with salt and pepper.
Turn it over to season the backside as well as under-
neath the wings and inside the cavity.

Brown the chicken.
Heat a large cast-iron skillet over medium-high heat,
add the olive oil, and cook the chicken, breast-side
down, until golden brown. Use tongs and a slotted
spoon to gently turn the chicken, being careful not
to tear the skin. Brown on all sides, 10 to 15 minutes
total, and transfer to a plate.

Prep the chicken for roasting.
In the same skillet, layer the onions in the center, so
they'll be underneath the chicken as you roast it.
They will soak up the fat and juices, which will make
them tender and super flavorful. Add the lemon
halves, cut-side down, and the garlic and thyme.
Drizzle everything with olive oil.

Roast the chicken.
Place the chicken back in the skillet, atop the onion
pile. Roast until a meat thermometer inserted into
the thickest part of the thigh registers 165°F, 35 to
40 minutes. Another way to see if the chicken is
ready is to cut into the thigh meat at the joint. If the
juices run clear, it's ready.

Taking the bird directly from the refrigerator to the flame will increase its roasting time and cause it to cook unevenly. Before cooking a chicken (or any meat), let it come to room temperature, about 30 minutes or so. Another frequent mistake is not properly drying the chicken before roasting it. There's no need to rinse the chicken if it's fresh—and doing so only increases your chances of getting a soggy skin. Instead, remove the chicken from any packaging and thoroughly pat it dry.

Serve.

Before cutting into the chicken, let it rest for 10 to 15 minutes, allowing the internal juices to reabsorb. The roasted chicken is great served alongside the tender caramelized veggies. Spoon the pan juices over all and enjoy!

![icon] HELPFUL HINT Not only does a generous sprinkling of salt make chicken taste good, it helps make for a crispy golden-brown skin.

mini pot pies

PREP TIME
15 minutes

COOK TIME
1 hour

TOTAL TIME
1 hour,
25 minutes

SERVES
4

**TOOLS/
EQUIPMENT**

Vegetable peeler

Rolling pin

Parchment paper

Baking sheet

Large cast-
iron skillet

Whisk

Ladle

4 ramekins

Pastry brush

1 sheet frozen puff pastry, such as Dufour brand, thawed in refrigerator

2 tablespoons all-purpose flour, plus more for dusting surface

4 tablespoons unsalted butter

1 shallot, finely chopped

2 teaspoons fresh thyme leaves

1 cup low-sodium chicken broth

1 cup whole milk

Kosher salt

Freshly ground black pepper

4 carrots, peeled and sliced

3 cups shredded or diced leftover chicken or turkey

1 cup frozen peas, thawed

1 cup white pearl onions, peeled

¼ cup chopped fresh flat-leaf parsley

Hot sauce, to taste

1 egg, lightly beaten

Preheat the oven to 400°F.

Roll out the pastry.
Unfold the pastry, and gently roll it out on a lightly floured work surface to ¼ inch thick. Cut it into 4 equal-size pieces slightly larger than the size of your ramekins. Lay them out onto parchment paper, transfer to a baking sheet, and refrigerate until ready to use.

Make the roux.
In a large cast-iron skillet over medium heat, heat the butter. When it is melted and bubbling, add the shallot and thyme, and cook until the shallot becomes translucent, about 4 minutes, stirring regularly. Add the flour and cook, whisking constantly, until the mixture is golden and fully incorporated, about 5 minutes.

Add the remaining ingredients.
Whisk in the broth gradually, incorporating the first half completely before adding the remainder. Whisk in the milk, and season with salt and pepper. Bring to a boil, then reduce heat and simmer, whisking occasionally, until the mixture is thick enough to coat a spoon, 10 to 12 minutes. Add the carrots and cook until just tender, 3 to 5 minutes. Add the chicken, peas, onions, and parsley. Season with hot sauce, salt, and pepper, and stir to combine.

Prepare the ramekins.

Ladle the mixture into 4 ramekins or mini casseroles assembled on a baking sheet. Drape puff pastry over filling, ensuring that it hangs over ramekin edges. Gently press on the edges to seal. Brush the pastry with the beaten egg, and make a slit in the centers with a sharp knife for steam to escape while baking.

Bake the pot pies.

Bake until the puff pastry surfaces are golden and the filling is bubbling through the slits, 15 to 20 minutes. Reduce the heat to 350°F, and bake until the puff pastry is deeply golden and cooked through, 10 to 15 minutes longer.

Serve.

Let sit for 10 minutes before serving on large plates.

> **PRO TIP** For an extra-special effect, use a small cookie cutter in place of cutting a simple steam vent. Press the cookie cutter into the center of the cold pastry sections. When assembling the pot pies, wet the back of the pastry cookie cutter shape with a little water and press into the pastry, next to its cutout.

turkey pan bagnat

PREP TIME
15 minutes
plus 20 minutes
to weight down

COOK TIME
none

SERVES
4

**TOOLS/
EQUIPMENT**

Small bowl

Bread knife

Whisk

Plastic wrap

Cast-iron skillet

FOR THE DRESSING

2 tablespoons Dijon mustard

1 tablespoon mayonnaise

1 teaspoon red wine vinegar

¼ cup chopped fresh parsley

1 tablespoon olive oil

FOR THE SANDWICH

1 (10-inch) loaf ciabatta bread

1 handful haricots verts, blanched, cut
into bite-size pieces

1 cup roasted red pepper strips

½ small red onion, sliced thin

Flake salt, such as Maldon

Freshly ground black pepper

8 ounces thinly sliced roasted
turkey breast

½ cup pesto (page 136)

Make the dressing.
In a small bowl, whisk together the mustard, mayonnaise, vinegar, parsley, and olive oil. Set aside.

Assemble the sandwich.
Slice the ciabatta in half horizontally. Partially hollow out the bottom half and set it on plastic wrap
large enough to wrap the sandwich. Place a layer
of each of the following on the bread in this order:
dressing, haricots verts, roasted pepper, and sliced
onion. Season with salt and pepper. Drizzle the
dressing all over, then add the turkey.

Weight down the sandwich.
Spread the top half with pesto, place it on to the
sandwich, and wrap tightly in plastic. Put the wrapped
sandwich in a resealable plastic bag, squeezing out
any air before sealing. Place a cast-iron skillet on the
sandwich to press for 10 minutes. Turn the sandwich
over and press it again for another 10 minutes.

Serve.
Before serving, remove the weight, unwrap the
sandwich, and let it come to room temperature, or
keep it wrapped and weighted in the refrigerator
for 8 hours or overnight. This extra time weighted
allows the flavors to meld. Cut into four sections.

TRY INSTEAD Swap the roasted peppers
for hard-cooked eggs, the turkey for
quality canned tuna, and the pesto for arti-
chokes. Voila! You have the traditional pan
bagnat, which literally means "bathed bread."

pulled pork sliders

PREP TIME
15 minutes plus
1 hour to rest

COOK TIME
3 hours,
40 minutes

TOTAL TIME
5 hours,
15 minutes

SERVES
8

**TOOLS/
EQUIPMENT**

Small cast-
iron skillet

Mortar and pestle

Small bowl

Plastic wrap

Tray

Aluminum foil

Baking sheet

Large bowl

Tongs

2 teaspoons whole coriander seeds

2 teaspoons whole cumin seeds

2 tablespoons dark brown sugar

1 tablespoon kosher salt

1 teaspoon freshly ground
black pepper

1 tablespoon paprika

1½ teaspoons dry mustard powder

¼ teaspoon ground cayenne pepper

1 (6- to 8-pound) bone-in pork shoulder,
preferably skin-on

½ cup apple cider vinegar

2 tablespoons cane sugar

Pinch red pepper flakes

Toasted buns, for serving

1 recipe Savory Cabbage Slaw
(page 110), for serving

Toast the spices.
In a small, dry cast-iron skillet over medium heat, toast the coriander and cumin until fragrant, about 1 to 2 minutes. Use a mortar and pestle to grind the toasted spices into a powder.

Assemble the spice rub.
In a small bowl, mix together the brown sugar, salt, pepper, coriander, cumin, paprika, mustard powder, and cayenne in a small bowl, mixing with your fingers or a fork until well combined.

Season the meat and let it rest.
Rub the spice mixture over the entire surface of the pork, caking as much of it onto the meat as you can. If you have time, let the meat rest 1 to 2 hours at room temperature before roasting, or refrigerate overnight, loosely wrapped in plastic and set on a tray.

Preheat the oven to 325°F.
But first, adjust the oven rack to the lower-middle position.

Roast the pork.
Place the pork on a foil-lined, rimmed baking sheet, skin-side-up, and roast for 3 to 3½ hours, or until the meat is pull-apart tender.

Let it rest.
Transfer the pork to a large bowl, and let it rest at least 20 minutes. ❯❯

TROUBLESHOOTING The shoulder is a hard-working muscle, which means it is a tough cut of meat. At a low, steady temperature, however, the collagen in the shoulder bastes the meat as it cooks, rendering it succulent. This is a process that cannot be rushed. You will know when it's ready: When pulled at with a fork, the meat will literally fall off the bone.

Roast the pork skin.
Use tongs to carefully lift the skin off. Raise the oven temperature to 500°F. Use a fork to scrape any clinging meat into the bowl. Remove the fat from the skin and discard, returning the skin to the baking sheet. Roast the skin for 5 to 10 minutes, until crisp and bubbly. Remove from the oven and set aside.

Shred the meat.
Shred the pork using two forks or your hands. Save bones for stock or discard. Finely chop the skin, and combine it with the meat, removing any visible fat. Season the meat with salt and pepper. Stir together the vinegar, cane sugar, and a pinch of red pepper flakes, and add to the mixture to taste.

Serve.
Serve the pulled pork hot, piled on toasted buns and topped with Savory Cabbage Slaw. Store the pulled pork for up to 4 days refrigerated in a sealed container. It also keeps frozen for up to 1 month.

DID YOU KNOW? This cut is often called "pork butt," even though it's actually the shoulder. The word *butt* comes from Old English and means "the widest part." On a pig, the widest part is the shoulder, not its actual hindquarters. And that's why it's called the butt!

minty lamb burgers

PREP TIME
10 minutes

COOK TIME
12–15 minutes

SERVES
4

**TOOLS /
EQUIPMENT**

Fine grater

Medium bowl

Pastry brush

Grill pan

Tongs

Bread knife

1 ½ pounds ground lamb

1 garlic clove, finely grated

3 tablespoons finely chopped
fresh mint

3 tablespoons finely chopped fresh
parsley

½ teaspoon cumin seeds, toasted
and ground in a mortar and pestle
(see No-Nonsense Guacamole,
page 101)

Kosher salt

Freshly ground black pepper

Olive oil, for brushing

Ciabatta rolls, for serving

Easy Tzatziki (page 95), for serving

Romaine lettuce leaves, for serving

delicious additions

Feta cheese, sliced thin

Red onion, sliced thin

Make the patties.
In a medium bowl, gently mix together the lamb
with the garlic, mint, parsley, cumin, and a pinch
each of salt and pepper. Divide the meat into
4 patties of equal size and thickness—about ½ inch
thick—and transfer to a plate. Press a small dimple
in the center of each patty with two fingers to offset
how it shrinks as it cooks. Lightly brush the burgers
with olive oil, and season again with salt and pepper.

Cook the burgers.
Heat the grill pan over high heat. When it's hot,
brush the grate lightly with olive oil. Grill the patties
over medium heat for 7 to 8 minutes for medium-
rare or 8 to 10 minutes for medium, turning halfway
through. Transfer them to a plate.

Grill the bread.
Slice the ciabatta in half horizontally, brush lightly
with olive oil, and place cut-side down on the grill
pan. Grill long enough to allow the bread to char in
spots, 3 to 5 minutes.

Serve.
Put the bread on plates and top with the burgers.
Garnish with the Easy Tzatziki, romaine, and any
delicious additions.

HELPFUL HINT Handle the ground lamb
lightly and don't pack the patty too
densely, or else the burger will be tough,
not tender.

savory beef ragù

PREP TIME
15 minutes

COOK TIME
1 hour
40 minutes

SERVES
4

**TOOLS/
EQUIPMENT**
Fine grater
Dutch oven
Wooden spoon

2 strips thick-cut bacon, diced

1 onion, chopped

2 carrots, scrubbed and chopped

2 celery stalks, chopped

4 garlic cloves, finely grated

1 fennel bulb, sliced

3 anchovy filets

1 pound ground beef

½ cup dry red wine

2 fresh thyme sprigs, leaves stripped
from stems

1 bay leaf

½ teaspoon red chili flakes

⅛ teaspoon freshly grated nutmeg

⅛ teaspoon ground cinnamon

1 (28-ounce) can whole plum tomatoes

1 tablespoon tomato paste

1 cup beef stock

2 teaspoons balsamic vinegar

2 teaspoons Worcestershire sauce

Kosher salt

Freshly ground black pepper

Cook the bacon.

In a Dutch oven or other heavy-bottomed pot over medium heat, cook the bacon until just crispy, about 7 minutes. Remove the bacon from the fat, and set aside.

Cook the vegetables.

Sauté the onion in the bacon fat until translucent, stirring occasionally, about 10 minutes. Add the carrots and celery, stir to combine, and cook for another 5 minutes or until lightly browned. Add the garlic, fennel, and anchovies, making a little room at the base of the pot for the anchovies. As they begin to sizzle, break the anchovies up with the edge of a wooden spoon and stir to incorporate.

Add the remaining ingredients.

Add the ground beef and bacon to the pot. Sauté until lightly browned, 5 to 7 minutes, stirring and breaking up meat as you did the anchovies. Add the wine, and as it bubbles, scrape the bottom of the pot to free up any browned bits. Reduce the wine by half, stirring occasionally, then add the thyme, bay leaf, chili flakes, nutmeg, cinnamon, tomatoes, tomato paste, beef stock, vinegar, and Worcestershire sauce. Give a good stir to bring the mixture together.

Bring the ragù to a simmer.

Taste, season with salt and pepper as needed, and cover. Turn the heat to low so that it bubbles slowly. After 10 minutes or so, break the softened tomatoes into chunks using the edge of a wooden spoon.

Continue to simmer.

Cover again and simmer for another 45 minutes to 1 hour, or until the ingredients have melded and the sauce has thickened. Season with salt and pepper.

Serve.

Serve hot directly from the pot set on a trivet at the table. This dish is fantastic tossed with cooked pasta or alongside crusty bread.

Coconut Ice Pops (page 179)

7

desserts

dreamy cheesecake

PREP TIME
20 minutes plus
3 hours to chill

COOK TIME
1 hour

SERVES
10

TOOLS / EQUIPMENT

Zester
Resealable bag
Rolling pin
Medium bowl
Rubber spatula
Springform pan
Electric mixer
Large bowl
Small bowl
Baking sheet

FOR THE CRUST

1 packet whole wheat graham crackers (9 crackers)

1 teaspoon ground cinnamon

3 tablespoons cane sugar

½ teaspoon kosher salt

⅓ cup butter, melted

FOR THE CAKE

2 (8-ounce) packages cream cheese, at room temperature

¼ teaspoon pure vanilla extract

1 teaspoon finely grated lemon zest

1¼ cups cane sugar

2 tablespoons all-purpose flour

¼ teaspoon kosher salt

5 whole eggs, plus 1 egg yolk

¼ cup heavy cream

Make the crust.
Put the graham crackers in a resealable plastic bag. With a rolling pin, crush the crackers into crumbs. If you prefer a finer crust, continue crushing the crackers until you've reached a texture you like. In a medium bowl, mix together the crushed graham crackers, cinnamon, sugar, and salt. Pour in the melted butter, and stir to combine.

Form and set the crust.
Use a rubber spatula or the back of a spoon to spread and compress the mixture evenly into a 9-inch springform pan. Press the crust a little up the sides of the pan, ensuring the crust is even at its base and thins as it goes up. Chill in the refrigerator to set while you make the filling.

Preheat the oven to 500°F.

Mix the filling.
In a large bowl, beat the cheese with an electric mixer until fluffy. Add the vanilla and lemon zest, and mix to combine.

Combine the remaining ingredients.
In a small bowl, stir together the sugar, flour, and salt. Gradually blend the dry ingredients into the cheese. One at a time, add the eggs and additional yolk, whipping to combine and pausing after each to scrape down the sides of the bowl. Gently incorporate the cream, and whip to combine.

Bake the cake.

Pour the mixture into the crust. Place on a baking sheet, and bake for 5 to 8 minutes. Lower the temperature to 200°F, and bake for about 45 to 55 minutes more, until the edges are golden and the center still jiggles. Turn the oven off, and with the door ajar, allow the cheesecake to cool inside for about an hour. Refrigerate for 3 hours, up to overnight.

Serve.

Remove the cake from the refrigerator. Run a butter knife around the inside edge to loosen the cake from the pan. Open the springform pan, remove the cake, and serve at once.

flognarde
(apple-custard bake)

PREP TIME
15 minutes

COOK TIME
30 minutes

SERVES
4

**TOOLS/
EQUIPMENT**

Zester

Vegetable peeler

Large cast-
iron skillet

Medium bowl

Whisk

4 tablespoons butter, cubed,
plus more for greasing the pan

5 tablespoons flour

4 tablespoons sugar

Zest of 2 Meyer lemons

⅔ cup whole milk

4 eggs

3 apples, peeled, cored, and cut
into ½-inch wedges

Confectioners' sugar, for dusting

Grease the pan.
Butter a cast-iron skillet.

Preheat the oven to 400°F.

Mix the ingredients:
In a medium bowl, mix together the flour, sugar,
lemon zest, and milk. Add the eggs and beat vigorously. Continue whisking as you pour the mixture
into the pan.

Arrange the fruit.
Fan the apple wedges and lay them onto the mixture.
It's okay if they slide a little as you arrange them.

Bake the custard.
Dot the surface with butter, and bake until the
custard puffs and has turned golden brown at
the edges, about 30 minutes.

Serve.
Dust confectioners' sugar onto the custard. Serve
hot or at room temperature, cut into wedges.

TRY INSTEAD Substitute sliced pears or
peaches for the apples. Or include a
scatter of raisins, grapes, or cherries in the mix.

DID YOU KNOW? *Flognarde* originated in
the Auvergne region of France. This
dessert goes by different names based on the
region it's made in and the toppings added.

peach-blueberry crisp

PREP TIME
10 minutes

COOK TIME
45 minutes

TOTAL TIME
1 hour
15 minutes

SERVES
4

TOOLS /
EQUIPMENT

Zester

Citrus reamer

2 large bowls

Ceramic or glass
baking dish

Baking sheet

Wire cooling rack

⅔ cup rolled oats

⅓ cup packed brown sugar, plus
3 tablespoons for fruit

¼ cup plus 2 tablespoons all-purpose
flour, divided

½ teaspoon ground cinnamon

2 teaspoons fresh ginger, finely grated

Kosher salt

¾ stick butter, freezer-cold and cubed

2 pounds peaches or nectarines,
cut into thin wedges

2 cups blueberries

2 teaspoons freshly squeezed
lemon juice

1 teaspoon lemon zest

Mix the dry ingredients.
In a large bowl, stir with a fork to combine the oats,
⅓ cup of brown sugar, ¼ cup plus 1 tablespoon of
flour, and the cinnamon. Add the ginger, a pinch of
salt, and the butter to the mixture, and work the
butter into the dry ingredients with your fingers
until pea-size crumbs remain. Refrigerate.

Preheat the oven to 375°F.

Mix the fruit.
In another large bowl, stir together the peaches
and blueberries with the lemon juice and zest,
the remaining 3 tablespoons of brown sugar, the
remaining tablespoon of flour, and a pinch of
salt. Toss all to combine.

Bake the crisp.
Pour the fruit mixture into a baking dish, then
spoon the oat mixture on top to coat. On a baking
sheet, bake the crisp until the topping is golden
and the juices bubble, 30 to 45 minutes. Allow
the crisp to cool on a wire cooling rack for at least
20 minutes.

Serve.
The crisp is delicious served warm, room temp,
or even cold. It's so virtuous you could even eat
it for breakfast! This fruity number is excellent
all by itself, but it would be amazing topped with
ice cream.

chocolate-pomegranate brownies

PREP TIME
10 minutes

COOK TIME
30 minutes

TOTAL TIME
50 minutes

MAKES

12

**TOOLS/
EQUIPMENT**

Double boiler
(see page 39)

Rubber spatula

Parchment paper

Baking dish

Large bowl

Electric mixer

Skewer or
toothpick

Wire cooling rack

12 ounces semisweet dark chocolate
(such as Callebaut), chopped, divided

1½ sticks butter, cut into cubes

4 eggs

1¼ cup light brown sugar

1 cup all-purpose flour

Seeds from ½ fresh pomegranate,
for topping

Preheat the oven to 350°F.

Melt the chocolate.
Using a double boiler, melt half the chocolate and
all the butter. Be careful that the water doesn't
bubble up into the top saucepan as you do so,
or it will ruin the chocolate. Remove the melted
chocolate pan from the hot water bath, wipe the
base with a dry dish towel to ensure no drips, stir the
butter-chocolate mixture together, and set aside.

Prep the baking dish.
Line a square or small rectangular baking dish with
parchment long enough that the paper extends
beyond edges by at least 2 inches on all sides.

Mix the remaining ingredients.
In a large bowl, use a fork or hand mixer to thoroughly combine the eggs, sugar, and flour. Add the
slightly cooled, melted chocolate mixture and the
remaining portion of chopped chocolate, stirring
to combine.

Bake the brownies.
Pour the mixture into the prepared baking dish,
and bake for 25 minutes, or until a skewer or toothpick comes out almost clean. If you jiggle the tin,
the center should move just a little. »

TRY INSTEAD If you cannot find a fresh pomegranate, top the brownies with fresh raspberries. They're just as delicious!

Let the brownies rest.
Cool the brownies on a wire cooling rack for 10 minutes in the pan; then, using the parchment tabs on either side, lift the brownies out.

Serve.
Cut the brownies into squares, and scatter the pomegranate seeds on top. Enjoy the delicious combo of still-molten chocolate and tart, juicy pomegranate!

coconut ice pops

PREP TIME
10 minutes
plus 4 hours to
freeze

COOK TIME
none

SERVES
4–8
DEPENDING
ON ICE POP
MOLD SIZE

**TOOLS/
EQUIPMENT**

Zester

Food processor
or blender

Rubber spatula

Ice pop molds or
small paper cups

Wooden ice-
pop sticks

Bobby pins

3 (5.4 ounce) cans unsweetened organic coconut cream

Juice and finely grated zest of 1 lime

⅓ cup maple syrup or honey

Blend the ingredients.
In a food processor, purée the coconut cream, lime zest and juice, and maple syrup.

Prep the ice pops.
Pour the puréed mixture into molds or small paper cups. Insert wooden ice-pop sticks, clipping bobby pins to the sticks and setting them across the mold to anchor the sticks in place.

Let the ice pops set.
Freeze the pops for at least 4 hours.

Serve.
To unmold, if using paper cups, simply peel the paper away and eat. If using ice pop molds, run briefly under warm water to loosen.

> TRY INSTEAD Swap seeds from a vanilla bean for the lime zest. If you add diced fresh young coconut, it will be a real treat!

very berry trifle

PREP TIME
20 minutes
plus 1 hour
to chill

COOK TIME
none

SERVES
4

TOOLS / EQUIPMENT

Citrus reamer

Medium bowl

Large bowl

Whisk or electric mixer

Rubber spatula

4 glasses

Plastic wrap

3 cups mixed berries of your choice

5 tablespoons cane sugar, divided

Juice of 1 lemon

Juice of ½ orange

1 cup mascarpone

2 cups heavy whipping cream

¼ teaspoon pure vanilla extract

Pinch kosher salt

8 ounces sponge, pound cake, or ladyfingers, sectioned into ½-inch slices to fit into glasses

Soak the berries.

In a medium bowl, soak the berries in half the sugar and the lemon and orange juices. Let the mixture soften for 10 minutes as you prep the cream.

Make the whipped cream.

In a large bowl, whisk together the mascarpone, heavy cream, vanilla extract, the remaining 2½ tablespoons of sugar, and the salt until soft peaks form. You can speed the process up by using a mixer here, but doing it by hand should take only a few minutes, thanks to the rich body of the mascarpone.

Assemble the trifle.

In 4 short cylindrical or wide-mouth glasses, arrange the ladyfingers or cake pieces to cover the bottom. Spoon the berry mixture onto the cake in an even layer. Use a rubber spatula to spread the whipped cream layer on top of the fruit, holding the glass and turning it in your hand as you spread the cream. Repeat layering each glass: cake, berry mixture, and cream, a couple times until the glasses are very full, ending with the cream on top. Chill, covered in plastic wrap, for 1 to 3 hours.

Serve.

Serve chilled with spoons long enough to reach to the bottom of all the layers, and enjoy. Yum!

banana "ice cream"

PREP TIME
7 minutes, plus
1 hour to freeze

COOK TIME
none

SERVES
4

TOOLS /
EQUIPMENT
Baking sheet
Food processor
Rubber spatula

1 bunch (5–8) ripe but firm bananas

Pinch kosher salt

delicious additions

Berries

Greek yogurt or crème fraîche

Ground cinnamon

Nut butters

Chocolate

Prep the bananas.

Peel the bananas, and cut them into chunky coins. Freeze for 1 to 2 hours (or overnight) on a baking sheet.

Blend the bananas.

Using a food processor, blend the bananas with just a pinch of salt until they become smooth and creamy, about 5 minutes. Stop periodically and scrape down the bowl. Watch the bananas transform, like magic, into ice cream! If you'd like to add in other flavors, do so now, and pulse again to combine.

Serve.

For best flavor, remove it from the freezer 10 minutes before serving. Cover and freeze any leftovers. Ice cream can be made 5 days ahead.

HELPFUL HINT If your freezer can't accommodate a baking sheet, a metal pie tin or baking dish works in a pinch.

strawberry-rhubarb mini tarts

PREP TIME
30 minutes
plus 1 hour
to chill

COOK TIME
45 minutes

MAKES
8
MINI TARTS

TOOLS / EQUIPMENT

Zester

Food processor

Plastic wrap

Large bowl

Rolling pin

2 baking sheets

Parchment paper

Pastry brush

Wire cooling rack

FOR THE DOUGH

2½ cups all-purpose flour

1 teaspoon cane sugar, plus 1 teaspoon for sprinkling

1 teaspoon kosher salt

2 sticks butter, freezer-cold and chopped into small cubes

¼ cup ice water

FOR THE FILLING

¾ pound rhubarb, rinsed, ends trimmed, cut into ¼-inch pieces

2 pints fresh strawberries, rinsed and hulled, cut into ¼-inch pieces

½ cup cane sugar

Zest of 1 orange

¼ cup orange juice

Pinch kosher salt

Make the dough.
In a food processor, pulse the flour, sugar, and salt to combine. Add the cold butter and pulse 5 to 7 times, until the butter mixes with the flour to form pea-size crumbs. In a slow stream, add the ice water while pulsing, stopping once the dough holds together.

Test the dough.
To test, unplug the food processor, open the lid, and press some dough together. If it holds together, it's ready. If it still crumbles, add a bit more ice water as you pulse a few more times. You may use slightly less or slightly more than ¼ cup of water.

Place the dough on a long sheet of plastic wrap.
Separate the dough into two mounds, then flatten each to form a disk. Cut the plastic wrap in two between the disks, and wrap each. Refrigerate for at least 20 minutes to let it firm up.

Make the filling.
In a large bowl, carefully mix together the rhubarb, strawberries, sugar, orange zest, orange juice, and salt. Cover with plastic wrap, and let the flavors meld, at least 15 minutes.

Roll the dough.
On a lightly floured surface, cut each disk into four. Chill the rest as you roll each one out. Roll from the center to the edge, turning an eighth turn with each pass of the rolling pin, until the dough is ⅛ inch thick. (They don't have to be perfect circles. Patch any large tears with dough pinched from the edge.) »

PRO TIPS:

- For the best results, cube cold butter and then place in a container in the freezer for 20 minutes. w
- For even baking, crimp a strip of foil over any parts that you don't want to brown further.
- You can make the dough ahead and keep it wrapped, refrigerated, for a few days, or it can be wrapped tightly and frozen for up to 3 weeks. To thaw, refrigerate overnight.
- The fruit mixture can also be made in advance and in fact benefits from a day or two of melding in the refrigerator.
- Cook any leftover fruit over low heat to make compote for yogurt, ice cream, muffins, or toast.

Assemble the tarts.
Line two baking sheets with parchment paper, and lay the rolled pastry 2 to 3 inches apart from each other. Spoon mounds of the fruit mixture into the center of each pastry, dividing the filling evenly and leaving a 1-inch border around the edge. Assemble one set of tarts at a time, leaving the other batch of pastry in the refrigerator.

Crimp the tart edges.
Gather the pastry edges, making pleats onto the piled fruit. Lightly brush water in between the folds to press the pastry together and keep it in place. If the dough becomes flabby, it needs to be rechilled.

Refrigerate the tarts.
Once you have filled and crimped the tarts, refrigerate them for at least 1 hour before baking.

Repeat steps 5 through 8 with the remaining dough.

Preheat the oven to 400°F.

Bake the tarts.
Very lightly brush the edges of the pastry with water, and sprinkle with the reserved 1 teaspoon of sugar. Bake for 30 minutes, or until the crusts are golden, then lower the temperature to 375°F and bake for 10 to 15 minutes, until the juices bubble and the crust is deeply golden. Transfer the tarts to a wire cooling rack to cool.

Serve.
Remove the tarts when they can be easily handled, and enjoy them warm. Store leftover tarts at room temperature, wrapped loosely in foil, for 2 days.

chocolate-cherry bark

PREP TIME
10 minutes
plus 15 minutes
to chill

COOK TIME
10 minutes

MAKES

1

SHEET

**TOOLS/
EQUIPMENT**

Double boiler
(see page 39)

Parchment paper

Baking sheet

Rubber spatula

1 pound bittersweet dark chocolate, cut into small pieces

2 cups granola of your choice

1 cup dried sour cherries, coarsely chopped

Flake salt, such as Maldon

Prep the chocolate and the sheet pan.
In a double boiler, melt the chocolate. Place parchment paper on a baking sheet, and pour the granola into a pile on it.

Mix the bark together.
Once the chocolate is molten, pour it onto the granola, and using a rubber spatula, mix the two together thoroughly. As you mix, spread the chocolate-covered granola into an even layer on the baking sheet. Keep spreading until the mixture reaches the edges, ending up about ¼ inch thick.

Add the sweet and salty accents.
Scatter the chopped cherries around, pressing them lightly into the bark, and then scatter on the salt. Use the salt as an accent more than a ground cover.

Let the bark set.
Place the baking sheet in a cool place to harden. Refrigerate for 15 minutes if you prefer to accelerate its cooling. Break the mixture into pieces. Refrigerate in a sealed container to store.

Serve.
Remove the bark from the refrigerator half an hour before serving to allow the flavors to fully bloom. Serve on a platter. It keeps for 2 weeks, refrigerated—if it lasts that long!

 HELPFUL HINT This delectable bark can be prepared 2 days in advance.

Appendix A
SETTING THE TABLE

The best part of preparing a meal is sharing it with family and friends: a little thoughtfulness on arranging the table and seating guests is worthwhile. A few simple guidelines will help you create a warm and welcoming feeling, whether for a casual lunch or a holiday feast.

Basic Table Setting A basic table is set with a knife, fork, and spoon framing the dinner plate. They are set out in the order of use: fork to the left of plate, knife to the right, and a soup- or dessertspoon to the right of the knife. A napkin can be rolled or folded and laid on the plate.

Glasses Each place setting should have all of the glasses needed for the meal. Water glasses sit on the right of each plate, just above the knife. For a meal with wine for grown-ups, place the wine glass above and to the left of the water glass.

Dishes On a daily basis, all you'll need is a single plate or large shallow bowl (for pasta, soup, or stew). For a more formal meal with many courses, add a bread plate to the left side of the setting, and a salad plate or soup bowl on top of the napkin and dinner plate, making an impressive display all guests will notice.

Silverware No matter how formal or casual your meal, set the silverware in the order of use, from the outside in. For multiple courses,

the fork for the first course (like salad) is the farthest to the left, followed by another fork for the main course. To the right of the plate, place a knife and if you need a soupspoon, place it on the far right. Lay dessert silverware horizontally above the plate, but for a casual meal, simply bring the silverware in with dessert.

Mix-and-Match Choosing plates and glasses from the same dish set automatically creates a harmonious table, but using different kinds of dishes, silverware, and glasses can be equally beautiful. An eclectic setting is more creative and lets your imagination guide the display. If you choose a mix-and-match theme, have one element tie everything together, such as the same napkin, the same scale for each plate, or a similar color scheme.

Extras There are infinite ways to make a table setting special. For example, an apple or leaf on top of each napkin, or a small vase with flowers transforms a regular meal into a special one. Place cards can make the table feel more formal. The twinkle of candles also makes for a great experience.

So, leave enough time during your food preparation to put these finishing touches in place. Then you can proudly watch your guests enjoy the fruits of your hard work, making the experience all the sweeter.

Appendix B
CONVERSION CHARTS

Volume Equivalents (Liquid)

US STANDARD	US STANDARD (OUNCES)	METRIC (APPROXIMATE)
2 tablespoons	1 fl. oz.	30 mL
¼ cup	2 fl. oz.	60 mL
½ cup	4 fl. oz.	120 mL
1 cup	8 fl. oz.	240 mL
1½ cups	12 fl. oz.	355 mL
2 cups or 1 pint	16 fl. oz.	475 mL
4 cups or 1 quart	32 fl. oz.	1 L
1 gallon	128 fl. oz.	4 L

Oven Temperatures

FAHRENHEIT (F)	CELSIUS (C) (APPROXIMATE)
250°F	120°C
300°F	150°C
325°F	165°C
350°F	180°C
375°F	190°C
400°F	200°C
425°F	220°C
450°F	230°C

Volume Equivalents (Dry)

US STANDARD	METRIC (APPROXIMATE)
⅛ teaspoon	0.5 mL
¼ teaspoon	1 mL
½ teaspoon	2 mL
¾ teaspoon	4 mL
1 teaspoon	5 mL
1 tablespoon	15 mL
¼ cup	59 mL
⅓ cup	79 mL
½ cup	118 mL
⅔ cup	156 mL
¾ cup	177 mL
1 cup	235 mL
2 cups or 1 pint	475 mL
3 cups	700 mL
4 cups or 1 quart	1 L

Weight Equivalents

US STANDARD	METRIC (APPROXIMATE)
½ ounce	15 g
1 ounce	30 g
2 ounces	60 g
4 ounces	115 g
8 ounces	225 g
12 ounces	340 g
16 ounces or 1 pound	455 g

GLOSSARY

Al dente This Italian term describes a food, usually pasta, when it is done but still firm—literally, "to the teeth."

Arugula Arugula is a dark green salad leaf with a mustardy, peppery flavor.

Basil Basil is a highly fragrant plant that is part of the mint family with more than 60 varieties. Whenever possible, choose fresh basil over the dried form. Basil leaves should look vibrant and free from darks spots or dried edges. It should be stored in the refrigerator wrapped between layers of slightly damp paper towels, sealed in a container or bag.

Bay leaf Bay leaves are aromatic laurel leaves and are used to flavor soups and stews. They do not soften when cooked and should not be eaten. Remove it when you find one. They keep dried for 6 months in a cool, dark place.

Blanch To blanch means to plunge food into boiling water for a brief amount of time. Most blanched foods are immediately transferred to an ice bath to stop the cooking process, also known as "shocking." Blanching raw vegetables brightens their color while maintaining a tender, crisp, barely cooked texture and flavor. Blanching also helps loosen the skin of tomatoes or stone fruit for peeling.

Bonito flakes Bonito is a kind of tuna, and bonito flakes (*katsuobushi* in Japanese, where the flakes originate) are the wispy shavings of dried and smoked bonito. Bonito flakes have a very savory, somewhat smoky taste, and are a great accent for all kinds of foods when you want to deepen the overall flavor.

Caramelize To caramelize is to cook something until it forms a deeply golden crust and the inherent sugars break down, intensifying a food's sweetness. For instance, caramelizing onions replaces their sharp flavor with a savory sweetness.

Cayenne pepper Hot and pungent cayenne pepper is one of the most widely used spicy ingredients. Avoid touching your eyes or other sensitive body parts after you've touched cayenne pepper, and wash your hands thoroughly with warm soapy water when you are finished. Dry peppers or cayenne powder can be stored at room temperature in a cool, dark place in an airtight container for several months.

Chile peppers Chile peppers are small peppers that make food spicy. Capsaicin is the chemical substance that makes chile peppers hot and the white membranes that hold the seeds contain the most. It highly irritates the skin and eyes, so always wash your hands immediately after cutting a chile.

Chili powder Chili powder is a spice blend for making chili that contains oregano, cumin, and garlic as well as dried hot chiles.

Chives Chives are part of the allium family. They impart a pleasantly subtle, onion-garlic flavor to savory foods. Chives are high in fiber, antioxidants, and vitamin K, which strengthens bones and maintains brain health. Chive stalks are hollow and quite slender, and look like lush bunches of foot-high grass. Their lavender blossoms are also edible.

Cilantro Cilantro has very green, papery, and tender leaves, and should be eaten fresh (the stems are edible, too). Season cooked foods at the last moment so the cilantro doesn't wilt. To store fresh cilantro, place them in a jar with water and cover with a plastic bag, and place in the refrigerator. Depending on its treatment at the market, cilantro should last up to a week in the refrigerator. Do not wash cilantro until you need it, since excess moisture can make the leaves slimy during storage.

Cinnamon Cinnamon is a fragrant, sweet-flavored spice used since biblical times for its medicinal and culinary benefits. It is the inner bark of a tropical evergreen tree, which curls into sticks when dried. Cinnamon is known to have antioxidant, antidiabetic, antiseptic, anti-inflammatory, and anti-flatulent properties.

Compost Compost is decomposed organic matter, a natural process of recycling organic material such as leaves and vegetable scraps. When you compost organic waste, nutrients are returned to the soil, nourishing everything that grows out of it.

Coriander Coriander is the dried round seed from the cilantro plant and has a spicy, citrus flavor. The seeds are often used toasted whole, which brings out their aromatic quality and essential oils, and then ground.

Cumin Cumin is a seed with a nutty, peppery flavor. It is an excellent source of iron, which helps keep the immune system healthy. It is a great seasoning for lentils, rice, chickpeas, and black beans, or as part of a spice mixture to roast meats, as well as boosting the flavors of salsas and sauces.

Dill Dill has green, wispy, fernlike leaves and imparts a tangy, sweet taste. Whenever possible, choose fresh dill over dried, which has little flavor. Dill stalks droop soon after being picked. Store fresh dill in the refrigerator, wrapped in layers of damp paper towel and then sealed in a container, or in a jar of water with a bag placed over the leaves. Since dill is very fragile, it will keep for only 3 to 4 days.

Divided Seen in ingredient lists, this term means that you won't use all of that ingredient at once. The instructions tell you how much to use and when.

Emulsify Emulsify means to combine two liquids together that do not ordinarily mix easily. The ingredients are usually oil or other type of fat and another liquid like water or broth. By constantly whisking these two different liquids together, the result is a thick, creamy liquid with a silky texture. Some familiar emulsions include hollandaise, mayonnaise or aioli, salad dressing, and crème anglaise.

English cucumber English cucumbers, also known as hothouse, greenhouse, or seedless cucumbers, are long and thin and have a milder, sweeter flavor. Its skin is thinner, and it contains smaller, less noticeable seeds. They are sold wrapped in plastic sleeves in the produce sections in grocery stores.

Flake salt Flake salt consists of sheer, lacy pyramid-like crystals, with a bright, clean, sparkly flavor. It is great on salads, fresh vegetables, roasted seafood, and fish. This salt dissolves quickly and should be added just before serving.

Ginger Ginger is an aromatic, pungent and spicy rhizome (root), prized for its medicinal and culinary properties. Fresh ginger has the best flavor and health benefits, and lasts up to 3 weeks unpeeled in the refrigerator. When purchasing fresh ginger, make sure the root is firm, smooth, and blemish free. If it is very young, it won't need peeling. Otherwise, the brown, papery skin on mature ginger root should be scraped off with a spoon.

GMO *GMO* stands for "genetically modified organism." It is produced by a laboratory process that uses genes from the DNA of one species and artificially combines them with the genes of another species of plant or animal. These genes may come from bacteria, viruses, insects, animals, or even humans. This process is often referred to as genetic engineering (GE) and operates in ways that are not possible or desirable in nature. This technique has not been lab-tested in a conclusive way before being planted in the field and leads to unpredictable changes in the DNA.

Gruyère Gruyere cheese is a traditional, unpasteurized, semi-hard cheese. It is an excellent melting cheese, used prominently in gratins, croques monsieurs and mesdames, and for grilled cheese, omelettes, and mac 'n' cheese.

Haloumi Haloumi cheese is a brined, slightly springy white cheese, traditionally made from sheep and goat milk. Its texture is similar to mozzarella or a firm feta. Haloumi can be easily fried or grilled, and is often served with watermelon and mint, or as part of *meze*, a Mediterranean appetizer platter of various savory foods.

Harissa Harissa is a spicy, aromatic chile paste widely used in North African and Middle Eastern cooking. It comes in tubes, jars, or cans, or you can choose a powdered spice version. Harissa is sold in Middle Eastern markets or in the specialty section of grocery stores.

Kosher salt Kosher salt has flaky white grains that dissolve slowly in cooking. Chefs favor it because its large grains make it easier to pinch between fingers, offering a tighter control on seasoning and because it also lacks the additives found in table salt, like iodine. Use kosher salt for general cooking, including recipes that specify coarse salt.

Labneh Labneh is a tangy, creamy Lebanese cheese made from strained yogurt. Custard-like in its consistency, it can be used in savory or sweet dishes. Look for labneh in Middle Eastern and specialty markets.

Meyer lemon Meyer lemons are sweeter in flavor than other lemons and have a floral aroma. Choose lemons that are deeply yellow, plump, and fragrant when you gently rub the skin.

Mint Mint is a hardy herb with vibrant green leaves and a fresh, sweet flavor with a cool aftertaste. There are more than 20 varieties, the most common being peppermint and spearmint. Use a sharp knife and slice mint leaves gently, as overchopping will bruise them. Store fresh mint in the refrigerator, carefully wrapped in damp paper towel and inside a loosely closed plastic bag. It should keep fresh for several days.

Mirin Mirin is a light golden wine that is a staple of Japanese cooking, lending its sweet flavor to contrast with other Asian sauces, such as soy sauce. Mirin is extremely versatile and a little goes a long way. Look for it in Asian markets or in the specialty section of the grocery store.

Miso Miso is fermented soybeans and is central to Japanese cooking. Usually a thick paste, its consistency is similar to peanut butter. Dark miso has a stronger, more pungent flavor, which enhances beef or lamb dishes. Light-colored miso is more delicate and used for soup, salad dressings, and sauces. Miso is one of the few nonmeat foods that contains all essential amino acids, which makes it a complete protein. It should be stored in the refrigerator in a tightly sealed container, and it keeps for up to one year.

Mustard seed Mustard seeds are the fruit pods from the mustard plant. There are many varieties of mustard plants, but the principal ones are black, white, and brown mustard. Black mustard seeds have a strong, pungent taste, while white mustard seeds (which are actually a soft yellow color) are milder.

Nutmeg Nutmeg is the inner kernel of a fruit from a tropical evergreen plant. Whole nutmeg grates easily and gives the best spicy flavor, and keeps indefinitely.

Oregano Oregano is a shrub with green oval leaves and white or pink edible flowers. It imparts a warm, peppery, and somewhat bitter flavor to foods. Whenever possible, choose fresh oregano over dried. Fresh oregano should be stored in the refrigerator wrapped in damp paper towel and sealed in a container.

Organic Certified organic foods are foods produced by farming methods that are free of synthetic additives like pesticides and chemical fertilizers and were not processed through genetic engineering, ionizing radiation, or industrial solvents. Eating organically grown food is a great way to limit exposure to cancer-causing contaminants and toxic heavy metals that are commonly found in foods grown using conventional agricultural practices. In addition to reducing exposure to these harmful substances, supporting growers of organically grown foods often means supporting local and small family farms.

Oxidation Oxidation occurs when foods are exposed to oxygen. When a food is peeled, sliced, diced, cut, mashed, or shredded, a reaction between their enzymes and oxygen in the air causes the food to turn brown. Apples, bananas, and avocados show oxidation whenever they are cut or peeled.

Paprika Paprika is made from ground bonnet pepper, a relative of chile peppers and bell peppers. It can be sweet, hot, or smoky. Fresh paprika has a lot of flavor, but it diminishes quickly as it ages.

Parsley The two most widely available types of parsley are curly and the broader Italian flat-leaf parsley. Italian parsley is more fragrant and holds up better in cooking. Choose fresh parsley that is deep green in color and looks crisp. Fresh parsley should be washed just before using and should be added toward the end of the cooking process to retain its taste, color, and nutritional value.

Persian cucumber Persian cucumbers have smooth, thin skin, and their flesh is very crisp and sweet. They have no developed seeds, and measure 4 to 6 inches in length. They can be used interchangeably with English or kirby cucumbers.

Quartered Seen in ingredient lists and instructions, this means to cut the ingredient into four pieces of roughly equal size.

Red pepper flakes Red pepper flakes and crushed red pepper are pulverized, dried red chile peppers, and impart a somewhat sharp, smoky flavor to foods.

Reduce This term is often used in reference to liquids. It means to cook down so that the liquid amount decreases. To "reduce by half" means to cook until you have half as much liquid as you started with, which concentrates flavor as the volume evaporates.

Rosemary Rosemary is an evergreen shrub with hardy quills that resemble flat pine needles. Most recipes call for the quills, or leaves, but you can also add a whole sprig to season a dish and remove it before serving. Quickly rinse rosemary under cool running water and pat dry before adding it to dishes.

Roux A flour-and-fat (usually butter) mixture used to thicken soups and sauces.

Sumac Sumac is a spice with a lemony flavor. It is used in dry rubs for lamb, chicken, and fish, marinades for meat or vegetable shish kabobs and sprinkled onto salads and dips.

Thyme Thyme is a fragrant herb with thin, woody stems and small, pungent leaves. You can add fresh thyme by adding whole sprigs or stripping leaves from the stems.

Trivet A trivet is an object placed beneath a hot serving dish, skillet, or roasting pan to protect a surface from heat or moisture damage. Trivets are made from metal, ceramic, wood, cork, or fabric such as felt.

Za'atar Za'atar is Arabic for "thyme." It is a Middle Eastern spice blend using thyme as well as toasted sesame seeds, sumac, and sea salt. Za'atar is used to add earthy savoriness to hearty soups and as a rub for chicken and lamb. A light sprinkling also enhances eggs, tomatoes, and feta cheese.

RECIPE INDEX

....

INDEX

ACKNOWLEDGMENTS

To Ma and Pa and Guiseppe, I love you so. Thank you for unconditionally loving me and believing in my creative spirit, and for your thoughtful feedback as I made this book. I am grateful to be part of such a wonderful family.

To Jim, my sweetheart and life partner, thank you for enthusiastically eating all my bright ideas and for compassionately sharing feedback and shaping who I've become. Happily, those bright ideas have gotten pretty good by now.

To Mark Tulloss, in that rickety apartment back in the early days in West Philadelphia, you sparked my interest in what delicious food could be.

To my editor Meg, you saw the potential of fantastic new work we could make together. I am so grateful you thought I should be the person to breathe life into this great book, and for our continued relationship.

To Katy, Maggie, Wendy, and the whole Callisto team, your vision and critical thinking have been a blessing. Thank you for working with me, brilliantly piecing together a written work for kids. And thanks for including children in the landscape of delicious, healthy cooking, aiding in their delicious futures.

Thank you for your generosity and support: Bryant Terry, Susan Spungen, Betty Fussell, Phyllis Grant, Aran Goyoaga, Jon Rowley, Graymarket Textile Design, Sorella Le Var, dear Instagram friends, and GIR silicone kitchen gear. Your support has fueled me on a continuous basis, often giving an extra boost to my day.

Thank you small family farmers, for producing the most beautiful produce, eggs, and meat for me to cook, style, photograph, and then, hungrily eat. Your tireless work makes the difference for more and more of us in the contemporary food landscape.

Big thanks to my kid chef recipe testers, Miles (10), Olivia (10), and Lili (7), who made my recipes at home and offered helpful suggestions for improvements. You helped make my recipes even clearer!

CPSIA information can be obtained
at www.ICGtesting.com
Printed in the USA
JSHW032251140821
17808JS00008B/8

9 781943 451203